# THE NEGRO IN FRANCE

*SHELBY T. McCLOY*

# THE NEGRO IN FRANCE

*UNIVERSITY OF KENTUCKY PRESS*

# FOREWORD

THE PURPOSE of this study is to present a history of the Negro who has come to France, the reasons for his coming, the record of his stay, and the reactions of the French to his presence. It is not a study of the Negro in the French colonies or of colonial conditions, for that is a different story. Occasionally, however, reference to colonial happenings is brought in as necessary to set forth the background. The author has tried assiduously to restrict his attention to those of whose Negroid blood he could be certain, but whenever the distinction has been significant, he has considered as mulattoes all those having any mixture of Negro and white blood. The study includes all aspects of life for those Negroes who have gone to France—social, economic, military, political, cultural. Fundamentally it may be considered a social history.

In the early 1940's, while working on a study of government assistance in eighteenth-century France, I came upon a number of references to Negroes in detention camps and hospitals. An article I wrote on these and other Negroes was published in the *Journal of Negro History* in 1945; the editor of this publication, the late Dr. Carter Woodson, encouraged me to pursue the study further. This I did at odd moments, and in 1954 I published in the same journal another article dealing further with Negroes and mulattoes of eighteenth-century France. Then came the Supreme Court decision of May 17, 1954, on the matter of school segregation in the United States, and the awakening of great public interest in the racial question. I thought once more of the Negro in France, and the committee administering Fulbright grants-in-aid enabled me to work in Paris for the academic year 1956-1957 on this subject.

It was not easy to find material. At the outset, a well-known authority on colonial history advised me to limit the study to

the eighteenth century, since the finding of material on Negroes
in records of the nineteenth and twentieth centuries is extremely difficult because references to color are generally
omitted. It was only after much thought and weighing of the
advantages and disadvantages of the two schemes that I
decided to attempt the more difficult route. The research has
proven slow and baffling, as predicted, for there has been only
negligible study made of this subject. The published works
of merit dealing with the topic in the nineteenth and twentieth
centuries are virtually limited to a small book by Professor
Mercer Cook entitled *Five French Negro Authors* (1943),
André Maurois' *Les trois Dumas* (1957), Roi Ottley's *No Green
Pastures* (1951), and J. A. Rogers' *The World's Great Men of
Color* (1947, 2 v.). For the eighteenth century, more material
is available, particularly in the archives, but even there it is not
abundant. This difficulty in finding material explains the
brevity of some of the later chapters. Despite the brevity,
however, I am convinced that they present a faithful outline
of a very interesting subject, a subject that will draw more
attention with the passage of time.

I have endeavored to be objective in treatment, but not
uncritical, for I have often ventured an opinion on matters, as I
think one who has studied a field should do. I hope that
throughout I have been fair.

There are many to whom I am indebted for aid in one form
or another. First and foremost is the Fulbright Commission
for the grant-in-aid that made possible a year's research in
Paris and several port cities in France. Next is the University
of Kentucky, for one semester of sabbatical aid during the same
academic year, for a subsequent summer free from teaching
duties for research and writing, and also for a trip to Washington in late 1959 for some final research. I am obligated to
many in France for interviews and aid on material for my
subject. They include M. Gaston Monnerville, Président du
Sénat de la République Française; Dr. Charles Braibant,
former Directeur des Archives de France; Professeur Emile G.

Léonard, of the Ecole des Hautes Etudes; Professeur Blanche Maurel, specialist on Santo Dominican history; M. C. LaRoche, Directeur des Archives de France Outre-Mer; M. Meyer, Archiviste des Archives Nationales; M. Jean Denizet, Chef de Service des Archives et de la Bibliothèque de la Marine; M. Audouy, Conservateur at the same institution; M. Allioun Diop, Rédacteur of *Présence Africaine;* Mr. O. Rudolph Aggrey, Youth Activities Officer in the United States Embassy; Mr. Robert L. Grière, Receptionist to the Vice President of the American Express Company; Dr. Robert O. Mead, Director of the Fondation des Etats-Unis at the Cité Universitaire; Madame la Générale Louis Hary; M. Villard, Directeur des Archives des Bouches-du-Rhône; Professeur André Ducasse, Marseille; M. Rebuffat, Directeur des Archives du Chambre de Commerce de Marseille; M. Betjé-Brezetz, Archiviste des Archives de la Gironde; M. Marcel Delafosse, Archiviste des Archives de la Charente-Inférieure; M. H. de Berranger, Archiviste des Archives de la Loire-Atlantique; M. Lecaudé, Archiviste, and M. Dodard, Commis d'Administration, Archives de la Ville du Havre; M. Le Bihan, Sous-Archiviste, Archives du Finistère; and M. E. Ravillef, Archiviste, Archives Municipales de Nantes. With all these the author had interviews and from each derived some aid. In addition, others have made valuable suggestions. M. Roger Vaurs and Mlle Yvonne Daumarie, Director and Assistant Director of the Service de Presse et d'Information of the French Embassy in New York, kindly supplied some useful information by letter. The courtesy of all these persons has been in accord with the high reputation of the French in this respect.

It was particularly in the Archives Nationales and the Bibliothèque Nationale, in Paris, that I gathered material, but there also was much valuable material in the Bibliothèque de la Marine at Paris, and in the departmental and municipal archives at Marseille, Bordeaux, Nantes, La Rochelle, Quimper, and Le Havre. In this country, in addition to the University of Kentucky Library, I have worked in the Library of Congress and Howard University Library. I acknowledge with thanks the courtesies of the staffs of these institutions, and particularly the kindness of Mrs. Dorothy B. Porter, Reference Librarian at Howard University. Several American libraries have placed books at my usage through interlibrary loan: the Library of Congress, Howard University, Fisk University, Stanford University, the Cleveland Public, the University of Missouri, and the University of Minnesota.

Last but not least of my obligations are those to my wife, who accompanied me to France and aided greatly in checking bibliography, examining newspapers for material, copying passages, typing the manuscript, and offering criticism.

# CONTENTS

# INTRODUCTION

*A* DISTINGUISHED Negro leader
in the United States has remarked that the outstanding problem
of the twentieth century is that of the "color line" (the relation-      D.B
ship of the light and dark races). Although it is not of the
gravity and scope of the world's struggle with nationalism and
communism, I do agree that our race problem is of gigantic
import.

The furor over racial integration in the United States of
America and the apartheid movement of the Union of South
Africa have brought the race issue most sharply to the fore in
recent years. To a lesser degree, but nonetheless keenly felt, it
has shown itself also in Great Britain, where eighty thousand
or more Negro colonials from Jamaica and Africa have come
as immigrants and settlers, and in Germany, where two or three
thousand "war babies" of mixed blood have been left by
American Negro soldiers in the aftermath of World War II
and that country's occupation. In Britain a few riots have
occurred in ports where the Negroes have settled; some
intermarriage between Negro men and British girls of the
lower classes has taken place; and there has been much alleged
labor discrimination and bitter ostracism of those whites
marrying Negroes. The problem has gained most force since
World War II and is an ugly one. It becomes worse as the
number of immigrants grows. In Germany no riots have
occurred; neither has there been economic rivalry or racial

intermarriage on a large scale. But there has been much ill feeling in regard to the mulatto babies, most of them born out of wedlock. They are not wanted, and the problem has been what to do with them. Happily, with the aid of the churches, the children are being sent to school with other children. Occasionally in other countries an incident occurs which reveals that racial feeling is not limited by geography, and that even in countries counted as friendly to the Negro there runs a current of aloofness or antagonism.

The subject has received much treatment in books and magazines by writers both white and Negro, from the United States, Britain, France, the French colonies, and elsewhere. Among these writers, only a few may be mentioned: J. A. Rogers, Walter White, James Baldwin, Kenneth Little, Michael Banton, John Otto Reineman, Robert Aron, Roi Ottley, and Sir Alan Burns. Their experiences and observations have by no means been uniform, and there has been variation of opinion both on the kind of treatment accorded the Negro in Europe and on the reasons for it. Overwhelmingly they report that the Negro is well treated in France, but some few writers, most of them Negroes, consider that not all Frenchmen are friendly toward him. Some, as Ottley, believe that the northern Europeans who have seen few Negroes are more cordial toward their race than the southern Europeans; others, like Baldwin, hold a different view. Some consider all Europeans friendly toward the Negro, but most of them concede that here and there cordiality is lacking.

These writers do not often state the reason for unfriendliness, although some have laid it at the door of white Americans traveling in Europe. Few try to analyze it. Baldwin thought that he discerned aloofness and hostility among some inhabitants of a Swiss mountain village who had never before seen a Negro; he even thought that he saw evidence of hostility on the part of some of the children who were reluctant to meet him or who called him in good German, "Neger! Neger!" Ottley, on the other hand, thought those Europeans who never had colonies to be free of racial prejudice; it is the colonizing experience that explains the matter. Of course it is generally recognized by everyone that color is the basic cause for whatever discrimination exists, and it may be added that the Negro's record as a slave race constitutes the second. Competition as a laborer often provides a third.

France is commonly known throughout the world for friendliness toward the Negro. It is doubtful whether any other country has a better record for having befriended the Negro or for the degree of hospitality which has been extended to him. This is not to credit all Frenchmen, either of the present or of times past, with freedom from racial bias. For two centuries or more, French planters of the West Indies, Guiana, and certain islands of the Indian Ocean enslaved and exploited the Negro, often treating him brutally. Some Frenchmen today dislike the Negro. Perhaps few French women of the middle and upper classes would entertain a proposal to marry a Negro. Thus there are some qualifications to be made, but despite them it can still be said that, generally speaking, the Negro is welcomed to France, and even embraced. He is given all the liberty of a French citizen (for such he is), and this liberty extends to all categories—economic, educational, social, and political.

This is not to say that the same conditions prevail in the colonies. The present book is a study only of the history of the Negro in Metropolitan France. In the colonies at present all natives are citizens and can vote in elections for parliamentary bodies that control them, but prior to the establishment of the Fourth Republic in 1947, citizenship was open only to a few. These few mingled with the white officials, for citizenship gave them social as well as political privileges. Theoretically, even racial intermarriage was possible in the colonies, but if I am correctly informed, it rarely took place. White officialdom stood at the peak of the social scale; after it came the native ruling class, and especially any mulattoes. In Africa, mulattoes were virtually nonexistent, but in the West

Indies they were fairly numerous, class conscious, and proud.
So they have always been, and they have tended to marry
within their own ranks. The Negroes, or blacks, have been left
largely to marry among themselves. This class snobbishness
shows itself also in the West Indian's treatment of the French
African. Similarly the American Negro in France has a tendency not to associate greatly with the French Negro. The
aloofness between these three groups is well understandable
when it is considered that each has a different cultural background. The West Indian alone of the lot has French as his
native language, and his history has long been associated
with that of France, so that he considers himself a Frenchman,
and French culture his culture. Reportedly he looks con-
descendingly on the French African as half barbarous, a
denizen of the jungle. This latter has learned French as a
second language. He is delighted with French civilization
insofar as it gives him a chance to acquire Western civilization
and the advantages that go with it. But it is only a means to
an end, for above everything else he craves independence.
The American Negro, who goes in amazing numbers to France,
regards it as the Mecca, the Oxford, the Stratford-on-Avon of
Negro aspiration and culture. There he finds all the intellectual
freedom and social equality that he has sought elsewhere and
too frequently missed. Many in all three groups decide to
settle in France, and this has gone on for decades.

Why France exerts such an appeal for the Negro is analyzed
in this book. It is not something that has come about by the
wave of a wand, but only after centuries in which the Negro
has found in France opportunity for service and advancement,
for comfort and pleasure, to a degree not found elsewhere.
There he has repeatedly been part of the record of French
history. When I first began this study in the 1940's, I had but
the faintest idea of the enormous part the Negro has played in
French history. I tackled it out of curiosity, but the subject
has opened up like an unexplored cave to larger and larger
treasure chambers.

The Negro's residence in France has been one of long duration, going back at least to the 1600's. The first Negroes to arrive perhaps were galley slaves, and these were followed, up to 1848, by a procession of colonial slaves, picked to attend sieur or madame while on a visit in France. They bunked in the hold of the ship and ate with other servants or with the crew. They knew not where they were going, but any change from slavery in the colonies was welcome. In France they found themselves in a strange world, with all men staring at them in turn as curiosities. Many were put into gay uniforms, as pages, butlers, valets, coachmen. This they liked, even if they were relegated to some attic for their lodging and to the servants' table for meals. When their stay was ended, they did not want to return home; the months or years had fled by all too quickly. The French were good to them, and they found companions in other slaves residing in the same cities—Paris and the large ports of Bordeaux, Le Havre, Rouen, Nantes, Rochefort, Marseilles, and Toulon, for the most part. It is difficult to revive the picture of those days, for the France of that period has departed entirely, with its lords and ladies, its elegant carriages, its powdered hair and lace jabots.

The only census of the Negro ever undertaken in France was made in that period—in 1777-1778, to be precise—and no complete figures even then were tabulated. Police officials estimated the number at 5,000, but that figure is preposterous; the sum of the figures by municipalities does not exceed 1,000. Perhaps the reason for negligence to compute the total was discovery that it was well-nigh impossible to get a report on all the Negroes. Their number was anything but constant; always some were arriving and some were leaving. It has been that way ever since; the Negro has commonly been a transient in France, staying only a few months or a few years, and then his place is taken by others. The normal French censuses, it should be mentioned, have considered the Negroes as citizens, and they give no data on racial or religious minorities.

Even in the early days the Negro had his friends in France. Sometimes for faithful service he was manumitted by his master or mistress; sometimes the church or a noble lady would take his part to prevent his return to the colonies. But these champions had limits to their zeal, and there arose no crusaders to espouse their cause before the Revolution, when the good Abbé Grégoire by accident took it up. He was never in the colonies and knew nothing at first hand about slavery. In fact, situated as he was in a small town in the hills of Alsace, he perhaps had never seen more than two or three Negroes. Even the church was split over the cause of slavery; some priests and religious orders had slaves. Thanks to the efforts of the Abbé Grégoire and others, however, both white and black, the Revolutionary government abolished slavery in early 1794. Theoreticaly this applied only to the colonies, since slavery was never recognized as existing in France; and yet, prior to 1794, slaves had been admitted to France, where they served their masters and mistresses, despite laws and regulations to the contrary.

Already by the time of the Revolution many Negroes were settled in France, as servants, innkeepers, or petty shopkeepers. Not a few had entered the army, some as freedmen, others as runaway slaves. Their most usual role was that of drummer or bugler. Prior to 1789 only one body of Negro troops in France had been sufficiently large to be a segregated or unified body —the guard of Maurice de Saxe—but with the outbreak of war during the Revolution a number of Negro and mulatto units came into being, some segregated, others intermingled with whites. Certain individual soldiers rose to high rank, even to that of general. They fought on all battlefronts in the Napoleonic wars, and some distinguished themselves for conspicuous bravery.

Others showed a facility for politics. During the Revolution the first Negro deputies came to Paris and sat in the French governing bodies. Others took an active part in the local Jacobin clubs. With only some rare exceptions, the Negroes realized the significance of the Revolution for their cause and came out strongly in its support. In their political activity, more violent in the colonies than in France, they revealed a proclivity for politics that has marked them ever since. Adroitly they saw their advantage in allying with one of the white factions, and thus they adopted the Machiavellian principle of dividing and conquering their enemies—if the whites can be so called. Following that tack, the Negroes have won victory after victory, both in that day and this.

Subsequent to the Revolution the Negro has traveled more and more to France as a freeman. Since 1848, when slavery was abolished for a second time and permanently, only as freemen have they gone to France, if we except the African soldiers, especially in the two World Wars; and yet, even for European service in these wars, the Negro soldiers volunteered.

More and more since the Revolution the Negro has gone to France for his education. Even previously a few natural sons were educated there, and there too all slaves accompanying their master or mistress were supposed to receive an education in the principles of Christianity. It was a state regulation, and the slaveowners on the one hand and the church on the other gave lipservice to this farcial requirement. In addition, the slaves, especially the boys, were to be taught a trade by some guildmaster. This was an education of practical value, and the colonies had need of it. In them white artisans could not compete with slave labor, and this made it essential for plantation owners to train their own needed skilled workmen.

With the outbreak of the Revolution, and even earlier, this trade education had broken down and was succeeded by literary and scientific training, which has continued in increasing degree until today. The professional men in the various French colonies have largely been educated in France—lawyers, physicians, engineers, priests, and others. After their training they have for the most part returned to the colonies. A few have remained in France. The extent of this educational activity today is so wide that it runs all the gamut from theology and law to technology and scientific agriculture. From the French angle perhaps the fact of greatest significance is that these students return home in most instances with happy memories of their days in France, and hence are friends. Most of them speak French fluently, continue to read French books, and thus promote French culture in the world. In a few rare instances these dusky students from the faraway colonies have done so well that they have been able to find opportunity for remaining to teach in lycée or university in France—an honor highly prized by the French themselves.

The Negro too has had his part to play in intercollegiate and municipal athletics which have developed so rapidly in the twentieth century. Athletic participation by Negro colonials in France also has increased, and it is to be observed that some of the leading French athletes have been Negroes. Their favorite sports have been mainly track, football, and boxing, activities demanding above all speed and coordination.

Since World War I the Negro has emerged in France as an entertainer—in music, dancing, and vaudeville. American Negro bands made a sensational impression on the French in late World War I, and from that day to this their popularity has only augmented. One may be surprised that the French who are such trained musical critics are fond of jazz, but they are; at least there are those who go in numbers to attend the jazz performances of the many American colored orchestras that visit France. They also like the spirituals and classic music, the latter sung by such a person as Marian Anderson. Some of the Negro singers and dancers have acquired widespread reputation. Josephine Baker, who established her fame largely in France, is a world-known artist.

In literature Negroes have taken an active role since the 1790's and have done remarkably well. In fact it can be pointed out as the field in which their most conspicuous success thus far has been achieved. In poetry, drama, and the novel—and especially historical fiction—they have made some remarkable productions. Among those contributing, several may be designated as major writers—the two Dumas and René Maran. In history, political thought, philosophy, theology, and science they have done less well, perhaps because these fields of endeavor demand longer and more rigorous education than most of the Negroes have received. That they do well in poetry and fiction is no doubt due to the fact that in these an elemental genius shines better than in the more demanding fields. The success of some has inspired the others, and no area of human endeavor has so attracted the Negro intellectual in France as the literary. All would be a Dumas *père*. Throughout the nineteenth century and subsequently, France has had its circle of Negro *littérateurs*.

It was in literature almost alone that the Negro in France in the latter half of the nineteenth century acquitted himself with distinction. During this period, or rather from about 1840 to 1914, little mention is made of Negro residents in the records. It was as if emancipation from slavery, which in March, 1848, came for the second time and permanently, was sufficient for his welfare and he needed no further attention. He was now treated as a common French citizen, losing racial identity, as indeed he wanted to be. But really it was unfortunate for him in that the historian has great difficulty in following his steps during this interval, and to a lesser degree even later.

Today the Negro writers are eclipsed in prestige by the politicians. Negro support to France in the two World Wars of the twentieth century has brought political recognition, and several Negroes have been named to French cabinets. Certain of them have become well known throughout France, as MM. Monnerville, Houphouet-Boigny, and Senghor. Establishment of the Union Française in 1946 and of the French Community in 1959 has set up a French league of nations, in which delegates from the colonies sit on relatively equal basis with those of France around the council table at Paris, Tananarive, Saint-Louis, or elsewhere to discuss problems of imperial concern. This of course places the respective delegates very much in the spotlight of French attention. It is a role which their representatives can fill with competency. Most of them have been educated either at the Colonial School in Paris or at one of the French universities and have read sufficiently to be well informed on national and world problems. The majority incline toward socialism or communism and have a keen knowledge of materialistic needs. Even more are they nationalist in spirit and desirous of independence for their countries. It appears moreover that most of them are well-to-do property owners at home and more capitalist at heart than communist, and that they really wish only political control of their colonies in their own hands.

The story seems like one from *Arabian Nights*—a tale of thousands of Negroes who came by boat from the colonies as slaves in the eighteenth century, of their remarkable part in the Revolutionary and Napoleonic armies, of their extraordinary contribution to French literature during the nineteenth and twentieth centuries, of their role as a savior of France in World War I and World War II, and now in their part as collaborators with France in its great imperial organization, the French Community of Nations. Is it not astounding that a Negro colonial from Africa was deemed significant enough to be buried, with highest honors, in the Pantheon, that Valhalla of French immortals? And the end of Negro achievement is not in sight.

ONE       EARLIEST NEGRO
ARRIVALS


*I*N EUROPE of the ancient Grae-
co-Roman world, Negroes were rarities; it was in the medieval
period that they first appeared in numbers. Many came to
Constantinople in the sixth and seventh centuries A.D., both
as freemen and as slaves. A black contingent served with the
Arab army that attacked Sicily in 902. In the eleventh century
several thousand black troops from Senegal, the Sudan, and
Morocco were used by the Arabs in Spain in their warfare with
the Christians; and in 1099 some Ethiopians served in the
defense of Jerusalem against the Crusaders. These first arrivals
were naturally seen in the southernmost countries, but by the
fifteenth and sixteenth centuries they were becoming somewhat
more numerous and more dispersed.[1] What is perhaps the
earliest painting of a Negro was a head drawn by Veronese
(1528-1588) which today forms part of the valuable Lehman
Art Collection of New York. Upon request of the French, this
collection was displayed in Paris in the summer of 1957.

[1] Thomas M. Jones, "East Indian Influences upon the Early Byzantine
Empire," *Journal of Negro History*, XLIII (1958), 57-58; Charles Mangin,
"Soldats noirs en Europe," *Questions diplomatiques et coloniales*, année 13
(Oct. 1909), 449-53; Fulcher of Chartres, quoted in Leon Bernard and
Theodore B. Hodges, *Readings in European History* (New York, 1958), p. 103;
Henry R. Hart, *Sea Road to the Indies* (New York, 1950), pp. 13-14;
*Cambridge Modern History*, I (New York, 1907), 349; Louis Battifol, *The
Century of the Renaissance* (New York, 1935), p. 69; *The Fugger News-
Letters . . .*, ed. by Victor von Klarwill (New York and London, 1925), p. 30;
and Jacob Christoph Burckhardt, *The Civilization of the Renaissance in Italy*, tr.
by C. G. C. Middlemore (London, 1878, 2 v.), II, 18 with n2.

Some Negroes brought to Bordeaux by a shipowner and placed on sale there in 1571 were ordered released by the parlement of that city on the ground that slavery did not exist in France. Thus, one of the earliest records of the presence of Negroes in France declared their right to freedom. Many other Negroes were in France or had been there by 1594 and spoke French well, reported a Portuguese writer, Alvarez d'Almada.[2]

This was before the French had entered the slave trade, in which they were relative latecomers. The Portuguese, the English, and the Dutch were all earlier participants, the Portuguese having made their start in the 1400's and the English in the 1500's. Though a company was formed at Rouen in 1639, the French did not enter the slave trade in earnest until 1670, through the West India Company.[3]

By this latter date, Negroes, though still rarities, were coming to Europe in greater numbers. One hundred and forty are reported to have been employed to form the impressive retinue of the French ambassador, the Comte d'Avaux, in peace negotiations at Munster in 1644—this at a time when the dignity of officials was reckoned in part by the display and ostentation they could afford. During the Holy Week of that year the Comte and his great black entourage attended the cathedral. The three Spanish envoys entering shortly afterward found the French already there in more impressive form and indignantly left to worship elsewhere. That so large a number of Negroes could be assembled at one spot in Europe as early as 1644 seems almost incredible, but the report of it comes from Saint-Romain, agent of the French ambassador who preceded him to Munster in 1643 and made arrangements there for him. It thus has a claim to reliability, although the reader is given no details as to how the Negroes were gathered or as to what became of them. Evidently they must have been

[2] Charles de la Roncière, *Nègres et négriers* (9th ed., Paris, 1933), p. 16.
[3] *Ibid.*, pp. 14-20.

enlisted in France and taken to Germany, but of this there is no certainty.[4]

Some Negroes were brought by the French for galley slaves to row their war vessels in the 1600's, but they were prone to die of tuberculosis and the practice ceased. Several hundred reportedly were brought from West Africa for this purpose in the 1670's. One hundred and forty Negroes arrived in one cargo, but 68 fell sick and 18 died. After this, none were actually put in the galleys.[5] That they were brought as mercenaries rather than as slaves seems apparent.

The Negro king of Dahomey in 1670 dispatched Matteo Lopez "as ambassador" to the court of Louis XIV, evidently to promote the slave trade. Lopez was accompanied by three wives and three sons, and also by five Negroes, a trumpeter and four valets or personal servants. They were received in dignity in Martinique and at Dieppe, and again, on December 19 of that year, at the Tuileries. This last reception was a pompous affair, large bodies of troops being drawn up to grace the occasion and the party of Lopez proceeding through long lines of soldiers.[6]

[4] M. E. T. Hamy, "Les cent quarante nègres de M. d'Avaux à Munster (1644). Anecdote ethnologique racontée," *Bulletins et mémoires de la Société d'Anthropologie de Paris* (Paris, 1906), pp. 271-73.

That the anecdote may be seriously questioned, however, is suggested by the fact that it is unmentioned by the almoner and secretary to the Comte d'Avaux, François Ogier, who accompanied the Comte to Munster and in his *Journal* records details of the trip and those of Easter week, 1644, without once mentioning the Negroes. See the *Journal du Congrès de Munster* by François Ogier, published by Auguste Boppe (Paris, 1893).

Ogier mentions the contest that developed over protocol and the ostentatious retinue of the Comte d'Avaux, but, clergyman that he was, he picks out the clergy of this convoy to discuss. Ogier himself preached once during the Easter week at Munster. His omission of the episode about the Negroes is not, of course, assurance that the story is untrue, but it does throw suspicion to that effect.

[5] Albert Rambaud, *Histoire de la civilisation française*, II (Paris, 1887), 242; Ernest Lavisse, "Sur les galères du roi," *Revue de Paris* (1897), 233-34; Paul Walden Bamford, "The Procurement of Oarsmen for the French Galleys, 1660-1748," *American Historical Review*, LXVI (1959), 31.

[6] Charles Bourd de la Roncière, *Histoire de la Marine française*, V (Paris, 1920), 495-96.

Shortly thereafter, in 1679, eighty-five Negroes were brought to Marseilles by a Captain Bonneau. The frigate carrying them had weathered a storm off the coast of Portugal, and some repairs had been necessary before it could proceed. No indication is given as to the destination of the Negroes, or whether they were slaves or freemen.[7]

On October 4, 1691, De Pontchartrain, Minister of the Marine, issued a declaration that thenceforth "Negroes brought into France would be free upon their arrival." This was rarely enforced during the following decades, however, because of the inconvenience it would have caused their owners, the West Indian planters, who brought them as their valets and maids.[8]

Michelet reports that Anne of Austria apparently gave her son, the Duc d'Orleans, brother of Louis XIV, as a mistress an old Negress who had been her chambermaid.[9] The story is also told by Saint-Simon and others that Louis XIV was fond of a Moorish mistress, the Mooress of Moret. She is sometimes referred to as a Negress, but this is a matter of uncertainty. She went into a convent in 1695, becoming a nun at Moret, and Madame de Maintenon there made visits to her from time to time. She was a person of much curiosity at the court, and various tales arose as to her background, she herself believing that she was the daughter of Louis XIV. She lived until 1732, and in her last years visited Maria Leczinska, queen of Louis XV.[10]

At the court of Louis XIV, Negroes were frequently seen, illustrating the quickening of French ties with Africa and

[7] Archives Nationales, Fonds de la Marine, B² 41, f 173. Cf. *ibid.*, ff 148 and 234.

[8] "Principes de la Marine, tirés des despêches et des ordres du roi, donnés sous les ministères de Colbert, de Seignelay, de Pontchartrain père et fils, du conseil de Marine et de Morville de 1669 à 1723," by Pidansat de Mairobert, MS. of 244 feuillets in Bibliothèque Historique de la Marine, f 118. This declaration is not to be found in the Code Noir, designed to regulate treatment of the Negro in the colonies.

[9] *Histoire de France au dix-septième siècle*, XIII (Paris, 1860), 21.

[10] J. Mathorez, *Les étrangers en France sous l'Ancien Régime* (Paris, 1919-21, 2 v.), I, 396.

the slave trade. Mathorez relates several instances of early Negroes to France.[11] Ten Negro slaves were sent by the King of Ethiopia to conduct to Louis XIV a present of horses and elephants. De Beaufort, a traveler to North Africa, brought back in 1663 as a gift to Queen Marie Theresa a little Negro boy, who became her frequent attendant. Another Negro boy at the court, given by an African prince in 1681 to Pontchartrain, was baptized at Fontainebleau, and Marie Theresa and the Comte de Brienne acted as his godparents on the occasion, holding him at the font. The baptism of a Negro child was a notable incident in France of this period, and was to continue so into the nineteenth century. On such occasions it was common for persons of distinction to attend the service and act as godparents.[12] This was not the first instance of Negro baptism in France; one occurred at Saint-Malo in 1597, when a little Negro boy aged ten to twelve, from Guinea, was baptized and received the Christian name of Antoine de Launay.[13]

In seventeenth-century France some Negro princes, actual or alleged, began to appear. One was Zaga-Christ, supposed son of the Negus of Ethiopia, Yacoub. He came to Paris in 1634, after a sojourn of several months in various Italian cities, where he received attention from French officials and even the Pope. In Turin, where he was a guest of the Duke of Savoy, he fell sick and was a ward of the Duke for eight months. At Paris he quickly built up a reputation as a devotee of Venus, and several incidents occurred in which he was embarrassed. He died in 1638, at Rueil, a guest of the Cardinal de Richelieu. Mathorez regards him as the genuine son of the Negus of Ethiopia, but some Frenchmen of the seventeenth century considered him an impostor, possibly because of his poverty. He was continually asking money of Richelieu and others whom he met.[14]

[11] *Ibid.*, I, 387-404.       [12] *Ibid.*, I, 394.
[13] *Ibid.*, I, 389. Mathorez also tells of one around 1676 at Ingrandes, a town in Anjou.
[14] *Ibid.*, I, 390-91.

# 16 THE NEGRO IN FRANCE

A prince or impostor of more interest was Aniaba, one of two Negroes sent back to France in 1687 by two French missionaries of the Dominican order to the Ivory Coast. C. W. Cole calls them slaves given the missionaries by the chief of Assinie. With the Negroes, Father Gonsalvez sent a letter saying that Aniaba was heir to the throne of that country. This erroneous statement, combined with Aniaba's high intelligence, enabled him to make a great impression in France. His popularity was increased by his willingness to receive the Christian faith and baptism. The French treated him as a prince. When he was baptized in 1692, the ceremony was held in Nôtre Dame and it was conducted by no less a dignitary than Bossuet; Louis himself acted as his godfather and gave him his own name. For his first communion he was instructed by the Cardinal de Noailles. Later he was created a captain in the French cavalry by Louis. When in 1700 news came that the chief of Assinie was dead, Louis hastened to send Aniaba on a French warship to assume charge of his kingdom, accompanied by a newly appointed apostolic prefect to the coast of Guinea. What was the surprise of the French on arriving but to find the natives of Assinie totally uninterested in Aniaba, considering him only as a former slave! The French then dropped him and did not press his claims.[15]

André Ducasse considers Aniaba as the genuine son of the chieftain of Assinie, and adds that homesickness was a factor in taking him back to Africa. There he reverted to nudity and shuffled off Christianity and French customs.[16] Simone Berbain, on the other hand, agrees with Cole in calling him a fake prince, but states that he was brought to France by Ducasse, who returned in 1687 from an official mission to the African coast, as a token of friendship on the part of the tribe.[17] There is archival evidence that the so-called prince ran up some debts

[15] Charles Woolsey Cole, *French Mercantilism, 1683-1700* (New York, 1943), p. 104.
[16] *Les négriers ou le traffic des esclaves* (Paris, 1948), pp. 48-49.
[17] *Etudes sur la traite des noirs au Golfe de Guinée: Le comptoir français de Juda (Ouidah) au XVIIIe siècle* (Paris, 1942), p. 38.

in France and was able to leave despite demand for their payment. At the time of his departure in 1701 he and Dumesnil, his French guardian, owed 31,500 livres, a considerable sum; the matter was brought to the attention of the Minister of the Marine in an effort to prevent them from leaving the country.[18] It is not clear how much of the debt was Aniaba's and how much Dumesnil's. The pressure was put on Dumesnil, but it appears that the creditors pursued him thinking they had a better chance of collecting from him than from Aniaba. It appears, moreover, that both left their debts unpaid.

The French government contracted in advance to pay the travel expenses of another African "prince" in 1701. This one came from Alexandria by boat to Marseilles, thence by coach to Paris. He was described as being from twenty-six to twenty-eight years old, handsome, "beautiful though black," with a mind "mature and refined" and "a desire to learn." It was also reported that "he likes wine, gets drunk, and is very brutal when he has drunk." Some fantastic tales were circulated concerning him. He was regarded very much as the "Grand Turk" in Molière's *Bourgeois gentilhomme*. This attitude, indeed, appears to have been taken toward the other "princes" as well. It will be recalled that Peter the Great on the occasion of his visit to Paris was given similar treatment. Molière had died in 1673, but he discerned and satirized well this French adulation of visiting aristocracy.[19]

Other African "princes" were to come to France in the decades that followed, some genuine, some impostors, for study and other purposes. They were perhaps the most interesting of the early Negro visitors to France, and in general their visits were to cement French ties with Africa and to further the development of the slave trade.

[18] Le Comte de Gacé to De Ponant, 2 April 1701, Archives Nationales, Fonds de la Marine, B³ 113. Part of this sum was owed to creditors at Lille and Isle-en-Flandre. See Du Gué de Bagnols to the Minister of the Marine, *ibid.*, B³ 111, ff 401, 402, 403.

[19] Gimbal to the Minister of the Marine, April 6, 12, and 13, 1701, Archives Nationales, Fonds de la Marine, B³ 114, ff 540, 541, 544.

The most noted of all such Negro visitors to France was
Abram Hannibal, son of the Negus of Ethiopia, who was
captured in an African war and sold in the slave market of
Constantinople at the age of eight. There a Russian nobleman
bought him and gave him as a present to Peter the Great, who
became fond of him and had him instructed in the Orthodox
faith. In 1707 he was baptized and given the name Abram
Hannibal. He was treated as a member of Peter's own family
and taken on trips with him. In 1716 Peter sent him to Paris
to study military engineering, in order that he might serve
in the Russian army. In Paris he attracted much attention,
remaining there until 1723 and serving for a time as an officer
in the French army. The Duc d'Orleans, to whom he had
become a favorite, tried to prevail on him to remain in
France, but he insisted on returning to Russia, where throughout Peter's lifetime he stood well, held high army posts, and
was so happy that he refused to return to his native country
even after receiving a request from his brother to do so.
After Peter's death, however, he fell from favor, and two years
later (1727) he was sent on a three years' exile to Siberia.
There he suffered great privations. At length in 1741 Peter's
daughter Elizabeth, now Czarina, restored him to favor, gave
him one high position and honor after another, and thus made
amends for his long neglect by previous rulers. Married to a
German girl, he became the father of five sons, descended
from one of whom was the great Russian literary figure
Alexander Pushkin.[20]

Prior to 1700 virtually every Negro visitor to France came
from Africa itself. Of these, some were from Ethiopia, a few
from the Barbary Coast, but the greater number were from
Guinea and the Ivory Coast. A few were from Madagascar.
Mathorez reports that for having brought to France some
Hovas from that island, an army captain named Regimont was

[20] Beatrice F. Fleming and Marion J. Pryde, *Distinguished Negroes Abroad*
(Washington, 1946), pp. 166-70; Henri Grégoire, *De la littérature des nègres,
ou recherches sur les facultés intellectuelles* . . . (Paris, 1808), pp. 197-98.

imprisoned in the Bastille in 1636 and left there several years. The reason for such action, when it was not forbidden to bring Negroes to France, is not explained. Other Madagascans were brought to France in 1648 and 1672. In the last group was one little girl of six or seven who was baptized.[21]

Negroes shared in the vicissitudes of the eighteenth-century European wars. In February, 1703, at the outset of the War of the Spanish Succession, a British vessel with 330 Negroes aboard was captured by the French near Ile du Prince, off Africa, but whether they were brought to France is not made clear. Later, on March 24, two other ships, one British, one Dutch, both laden with Negroes, were captured.[22] The French appear to have lost more Negroes at sea in these wars than they captured, however, for there are repeated mentions of their losses. Generally the French reduced or brought their slave trade operations to an end at the outbreak of hostilities, but it was impossible to do anything about cargoes already under sail. Immediately on restoration of peace the slave trade hummed again. In the first quarter of the eighteenth century, vessels from Nantes had the lion's share of the French slave trade. Of the 75 vessels transporting 11,833 Negroes to Martinique in the years 1714-1721, 59 were Nantais.[23]

Even early in the 1700's an occasional Negro ran afoul of the law. A Negro named Julien, who called himself a son of the "King of the Congo," was condemned to the French galleys for robbery and placed in the hospital for galley slaves at Toulon. There he proved to be a troublemaker. Using a knife to saw off his chains, he wounded or killed his guards and set fire to some bedclothes. The fire was extinguished by some

[21] Mathorez, *Les étrangers en France*, I, 392-93.

[22] *Inventaire-sommaire des archives départementales antérieures à 1790. Département du Finistère. Série B. Amirauté de Léon à Brest*, p. 19.

[23] Léon Vignols, "La piraterie sur l'Atlantique au XVIIIe siècle," *Annales de Bretagne*, V (Rennes, 1889-90), 244. The intendant of Santo Domingo in February, 1781, stated that no Negroes had been sent back from France since 1778. But in March, 1783, they were landing almost daily in France. Léon Vignols, *Les esclaves coloniaux en France au XVIIe et XVIIIe siècle et leur retour aux Antilles* (Rennes, 1927), p. 5.

Protestant fellow slaves. Julien was tried for this action and strangely enough exonerated, but shortly afterward he committed suicide. During this trial he admitted that he was not, as he had claimed to be, the son of a chieftain.[24]

In that same year (1706) a free Negro born in Havana, named Michel Joseph, on his third voyage to France had shipped as a stowaway aboard *Le Conventry* after a fight in Havana with another Negro. Fearing punishment, he had slipped into the ship's hold and hid until the vessel was out at sea. On landing at Port Louis, near Lorient, he was taken ashore, and his case was reported to the Ministry of the Marine at Paris for disposition. Clairambault, the Marine official at Lorient, stated that Michel Joseph wished to spend a year in France and afterward to rejoin his father, Jean François, in Havana. Mentioned in his favor was the fact that both he and his father were "bon catholique apostolique et Romain." What disposition was made of the case is not reported. It was the first of many stowaway cases noticed in the Archives.[25]

The Negro was not only occasionally a law violator but sometimes a victim. A Negress named Marie Isabelle claimed that her mistress, the Demoiselle Accard, had given her a discharge in writing but afterward refused to pay her her dues or to let her cease work and wished to take her back to Martinique. The case was referred to the Ministry of the Marine, and the Negress was ordered freed and paid for her labor from the time that she had arrived in France, on the ground that Negroes were legally entitled to the same freedom in France as other subjects.[26]

In 1711 a Negro reported sold by the jailer of Dinant, Brittany, to some Irish officers of that city was the cause of quite a stir. The jailer was threatened with imprisonment,

[24] Etienne Creisel, *Pierre, David et Jean Serres: galériens protestants, 1685-1714* (Cahors, 1900), pp. 107-108. Creisel says that Louis considered some Protestants as responsible for the fire and confined them to the Château d'If.

[25] Clairabault to De Ponant, Archives Nationales, Fonds de la Marine, B3 137, f 679.

[26] De Ponant to Lombard, 9 July 1710, Archives Nationales, Fonds de la Marine, B2 222, f 57.

but no one could be found to jail him and so he remained at freedom. The charge, moreover, could not be proved, so that the local official could only threaten to force the jailer to pay the Negro's expenses to the colonies. This official reported to the Ministry of the Marine that he had the jailer frightened, as was very likely the case, but there is no evidence that the jailer admitted guilt or paid the money or that the Negro gained his freedom.[27]

These were but precursors of many similar cases yet to come, for the status of the Negro in eighteenth-century France was confused. Freedom from slavery was recognized by French laws as a heritage of long standing, and no Frenchman could be enslaved. Nor could anyone in France be bought or sold. But if a planter wanted to bring a valet or a maid for service to his family while in France, could he not bring a slave from the colonies? And could he not take this slave back on his return? For slavery in the colonies had official recognition. The matter was a thorny one, and it was brought to the fore in 1715 when a Negro girl was freed, thanks to some nuns at Nantes. The girl's mistress had placed her with the nuns of Calvary at Nantes while she made a trip to Paris. On her return, the nuns refused to release the girl. The matter was taken into court and sharply debated for some time, with an ultimate decision of liberty for the girl on the ground that the owner had failed to declare her a slave when entering France. The decision was thus rendered on a legal technicality.[28]

Shortly afterward Gérard Mellier, mayor of Nantes, sent a several-page memoir to the Royal Council of the Marine, which itself was a reply to an earlier memoir by another party in regard to the status of slaves in France and the policy which the government should adopt toward them. Evidently the earlier memoir had proposed their complete liberation when they set foot on French soil; Mellier took a different view.

[27] Letters from l'Empéreur to De Ponant, Archives Nationales, Fonds de la Marine, B³ 195, ff 237, 240, 270.

[28] See the very interesting "Mémoire de Gérard Mellier, maire de Nantes, justifiant la traite des nègres," Archives de la Loire-Inférieure, C 741.

He set forth the current policy followed by officials of the Marine in the various French ports and advocated its continuance. This practice enabled colonists to retain ownership of their slaves while in France provided that they registered them properly with port officials on their arrival. They might thereby claim their service while in the country and on their departure take the slaves back with them. Failure to carry out this legal technicality was sufficient ground to justify a slave to claim his freedom. Mellier cited the case of the girl left with the nuns of Calvary at Nantes.

Mellier proceeded to justify his position. He stated that the African tribes, who were continually at war with one another, normally killed their prisoners; but they would sell them to Europeans, a more desirable fate than death. Secondly, he said that if the planters were not permitted to bring their slaves into France, they would be obliged to bring whites to serve as domestics, and this would operate against French hopes of building up a white population in the colonies. Thirdly, if planters were not permitted to retain the service of their slaves in France, they would cease to bring them for apprenticeship in the various trades as they had been doing. This training of the slaves was of value both to the planters and to the colonies. Finally, it was important that the Negroes learn something of France and French culture and return to report on it to their fellows. He referred to the son of the "King of Albany" who had been sent to France by his father for an education, and said that it was customary for the shipowners and captains engaged in the slave trade "to bring one or two to France by each vessel, at their own expense, in order that they might learn the language and later be sent back" to serve as interpreters and inform their people better concerning French ways. For example, he said, the blacks of Africa were of the opinion that the red wine drunk by the French was the blood of their fellow Negroes. This was a great deterrent to the slave trade, since it made captured Negroes morbid and induced them to commit suicide en route to America.

Mellier advocated strongly the retention of the current French practices regarding planters and their slaves.

On the other hand, he was not in favor of the Negro being permitted to marry while in France. For children born to slaves from union with whites he favored freedom. Moreover, he was of the opinion that planters should not be allowed to rush to France with their slaves to escape their creditors in the colonies. In such cases he insisted that creditors should be privileged to seize the slaves and take them back to the colonies for sale and reimbursement. No Negroes, however, should be sold or traded in France; if a master wished to dispose of a slave, he should be obliged to return him to the colonies for that purpose.

Mellier asked for a new declaration or statement of policy by the government which would clear up the confusion on these points.[29] From time to time in the eighteenth century, declarations were made which expressed Mellier's views, but the position of the Negro was never entirely clarified, and down to the end of the Old Regime there continued to arise those who, like the nuns of Calvary, became champions of liberty for the slaves brought to French soil.

By 1716 planters were bringing Negroes in fair numbers on their trips to France. They were not only servants but ornaments, for to cut a good figure in French society on his return from the colonies, a planter must be accompanied by one or more blacks. The eighteenth century was to see an ever-increasing tide of them, until in time the government itself was to become alarmed at their numbers and what they portended for the future population and manners.

The information given in the sources concerning these "earliest arrivals" of the Negro race in France is limited indeed. The historian wishes that more details were available, but those who mentioned the Negroes in official correspondence and other writings were concerned principally with other matters. We have only a hazy picture of the dress of the early

[29] *Ibid.*

Negro visitors, of their rooms and food, of their social contacts, of their difficulties. No marriages while in France are reported. The Negroes appear to have been received without prejudice, to have obtained much more attention than French visitors would have obtained from their fellows, and to have enjoyed their stay in the country. All apparently were "birds of passage," returning home after a period of residence; but of this there is no certainty. They were as much curiosities as the parrots and tropical birds brought back by travelers to faraway lands.

# TWO INFLUX OF COLONIAL SLAVES

*T*HE MEMOIR of Mellier, written in the spring of 1716, was one of several submitted to the government, possibly at its own solicitation. Remarkably enough, all of its suggestions were set forth in an Edict of October, 1716, by the Royal Council of State. This edict clarifying government policy in regard to the importation of Negro slaves in France by colonial slaveowners became the standard of action for more than two decades, and then it was but slightly modified by the Declaration of December, 1738. The Edict of 1716 gave significant concessions to slaveowners, who were allowed to bring their slaves to France, retain their services, and after an indefinite time return them to the colonies in the status of slavery, provided only that they scrupulously fulfilled certain procedures. They must obtain permission of the governor or commandant in the colony to bring the slave to France; they must register the slave within eight days after landing, and afterward in Paris at the Admiralty. Failure to conform to these regulations would make the owner liable to the heavy fine of 1,000 livres and the loss of the slave, who would be given his freedom. No slave might marry while in France without his master's consent, and if the master did consent, the slave would be regarded thenceforth as free. The master was responsible for maintenance of the slave; also, he was to receive any pay that might come from the slave's work for another party. The master was also to inherit any money belonging to a slave who died while in France.

Not without justifiable reason, however, might a master bring his slave to France. The owner must state in writing that it was for the purpose of teaching him a trade or of instructing him in the principles of the Christian religion as represented in the Catholic faith. Thenceforth until the Revolution this demand continued and was scrupulously followed. In virtually all the thousands of registrations of slaves with port authorities on entering France one finds the statement made that the slave under consideration (his name and age given) was to be taught a specified trade and instructed in the tenets of Catholicism. In this way the state justified slavery.[1]

In consequence of the protection under this law, slaveowners brought their slaves to France in ever-increasing numbers. However, it was reported that "most of the Negroes" developed in France a spirit of independence, while their master neglected to see that they learned a trade and in many cases even became indifferent to their return, "finding them most commonly useless and dangerous." To correct these and other undesirable tendencies resulting from the Edict of 1716, the Declaration of 1738 was promulgated. This act required the advance deposit with the Admiralty of 1,000 livres in caution money to assure the return of the slave to the colonies within three years; failure to take the slave back within this time limit would bring default of the sum to the government. The slave moreover must be registered on the day of his arrival in France. Neither might the slave marry while in France, even with his master's consent, and he might be freed only by testament or by the death of the owner before the time to return the slave to the colonies. It was required furthermore that the particular trade in which the slave was to be instructed must be stipulated, as well as the name of his instructor. Like the previous act, it stated that the slave must be reared in the Catholic faith. Slaves to be taken to Paris must be registered there, and slaves already in France must be registered anew

[1] The Edict of 1716 is found in the *Recueil général des anciennes lois françaises* . . . , ed. by F. A. Isambert *et al.* (Paris, 1822-33, 29 v.), XXI, 122-26.

within three months. The act was not greatly different from that of 1716; if anything, it imposed conditions slightly more severe on the slave, by forbidding marriage and endeavoring to make certain his return to the colonies. On the other hand, the measure was designed to assure his acquisition of technical knowledge and his greater service to society.[2]

The act was not designed to decrease the number of slaves brought to France, but merely to assure better control of their movement and actions and to make certain their return to the colonies. There was also the expressed desire that they not be allowed to marry into the French population. No limitation was placed upon the number of slaves that a master might bring, and for many years after 1738 it was not uncommon for an owner to bring two, three, or even more slaves, of one or both sexes. Registered with the Admiralty office at Nantes in 1742 were five slaves of one planter, Jean Jacques Lefebvre of Cap Français, Santo Domingo.[3]

In almost every instance the name, age, and a description of the slave were recorded, as prescribed by the laws of 1716 and 1738. The place of birth was usually noted, whether Africa or the colonies, and if the slave was branded, as was often the case, this fact too was reported. Usually the mark of his branding was designated.[4] Branding, as well known, was

[2] Paul Trayer, *Etude historique sur la condition légale des esclaves dans les colonies françaises* (Paris, 1887), pp. 93-94; Lucien Peytraud, *L'esclavage aux Antilles françaises avant 1789* (Paris, 1897), pp. 380-81; *Code noir, ou recueil des règlemens rendus jusqu'à présent* . . . (Paris, 1767), pp. 371-85. (This last gives the entire wording of the Declaration.)

[3] These were Thomas an eighteen-year-old Jamaican-born Negro; François, a seventeen-year-old Congo-born Negro; Thérèse, a twenty-four-year-old Creole (born in the colonies); Thérèse, twelve-year-old daughter of the above; and Jeanneton, a nineteen-year-old Creole. "Registre des receptions . . . commencé le 5 aoust et fini le deux mars 1741," Archives de la Loire-Inférieure, C 4515, pp. 163-64.

[4] *Ibid.*, pp. 89, 116. Among nineteen slaves registered at Nantes from June 30 to December 28, 1741, eight were branded. All save one were African-born. Branding was commonly done by the slave traders, and sometimes by the owners. Yet in this list certain slaves born in Africa were not branded, while at least one Creole, Marie Roze, twenty years old, was branded. *Ibid.*, pp. 110, 112, 122. Cf. Gaston Martin, *Négriers et bois d'ébène* (Grenoble, 1934), pp. 72-73; "Affiches américaines," Archives Nationales, Colonies, F[3] 150.

commonly employed in eighteenth-century France for those sent to the galleys and for repeated beggary. That anyone should have been branded, whether for legal infraction or as an indication of chattelism, is revolting to our conscience today, but it must be remembered that in the eighteenth century it provoked little criticism.

The names given slaves by their master are a feature of much interest. In rare instances the African names were retained, but in perhaps nineteen-twentieths or more of the cases the names were altered to meet European standards of taste. First and most heavily to be drawn upon was the great Biblical repository of names, like Pierre, Jacques, and Jean, for the men; and Marie, Anne, and Catherine for the women. Not infrequently a combination of two names was given, like Jean Jacques or Marie Anne. One can only surmise that in giving them these names, which commonly came at baptism, the owners placed them under the special protection of the saints invoked. Their continued use afterward, however, depended, it would seem, upon the religious temperament of the owners. A second great reservoir of names was classical, drawn from Greek and Roman history and mythology. Thus one meets repeatedly among the French slaves Jupiter, Apollo, Mercury, Priam, Hector, Achille, César, Pompée, Scipio, Télémaque, and Zephir, as recorded in the passenger lists of the vessels and in the registry lists of Negroes left by the Admiralty offices. There were also many names of French origin, a few coined by the owners, and a few of celebrated contemporaries. It is apparent that the owners found much amusement in bestowing some of these names—names like Jupiter, Pompée, César, Décembre, or Lamour. It is also evident that the masters held many of these slaves in great affection. In fact, when the masters and mistresses possessed many slaves, affection for a particular slave was probably the reason for his selection to make the trip to France—the equivalent in the life of the slave to the Grand Tour for the son of the English noble. A trip to France was certainly the greatest thing that a slave of that day could wish. It gave him a chance to see the great world of Europe, and he could never be quite the same person again.

Many were the trades that the slave would learn. Most frequently designated were those of barber, wigmaker, cooper, tailor, cook, painter, carpenter, and baker. Saltmaking, plow-making, and other occupations were sometimes named. For the women, the most frequently named trade was that of seamstress, but tailoring, wardrobe-keeping, and other skills were mentioned. Most girls and women, however, made the trip as nurses for their mistress and her children. None was listed as mistress for her master, but there can be little doubt that some served in that capacity.

As for age, the overwhelming majority of the slaves brought to France were less than thirty-five, but some were older. In reality, they ran the gamut from five to sixty. Almost as many were African-born as Creole, indicating that the Africans showed facility at learning the French language, although the Creoles possessed an advantage in having it as their native tongue. The large number of mulattoes brought over as the century advanced revealed that no seeming discrimination was displayed by the master between Negroes and mixed bloods. Many of the latter were brought and mentioned as quadroons, mulattoes, métis. M. Debien, one of the leading contemporary scholars on the history of the French West Indies, has pointed out that the colonists did not scruple to acknowledge their mixed-blood children.[5]

It was a period when the West Indian planters ranked among the rich people of France.[6] Perhaps none had more money to

[5] G. Debien, "Les travaux d'histoire sur Saint-Domingue. Chronique bibliographique (1950-1952)," *Revue de l'histoire des colonies françaises,* XL (1953), 455.

[6] A large coffee plantation in Santo Domingo, with ninety slaves, was sold in 1787 by Mardoché Mendes France (very likely an ancestor of M. Mendes France of our day) for the sum of 1,060,000 livres. An inventory of the property has been typed and is found in the Archives de la Ville du Havre, Période historique, série HH, liasse 71, Colonies 1787-1792. Another plantation which has come to the author's attention was valued at 2,500,000 livres. These were among the larger estates and give some idea of the wealth of the big planters.

display or to spend except princes of the blood and the high aristocracy. Society bowed before these planters, and the government in its legislation was constantly solicitous of their welfare, for some in fact were enobled.[7]

But life in the colonies was precarious because of the hazards of health. Neither slave nor planter could live there long. The supply of slaves was kept up by constant renewals; the planters were obliged to return with their families every few years to France for restoration of their health. No doubt boredom with the wilderness and desire for display also motivated their return. Certainly there was a constant movement of the richer colonists between the colonies and France, and many brought along one or more slaves. There was a maid for madame, a valet for monsieur, and a nurse or two for the children. Sometimes there were two or three male slaves. All were to be instructed in the Catholic faith and taught a trade, although mention of a trade was often omitted for the female slaves.

In France it was the day of the exotic. Dress, furniture, decorations, foods and drinks, books, and plays smacked of the faraway—of the Orient and America—and a sure way to prestige was to have a black in livery to open the door for madame's friends and to drive her carriage. How many were dressed in livery unfortunately is not stated in the records of the time. Many were not, for such conspicuous clothes would have handicapped them in their runnings away, but we can be sure that a large portion were. Little Negro boys were often presented as gifts to persons of prominence in France by officials and planters abroad. One boy of five or six years was sent to Marie Antoinette in 1787 by the Comte de Boufflers, governor of Senegal. He was baptized at Versailles, given the name of Jean Almicar, and placed under a teacher at the Queen's expense.[8] A little boy from India designated a Negro,

---

[7] For a study of this aspect, see Carl Ludwig Lokke, *France and the Colonial Question* . . . (New York, 1932).

[8] Mathorez, *Les étrangers en France*, I, 402.

named Zamore, was sent by another official to Madame du Barry. Little Negroes of this type, dressed in gaudy uniform, carried a parasol or fan for their mistress and threw down a rug for her to walk on when she descended from her carriage. They might also be called in to do tumbling as amusement for her friends. In short, they were curiosities from abroad, along with monkeys and parrots. Some of these little boys became spoiled and impudent. One named Scipio at the Palais Royal, accustomed to walking on his hands for the entertainment of the public, is reported to have accosted a princess, asking her, "Madame, why have you such a big nose?"[9] Apparently he escaped a caning, for little Negro boys were favored creatures. We are told that the Duchess of Chartres, wife of Louis Philippe, often took Scipio with her in her carriage and one evening took him to the theater. Because he was spoiled, there was some talk of sending him away from France, but he liked France and wanted to remain.[10]

Some instances of great affection for little Negroes were noted. Elie Germon, the hard, crusty captain of a slave ship carrying a load of six hundred Negroes from Angola to Santo Domingo in 1732, became so fond of a small Negro boy he attached to himself in the crossing that he decided not to put him ashore in Santo Domingo but to take him on to France. The captain became sick and died before reaching Santo Domingo, but before his death he communicated his intention to Sieur Baillou, his second in command, who carried out his wishes. The little boy was taken to La Rochelle, baptized under the name of André, and a curé named Jaillot was engaged to educate him and to instruct him in the Catholic faith. André became a domestic. In 1742 some question about his status must have arisen, for two citizens testified to this

---

[9] *Mémoires inédits de Madame la Comtesse de Genlis* . . . (2nd ed., Paris, 1825, 10 v.), IX, 308-309.

[10] *Ibid.* Richard Strauss in his opera *Rosenkavalier* introduces a little Negro boy into the cast as servant to his mistress. The setting is eighteenth century, though not French.

story at the office of the Admiralty in La Rochelle, insisting
that André should be free because the ship captain had so
intended.[11]

There is a similar story of the same time and city. The
Negro boy in this instance was Jean Medord, taken from
Guinea to Santo Domingo in 1735 when twelve years of age.
But he was not put ashore in Santo Domingo; rather he was
taken to France, baptized, and afterward received into the
Catholic church. He became chief servant in the home of a
prominent family on the Isle de Ré, a few miles from La
Rochelle. In consequence of the Declaration of 1738 he was
obliged to register at La Rochelle. A merchant of La Rochelle
named Regnaud de Beaulieu wrote in his behalf to Maurepas,
Minister of the Marine, giving details in the case and testifying
that he was not and never had been a slave.[12] The Negro in
this case had been brought from Africa by the father-in-law
of a wholesale merchant named Elie Dujardin. The story is so
close to that already related as to appear a variant, but the
deviations are too great and it must be regarded as a different
case.

Numerous instances of emancipation of slaves by their
masters and mistresses are recorded. Some were freed when
the slave was still young, others when he was well along in
years.[13] It does not appear that emancipation was employed
in these cases to escape expense and responsibility for the slave
in his declining years. No doubt there were some such
instances, but in most cases deep affection for the slave was
expressed. One reason that even more instances of emancipation did not occur was that the government imposed the high

11 "Extrait du registre de la Majesté du siège de l'amirauté de la Rochelle,"
Archives Nationales, Fonds de la Marine, B³ 412, ff 192, 193.

12 Ibid., B³ 412, ff 196, 197. Still a third instance at La Rochelle in 1742
occurred concerning a Negro boy named Jean Cascarin. Ibid., ff 162, 163.

13 For an instance of a slave Negress being freed after five years of service,
in 1739, see Archives de la Charente-Inférieure, Registre B 226, p. 38. Another,
concerning a quadroon, evidently young, is recorded by Hervé de Halcourt,
"Inventaire d'une habitation à Saint-Domingue," Revue de l'histoire des
colonies françaises, année 21 XXVI (1933), 236.

fee of 1,000 to 2,000 livres,[14] which would have the value of the same amount in dollars in today's money. No fee was charged, however, if emancipation came through the will of the master or mistress. It is suspected that the willingness to see the slave receive his freedom was in part responsible for the large number of runaway slaves, often shortly before the time for return to the colonies. A large percentage of the fugitives were never apprehended. When arrested and interrogated by the police in other cities, perhaps months or years later, they had ready stories to give of alleged liberation by a master who had died or returned to the colonies without them. In either case this commonly meant freedom for the slave. Official correspondence of the period reveals that many planters in France did not keep up with their slaves and knew not where they were nor seemed to care greatly. On the motives that operated in such cases, however, one can only speculate.

Rarely a master might go beyond emancipation of his slave. A Senegalese girl named Ourika was adopted by the Chevalier de Boufflers. A novel, *Ourika*, in which she was the heroine, was later written by Madame de Duras. Also a painting was made of her which still hung in 1919 at the Château de Mouchy.[15]

The Negroes were in some cases equally affectionate. Such a story is related concerning a baker named Louis, who accompanied his master, a wealthy but stern slave trader, to France. His growing insolence led his master to return him to Santo Domingo, but instead of selling him, he freed him. Sometime later the master, returned to the colony, lost both his health and his money. Learning of the circumstances, the Negro came to him, prevailed on him to return to France, paying his expenses, and maintained him financially thereafter. Accord-

---

[14] An ordinance of 22 May 1775 set a tax of 1,000 livres for the emancipation of a Negro man, and a minimum of 2,000 livres for that of a Negro woman less than forty years old. G. Debien, "Gens de couleur libres et colons de Saint-Domingue devant la Constituant," *Revue d'histoire de l'Amérique française*, IV (1950-51), 411.

[15] Mathorez, *Les étrangers en France*, I, 402.

ing to one version, he was at Nantes; according to another, at Bordeaux. One version moreover says that the Negro remained at Cap Français in Santo Domingo, while the other reports that he too went to France. While details vary, there doubtless was a foundation for the story.[16] Many cases of warm affection on the part of former slaves existed in the late 1790's and early 1800's, when they remained on in service, despite emancipation.

By no means were all the Negro slaves brought to France by planters. Many were brought by government officials, military officers, and ship captains returning from overseas service, for Negro servants were the fashion of the day in Europe. It is related that there were fourteen thousand Negro servants in England in the late eighteenth century, a number that seems excessive to this author but nevertheless reveals the tendency.[17] Even Dr. Samuel Johnson, whom no one will accuse of being a man of fashion, had his Negro servant, Francis.[18] One reason alleged for the popularity of Negro servants in England was their greater docility than white servants. This has not been said of the Negro servants in France; on the contrary, many are reported to have become infected with a spirit of independence and impudence. Mathorez reports the story of one Negro coachman who so scorned the public that he rode his horse over the body of the Duc de Choiseul-Praslin, badly injuring him. The Negro was the servant of a great Bordelaise shipowner, Abraham Gradis, and was dressed in livery. Naturally, complaint was made to Gradis.[19]

Reflecting the importance of the slave trade and the importation of Negroes to France in the latter part of the century

[16] See the accounts by Michel René Hilliard d'Auberteuil, *Considérations sur l'état présent de la colonie française de Saint-Domingue* . . . (Paris, 1776-77, 2 v.), I, 142 n. 1; Grégoire, *De la littérature des nègres*, pp. 121-23; Pahin de Blancherie, *Extrait du journal de mes voyages* . . . (Paris, 1775, 2 v.), I, 352-58.

[17] *Journal of the History of Ideas*, II (1941), 237.

[18] A. S. Turberville, ed., *Johnson's England: An Account of the Life and Manners of his Age* (Oxford, 1933, 2 v.), I, 342.

[19] *Les étrangers en France*, I, 400.

were names of ships in the colonial service like "The Negro King," "The African," and "The Black Princess," all operating out of Nantes.[20]

Among other cases of Negroes making themselves troublesome was one in which a Negro was hired in 1754 by the Comte de Clermont, cousin of the King, to administer a beating to the poet Pierre Charles Roy (1683-1764) for writing some slurring verse on him. Roy and the Comte had been competitors for election to the Académie Française, and with no claim to merit the Comte had won. Roy took revenge by writing some verse on the matter, in which he held up the Comte to ridicule, calling him a nonentity. The Comte in turn hired the Negro to administer to Roy a beating, which he did so well that for some days Roy's life was in danger.[21]

In another instance a Negro and his family (it was rare for a Negro family to be brought from the colonies) were imprisoned at Bayonne for making themselves a nuisance. Their master had died, and the Negroes claimed their liberty in consequence of having resided in France. The judge of the Admiralty decided in their favor, but the master's heir contested the matter and appealed to the Parlement of Bordeaux, hoping to be enabled to take them back to the colonies. During the period of the appeal came the imprisonment, the Negroes being charged by their neighbors with scandalous living. The neighbors professed to be horrified at some of their actions. Unfortunately, these are not described.[22]

The Negro in this case is reported to have called himself Nicholas Bertier, which is a matter of interest inasmuch as Bertier is a surname in France and, by the Code Noir which regulated life for the slaves in the colonies, no Negro was permitted to take a surname. However, after a Negro estab-

[20] See "Registre des soumissions d'armateurs et réceptions de capitaines . . . ," Archives de la Loire-Inférieure, B 4522, entries for 14 Oct. 1768 and 9 March 1771; and the Registre for the years 1783-87, ibid., B 4527, entry for 30 Sept. 1783.

[21] Nouvelle biographie générale, ed. by Hoefer, XLII, 805-806.

[22] De Baslore to Maurepas, 10 Feb. 1737, Archives Nationales, Fonds de la Marine, B³ 383, f 292.

lished his freedom, he had the liberty of taking one. There were no doubt many instances of slaves who were taken to France running away, claiming freedom, and assuming surnames.

This practice regarding surnames facilitates the recognition of slaves in the registers and other manuscript records of the 1700's, although generally they are designated by the term "nègre," "noir," or "esclave." This writer is strongly inclined to consider as a Negro, because of his name in large part, a certain peasant named Annibal, living in Provence in 1754. He allegedly was 116 years old, and a certain wigmaker of Marseilles conceived of the scheme of taking him to Paris and presenting him at court. How the wigmaker was to profit from the enterprise is not mentioned. But he went about the matter very zealously, applying, as necessary, to the intendant of Provence, who in turn appealed to the Minister of the Marine, the official having supreme custody over the Negroes in France. The intendant argued against permission being accorded, saying that the old man had led a simple life and that the rigors of the long journey would be too much for him. The decision was not recorded, but if typical of most cases of this type, it followed the recommendations of the lower official. The fact that the matter had to go to the Minister of the Marine is strong supporting evidence that the old man was a Negro, for peasants in France in that day did not have to obtain leave to travel. On the contrary, Negroes had to register with local police officials and could not legally move their residence without permission.[23]

Among the slaves brought to France by ship captains was a ten-year-old Negro boy named Lubin, resident at La Rochelle in 1777. Trained in French for future use as interpreter on the Guinea coast, he had been given the captain as a hostage by his tribe but never redeemed.[24]

23 Archives Nationales, Fonds de la Marine, B3 512, f 312.
24 "Police des gens de couleur transportés en France et de France aux colonies, 1778," Archives Nationales, Colonies, F1B4.

Sometimes slaves were brought to France by pirates and privateers. Negro war prisoners were sometimes so brought. Several Negroes were captured on British vessels in 1746-1747 and taken to Le Havre, and some correspondence exists in the archives there concerning them. Much concern was taken to see that one of these Negroes was indoctrinated in the Christian religion.[25]

In 1729 fifteen Negro slaves were brought to Nantes and turned over to the French government by the pirate Dulain and his band, who laid down their arms under terms of amnesty. Fourteen of the Negroes were imprisoned at Nantes; the fifteenth, being sick, was sent to the Hôtel-Dieu.[26] Slaves of this sort that became the property of the government were sent back to the colonies for sale and the government received the money.

Occasionally foreigners brought Negroes to France, but only after governmental permission had been obtained. In 1779 an English noble brought to La Rochelle two young Negroes, and afterward he obtained permission of the Minister of the Marine to take them by ship to Amsterdam.[27]

A few independent Negroes came during this period from Africa and the colonies, either at their own expense or at that of the government.[28] Among them were several chieftains' sons. One old chief sent his grandson, Cremon or Télémaque, in 1743 to France that he might learn to speak French and then return to rule after him.[29] The chief of Anamabou, on the Guinea coast, sent his son for a similar reason, and in 1752

[25] Letters from Maurepas to Derchigny of 6 Feb. 1746, 27 March and 11 Dec. 1747, in "Colonies, Traite des Noirs, 1713-1750," Archives de la Ville du Havre, Fonds Marine. Also letter of same to same, 10 Dec. 1750, *ibid.*

[26] Vignols, "La piraterie sur l'Atlantique," 373-74 with n.

[27] De Castries to Macartney, 1779, Archives de la Charente Inférieure, B 5592.

[28] There were several cases of free Negroes and mulattoes at Le Havre gaining permission in the 1760's and 1770's to return to the colonies at their own expense. Also there was one instance of a free Negro being returned at government expense. "Nègres et esclaves 1763/76," Archives de la Ville du Havre, Fonds Marine.

[29] Ducasse, *Les négriers*, pp. 92-93.

the boy was enrolled at the Jesuit College of Louis-le-Grand at the expense of the French government. So at least reported D'Argenson, who stated that the boy's expenses attained the extravagant rate of 100 livres a day—a large sum for that era.[30] Another author reports the sons of two Fanti chiefs as being in France in 1752, and implies that the French defrayed their expenses in order to curry favor with their tribes. In 1786 another chieftain's son was in France, this time a shipping firm in Saint-Malo serving as patron.[31]

Among the free Negroes in France in this century were two albinos, who created much curiosity. One was a small boy of four or five years, at Paris in 1744, of whom Voltaire has left a description; the other, a fourteen-year-old chieftain's daughter, Quircana, was sent to France for an education in 1787. The latter was at Honfleurs, and her tutor planned to take her to Paris. The *Mercure de France* gave a somewhat detailed description of her.[32] It would be very interesting indeed to know how these students acquitted themselves and what interest and capacity for learning they revealed. The records are mute. Their study no doubt was limited largely to the French language and customs, and their intellectual development to what they saw as visitors.

In the French colonies the schools and professions were closed to Negroes. One never reads of a Negro priest, lawyer, or physician. And yet there was a Negro surgeon, or rather surgeon-apprentice, in Louisiana and France in the mid-eighteenth century. He was a Creole, François Antoine, a slave it appears of the Capuchin order in New Orleans. Père Hilaire of this order had caused the Negro to learn surgery in the hospital at New Orleans, with the view to serving there as a surgeon in time. In June, 1756, he set out for France with the Negro, but en route to La Rochelle the vessel was captured

[30] *Journal et mémoires du Marquis d'Argenson, publiés pour la première fois* . . . , ed. by E. J. B. Rathery (Paris, 1859-67, 9 v.), VII, 257.

[31] Ducasse, *Les négriers*, p. 165.

[32] Nicolas Le Cat, *Traité de la couleur de la peau humaine* . . . (Amsterdam, 1765), 102-104; *Mercure de France*, 22 March 1788, pp. 183-85.

by the British and François Antoine was disembarked at Portsmouth and made to serve there in the hospital and at a so-called Château of Lizinghuet until 1758, when he was freed or exchanged and brought from England to Calais. Thence he should have proceeded to La Rochelle, for embarkation to New Orleans with Père Haury, but in passing through Dieppe he was persuaded (the record says "taken") by the Prince de Turenne to enter his service at the Hôtel de Bouillon in Paris. There he remained until 1760, when Père Hilaire made petition through the Admiralty officials that the Prince de Turenne be required to release François Antoine in order that he might be taken back to New Orleans where the Capuchins needed him in their hospital. Nothing more on the matter is reported. That a Negro in the French colony of Louisiana had been apprenticed or otherwise trained in surgery in the 1700's, when this was forbidden or shortly came to be forbidden by the law, is of great interest, as also is the fact that his services were in demand by the British and the Prince de Turenne. We are not told whether he served Turenne as a surgeon or surgeon-apprentice or in some lesser capacity. He must have had personal qualities or training that made him attractive, and from the fact that the Capuchins were solicitous for him to serve in their hospital, it may be concluded that he was fairly skillful.[33]

The presence in France of so many Negroes and mixed bloods in the latter part of the century very naturally provoked

[33] "Troisième registre servant aux declarations de nègres, Paris, ce 22 aoust 1756," Archives Nationales, Z¹D139, f 18. The Capuchins did own slaves. See V. P. Malouet, *Collection de mémoires sur les colonies* . . . (Paris, an X), IV, 94-95.

A royal ordinance of 30 April 1763 forbade any Negro or man of color, whether slave or free, to practice medicine or surgery in the colonies for any ailment whatever. "Extraits de l'ouvrage de M. Moreau de St. Méry," Archives Nationales, Colonies, C⁹C4. This writer does not find an earlier prohibition, but the spirit in the colonies was to deprive the Negro of professional training.

A mulatto from Peru named Dávalos also received medical training in France in colonial days. Irene Diggs, "Color in Colonial Spanish America," *Journal of Negro History*, XXXVIII (1953), 423.

reflection on the difference of color in races. Why should one
man be white and another black? Was there any other difference between races than the color of the skin? And what
caused the Negro's skin to be black? Curiosity was increased
by the fact that an occasional albino was to be found among
the Negroes. Several eighteenth-century scholars wrote treatises
on the subject of skin color. The earliest apparently was an
elaborate brochure of 191 pages by a famous Rouen surgeon
named Nicolas Le Cat, published at Amsterdam in 1765. He
told of autopsies which he had made on two Negroes that had
died at the Hôtel-Dieu of Rouen. He had examined with
great care the flesh, brain, and skin. He had examined
minutely the blood of other Negro patients, and compared it
to that of the whites. He had made similar studies on white
and black rabbits and on black and white sheep. The seat of
color, he found, lay in the lymph, beneath the skin. White
people had white lymph, Negroes black. Why the difference?
Le Cat scouted the idea that climate could have caused it;
rather, it could have been caused by the imagination of
mothers, both in humans and animals. He related the Biblical
experience of Jacob with Laban's flocks, and the similar
experiment with dogs by one of his friends. This famous
surgeon, who was a member of nine scientific academies in
Europe, including those of London, Paris, Berlin, and Bologna,
appears ridiculous to readers of the twentieth century, but his
little treatise was the result of much medical research, reading,
and thought. His error lay in depending on the book of Genesis
for scientific purposes.[34] Shortly after Le Cat, a German
physiologist and anthropologist at Göttingen, Johann F. Blu-
menbach, likewise of great reputation, published a study on
the variations in races; and he, in turn, was followed in a
treatise in 1787 by the Princeton professor, and later president,
Samuel S. Smith. Finally, in this connection should be men-

[34] *Traité de la couleur de la peau humaine*, pp. 8, 17, 18-23, 53-54.
Interestingly enough, while Le Cat accepts the Biblical story of Jacob as
plausible, he rejects that of Noah's curse on Ham.

tioned some discussion of the subject at the conclusion of two-volume treatise on Africa published in 1767 by the French ecclesiastical traveler Demanet, who insisted that climate was the cause of racial differences. No doubt the matter of racial differences, which to some extent had been set off by the publication of Montesquieu's *Esprit des lois* in the midcentury, must have become a common topic of conversation. The government itself became interested, and some legislation was enacted in the 1760's and 1770's, to be discussed in the next chapter.

It is regrettable that so little is known of the eighteenth-century Negroes in France. Our chief sources of information are the ship and Admiralty and police records. The entries for the most part are brief, giving name, sex, age, place of birth, owner, and trade in which to be apprenticed. Sometimes happily more is recorded. Occasionally there is the story of a runaway slave or of one protesting return to the colonies. These generally necessitated some investigation and more elaborate reports. It is such reports that give us the best information. It can be stated without qualification that the Negroes were pleased with France—it was heaven to them—and many endeavored to remain. There were no suicides, as reportedly took place on slave ships from Africa en route to the colonies, and this despite the fact that the slaves must have been housed miserably in garrets of their masters' hotels, in the homes of their instructors, or with poor families. On the ships they received the poorest accommodations, and in France their lodging and food must have been of a low standard, save for those eating in the kitchens of their masters' hotels. There was no animus against them by the populace, and socially they might mix with the French, save that there was a class barrier among the French themselves. Yet the Negroes had little in common with the French. They went to church, were baptized, and in many cases were confirmed. A few married—some to whites—and these generally remained in France and found employment of some sort, as domestics, carpenters, tavern assistants, or even as tavernkeepers. A few became prosperous.

Generally, even in the cases of free Negroes, they were servants. This was the most significant feature of the Negroes as a group in eighteenth-century France. Most of them were servants of the planters, or of the army and navy officials who had seen service in the colonies. A few were presented as gifts to friends in France by returning colonials. They were left to associate with white servants in France, and there appears to have been no friction between the two. If the Negroes of that day were gifted at song or musical instrument of any kind, there is no mention of it. They were entirely different from the Negroes seen in Paris today—as different as the Old Regime was from twentieth-century France.

*skillful recreation of 18ᵗʰ century atmosphere of Fr*

# THREE  A NEGRO PROBLEM
IN FRANCE

*H*OW DID one reconcile the internal policy on slavery and the policy for the colonies which France pursued during the 1700's? This was a live question and many felt very strongly about it. Slavery in theory had not existed in France since the Middle Ages, and slaves could not be bought and sold on French soil. But it had been recognized as necessary and legal in the colonies, where labor was scarce and the climate severe and conditions prevailed which were considered beyond the strength of the white man. Could the colonist bring his slave to France, where slavery did not exist, and treat him there as a slave? Yes, under certain conditions, was the answer of some; no, under no circumstances, was the answer of others; and even the law courts of France were divided on the matter. The Parlement of Paris, most important tribunal in France, ever was ready to recognize the claim to freedom of a slave that came within its jurisdiction. It did not recognize the constitutionality of the Declaration of 1738.

There were suits for freedom in the eighteenth century. That of the slave girl at Nantes who was aided by the nuns of Calvary in 1715 was apparently the earliest. She was granted her freedom. In 1728 a Negro appealed against return to Martinique, after being allowed to run at liberty since 1720, and Maurepas, Minister of the Marine, granted his request.[1]

[1] Maurepas to Rigaud, 23 June 1728, Archives de la Charente Inférieure, B 5590.

In 1743 there came up the case of César, slave of the Danish consul at La Rochelle, who had run away and joined the French army. The consul wanted to send him back to the colonies. Maurepas was called upon to make the decision, and upon technical grounds he decided that César should become the property of the government.[2] In 1747 a slave named Catherine likewise was confiscated by the state after her master, at Nantes, became so brutal that a lawyer named Terrien espoused her cause. The state sent her back to Santo Domingo and sold her.[3]

None of these cases, however, set a precedent. Each was decided on its own merits, and to a large extent all the cases of the eighteenth century were settled on merit. Nevertheless, a case in 1762 did much in setting a precedent, was often cited thereafter, and came to affect French legislative policy. This was the case of Louis, a mulatto slave from Santo Domingo, against his master, Jean Jacques de Febre, a bourgeois of Paris. Louis appealed to the Court of the Admiralty for the right to go free since he had been brought on French soil, and won his case, which is sometimes referred to as Lestaing *versus* Hutteau (the two lawyers involved). Decision was rendered on March 31, 1762. The Royal Procurator, Guillaume Poncet de la Grave, drew up an elaborate report on the case. Tracing the development of personal liberty in France, he stated that since the late Middle Ages, and particularly since 1552, no corporal bondage had existed in France. But while he championed the right of the individual to freedom within France, he related how slavery had developed in the colonies with government protection. He asked if the slaveowner might bring his slave to France, and under what conditions. The Edict of 1716 became necessary, and then the Declaration of 1738. As a result, France, and particularly Paris, had become inundated with slaves. He charged that men were bought and sold in

[2] Archives Nationales, Fonds de la Marine, B³ 420, ff 75-79, 179, 181, 182, 186, 188.
[3] *Ibid.*, B³ 455, ff 130-38.

Paris, and that "there is not a bourgeois or worker who has not his Negro slave." He charged, further, that Negroes were constantly being thrown into prison on no other ground than the whim of their masters. But the Negroes, on their part, had become entirely too numerous, and the consequence would be "dangerous." He feared that they would "soon see the French nation disfigured." He declared that "the Negroes in general are some dangerous men," adding that almost every one given his liberty had "abused it." The Negroes were considered "dangerous for society." He then proceeded to declare the freedom of Louis and the decision that his master must pay him 750 livres in back wages in consideration of his work as a freedman, at the rate of 100 livres a year from the date of his arrival in France to the present.[4] This decision was followed in some subsequent cases. So, too, were the sentiments toward the Negroes. Indeed, this seems to be the first expression of fear in regard to the Negroes, and it was to have important consequences in legislation.

An ordinance bearing the date of March 31–April 3, 1762, issued at the very time of this decision, was sent out to the various Admiralty offices in France, requiring the immediate registration of all Negroes and mulattoes, whether slaves or free, within a month. It repeated verbatim those parts of the report on the case of Lestaing *versus* Hutteau charging that every bourgeois and worker had his Negro, that Negroes were flagrantly bought and sold in France, that the Negroes had become numerous and were a danger to French society.[5]

On June 30 of the next year the government sent out a letter to officials in the colonies ordering them to permit no sailings for France thenceforth by Negroes, whether free or slave. It expressed disappointment with the training of slaves in religion and for trades, permitted by the laws of 1716 and 1738, saying that little was being accomplished in these

[4] Document entitled "5 avril 1762. Sentence de règlement rendue en amirauté de France concernant les declarations à passer pour les nègres et mulâtres," Archives Nationales, Z¹D139.

[5] A printed copy is in the Archives de la Charente Inférieure, B 5592.

respects. It also directed that the slaves in France be returned
to the colonies by October 1, to stop the mixing of blood and
the debasement of culture. The government, however, shortly
afterward countermanded the order, and no attempt apparently was made toward the expulsion.[6]

Government discontent with the increased number of Negroes continued to find expression, and in 1776 steps were
being taken to draw up legislation anew to deal with the
situation. It drew the attention of a committee on legislation,
and some sharp criticism of existing conditions was expressed
in reports to it by Poncet de la Grave, Royal Procurator of the
Admiralty at Paris, and Miromesnil, Keeper of the Seals. Poncet
remarked that the laws of 1716 and 1738 had not been accepted
by the Parlement of Paris and certain other courts (thus
refusing to recognize slavery in France), so that any Negroes
who appealed to them obtained their freedom. This brought
confusion, and there was need of a new, more comprehensive
law. He complained that the Negroes "multiply each day in
France," that "their marriages with Europeans" were favored,
that "the colors mix" and "the blood is altered," that agriculture
in the colonies suffered by their absence, that they contracted
in France "the spirit of liberty, independence, and equality,
which they communicate to the others," and that as a result
of their development of insubordination they "prepare thus
a revolution." (Is this the first suggestion of the Revolution of
1789?) He scoffed at the grounds of bringing Negroes to
France for instruction in religion and the trades. They could
learn religion better in the colonies, and as for the trades,
enough persons were already trained for them—they should be
in the hands of whites anyway. There was no longer any
reason for bringing Negroes to France. Yet, since white
servants were not available in the colonies, he would permit
planters or officials coming to France to bring a single slave
for service during the voyage, and to send the slave back on

[6] *Inventaire sommaire . . . Bouches-du-Rhône*, C 2561; Peytraud, *L'esclavage
aux Antilles françaises avant 1789*, pp. 387-88.

arrival in the French port. He would permit the slave to be kept "in a public depot," a sort of concentration camp, at the master's expense, until he could be embarked for return. As for the Negroes already in France, both slave and free, he would send them back to the colonies were it not that they would create more trouble there than in France; but he did think that their life could be more controlled by legislation. Particularly should no Negro be traded or sold in France. Miromesnil, who had read the proposals of Poncet, made a report approving them in virtually all respects.[7]

The ideas of Poncet were to be incorporated to a remarkable degree in a royal declaration of August 9, 1777, an enactment in large part replacing that of 1738, and these terms with faint modification were to continue in operation down to the end of the Old Regime. This law, consisting of thirteen articles, repeated the charges that Negroes had become too numerous in French cities, and especially in Paris, that they were "the cause of the greatest disorders," and that they returned to the colonies with a "spirit of independence and insubordination" that rendered them "more harmful than useful." It was therefore provided that thenceforth no "Negroes, mulattoes, or other men of color" might be taken into France, whether male or female, free or slave, on penalty of a fine of 3,000 livres. Colonists coming to France might bring with them a single slave to serve them during the sea passage, but this slave must be left at the port confined in a depot at the owner's expense for return to the colonies. Should the owner wish to keep the slave at the port until his return, he might do so by registering him with the port officials and, as surety for maintenance expenses, by making a deposit, the residue of which would be returned to the owner upon departure. It was similarly forbidden that ship captains transport "any Negro, mulatto, or other men of color" to France, on penalty of a fine of 1,000

[7] Poncet's memoir of 24 Feb. 1776 to the Conseil des Depêches, Archives Nationales, Colonies, F¹B3; Miromesnil's letter to De Sartine, 12 Feb. 1776, ibid., F¹B4. Despite the priority of date of the latter report, Miromesnil states that he has read that by Poncet.

livres for each person so transported, and double that sum
for a repeated offense. The act also required that all slaveowners already in France must report at the nearest Admiralty
office within the next month and register their slaves. Similarly
it ordered all free "Negroes, mulattoes, or other men of color"
living in France to report within the same period of time to
the Admiralty officials. Such were the terms of the important
acts that were to regulate this new "problem" that already was
giving the government much trouble.[8]

Several delays prevented the law from going into operation
until 1778, one of them being the necessity of each of the
thirteen parlements to enter it on its books. By the last of
January, 1778, eleven had so registered it. These did not
include that of Paris, which appears however to have observed
its terms.[9]

The act stated that all Negroes who were registered would
be provided gratis with a certificate, carrying a description
of them, their name, age, trade or employment, and name of
master. All Negroes, slave or free, found without such a certificate would be arrested, conducted to Le Havre (if resident
in Paris), and sent to the colonies.

Officials in the colonies were concerned about certain provisions of the act. Two intendants in Santo Domingo wrote
the Minister of the Marine, De Sartine, insisting that the nurse
for a child or a pregnant mother or for a sick master or mistress
should not be turned back at the port, but should be granted
entry into France. The Admiralty agreed that the nurses for
children and pregnant mothers would be granted entry but
sent home as soon as the need for their nursing was ended.
In the other case, it was refused.[10] A later letter by one of the

8 The terms of this law are to be found in *Recueil général des anciennes lois
françaises*, XXV, 81-84; Maurice Besson, "La police des noirs sous Louis XVI
en France," *Revue de l'histoire des colonies françaises*, année 16, XXI (1928),
436-41.

9 Archives Nationales, Colonies, F1B3; Besson, "La police des noirs," 441-43;
Arrêt de conseil of 19 Oct. 1777, Archives Nationales, Colonies, F1B4.

10 Dargout and Devaivre to De Sartine, 23 Dec. 1777, Archives Nationales,
Colonies, F1B4.

same intendants requested that the Negroes in France be sent back to the colonies in small numbers, inasmuch as they were "a crowd of bad subjects, spoiled, corrupted, instructed in more than is necessary for them, by their sojourn in Europe." The return of too many at once might "lead to the greatest disorders."[11] It turned out that the intendant was not to worry long over this matter, for the outbreak of war took care of that.

Before considering, however, the enforcement of this important law, it is proper to describe certain other bits of legislation enacted by the government in early 1778 aimed at reducing the Negro problem in France. One was an Order of the Council of State, drawn up in January, 1778, consisting of nine articles, directing all Negroes and persons of color in France who had not already registered with an office of the Admiralty to do so at once, or run the risk of being arrested, imprisoned in a depot at the nearest port, and sent to the colonies. They were told that they must carry with them at all times their *cartouche* or identification paper.[12] This was followed on April 5 by a similar Order of the Council of State forbidding all marriages between whites and blacks in France, on penalty of being expelled at once to the colonies. All notaries were ordered to refuse to issue marriage licenses in such cases, else they were to be subject to a fine. In Paris enforcement was placed in the hands of Lenoir, lieutenant general of police, and in the provinces, in the hands of intendants and officials of the Admiralty.[13]

In view of the fact that so much had previously been said about the menace of intermarriage between the races, it is surprising that no step to this effect had been taken in the act of August 9, 1777. In actuality it was already forbidden by one of the clauses of the Declaration of 1738, which denied any Negro residing in France the right to marry. The new prohibition was to be observed no better than the older one. The bishops were informed of the new order regarding mar-

---

[11] Devaivre to De Sartine, 15 Jan. 1778, *ibid.*
[12] *Ibid.*           [13] *Ibid.*

riage and requested to enforce it. Their attitude on the matter is not recorded, but the fact that marriages of this type had been celebrated despite the prohibition of 1738 is evidence of their indifference. The church authorities throughout the eighteenth century were interested in the Negro's religious training and development, and made little or no distinction between him and other individuals save perhaps to give him special attention because of his poverty. The church did not openly combat slavery, either within France or in the colonies —actually it accepted slavery as an opportunity to christianize the slave, and some religious orders even owned slaves—but it often seized opportunities to aid slaves seeking freedom.[14]

For all this legislation to present interracial marriages and to keep Negroes out of France there appears to have been no demand whatever on the part of the French populace. It came entirely from certain leading officials in the government. No doubt the colonists and their friends among the upper circles in France shared these views of racial distinction, but it happened that the colonists were disturbed by the endeavor to exclude Negroes from France. They preferred to be left the freedom to bring in their slaves. The provincial intendants did not at first take the matter seriously, and they had to be warned by special letters from Versailles. They were asked to supply the government with elaborate reports on the Negroes, mulattoes, and other men of color resident within their jurisdiction. De Crosne, intendant at Rouen, a man of no mean merit, was given a sharp reprimand for stating hastily and erroneously that there were no Negroes resident in his city. The Admiralty official wrote back that a Negro woman was living at that very moment just behind his garden, and that a family of Negroes lived on a designated street. He then asked De Crosne to send in their names and other information as demanded. To De Crosne's response that seventeen in-

[14] Letter from De Sartine to the bishops, in April 1778, Archives des Bouches-du-Rhône, C 4621; Gaston Martin, *Nantes au XVIII siècle*, II (Paris, 1931), 163-64; Martin, *Négriers et bois d'ébène*, p. 50.

habitants of Rouen had neglected to furnish him with the desired information, the official replied that he knew how to handle cases of this sort. Very clearly De Crosne had considered it some legislation of little consequence; he learned otherwise.[15] Certain other intendants, too, had to be called on for additional information.[16] The result was that in 1777 elaborate reports for all of France were sent in to Paris or Versailles concerning the Negroes and other men of color in France, with a description of each person so listed, his name, age, sex, trade, family status, place of birth, date of entry into France, status of slave or freedman, and other details. Such full information had never been set forth previously, not even on the shipping or Admiralty lists, and this valuable collection of documents reposes in the Archives Nationales under the designation of "Police des Noirs."[17]

These reports from the intendants were made out by city and town, so that it is possible to ascertain with relative precision the geographical distribution of Negroes in France. As already stated, they were most densely settled at Paris, and after it in the seaports, especially those of the west coast, like Bordeaux and Nantes. Yet even in the mountains of Burgundy and the Pyrenees were to be found a few stragglers. The register of those residing in Paris was at first imperfectly done; it contained only the names of slaves registered with officials by their owners since 1760. The total was 256. Later a second and more complete report for Paris was submitted. It contained about four hundred entries, on eighty pages, with occasional entries describing more than one individual. Perhaps 450 are listed in this register, which incorporated the

---

[15] Chardin to De Crosne, 29 Sept. 1777, Archives Nationales, Colonies, F¹B3.

[16] De Sartine, for example, criticized the careless report of De la Tour, intendant of Aix, and asked for the names of the Negroes he listed only in figures; later he acknowledged the receipt of the additional reports, saying that they "respond perfectly to the intentions of his Majesty." Archives des Bouches-du-Rhône, C 4622.

[17] Archives Nationales, Colonies, F¹B4.

names of free Negroes as well as those of slaves.[18] The report for Bordeaux gave the number of 121 as residing within the city, and of 37 others living in other designated towns in the generality, for a total of 158 in Guienne.[19] Another report, for 1778, including both slaves and freedmen, gave the number residing in Bordeaux as 174. From the large variation, one may conclude that the earlier report was not made with the same care as the second.[20] At La Rochelle 65 slaves were declared, 15 at Bayonne, 13 at Marseilles, 3 at Dieppe, 6 at Honfleur, 5 at Calais, 6 at Agde, and 9 in Burgundy. Many were declared in other towns and cities. The Committee on Legislation, in a report of 1782, estimated the number of Negro slaves residing in France at four to five thousand.[21] This figure appears fantastic. There can hardly have been more than a thousand Negroes, free and slave, in France either in 1777 or at any later date in the eighteenth century. One may add the figures in the reports of 1777; he may also consult the "Table alphabétique des nègres" for all France during the period 1777-1787, consisting of three large notebooks or registers, and find only 770 names listed.[22] This last is perhaps the most summary set of figures for the era.

In attempting to arrive at statistics, however, it must be recalled that the French did not take a census of their own people until 1800, relying prior to that time on estimates, which were not badly wrong. The problem of deriving sum-

[18] The second register is entitled "Registre des declarations des nègres et mulâtres commencé le 3 may 1777 et fini en 8bre suivant," Archives Nationales, Z¹D138. A third register for Paris, found in this same carton, begun in 1777 and continued until 1790, has about 540 entries on its 90 pages and contains listings of 700 or more Negroes. Since some were always coming and others always leaving, it was difficult to designate the precise number at any particular date.

[19] "Etat des noirs esclaves de l'un et de l'autre sexe, généralité de Bordeaux, année 1777," Archives Nationales, Colonies, F¹B4.

[20] "Amirauté de Bordeaux. Etat des noirs, mulâtres et autres gens de couleur qui ont été déclarés en exécution de l'art. 9 de la déclaration du Roy du 9 août dernier," ibid.

[21] "Avis du comité de législation sur les deux questions de Monsieur le Marquis de Castries au sujet des noirs et mulâtres qui se trouvent actuellement en France," ibid.

[22] Archives Nationales, Z¹D138.

mary figures for the Negroes and mulattoes for any moment in that period in France is complicated by the fact that there was a constant flow of arrivals and departures. Moreover, the colonists moved about in France with them, and also there were Negro runaways. It was hard to check on a floating population.

That there were perhaps less than a thousand in France at any time before the Revolution makes the fear of a Negro problem seem a bit strange. Could there have been grounds for alarm that the blood of France would be altered? A reader of today may consider the fears to have been without foundation, but it must be recalled that the tide of incoming Negroes had been steadily rising. Reports of 1777 and later years did reveal that two or three score Negroes and mulattoes were intermarried with whites, more commonly Negro men being married to white wives, and in numerous instances their union had been fruitful with children.[23] The revelation might have been disturbing to the officials at Paris, but in the provinces it was clearly regarded without concern. The inhabitants of the town of Cassis, in Provence, were reportedly much disturbed lest a Negro dwelling there and recently married to a white girl be arrested and sent back to the colonies. The subdelegate wrote that the Negro (named Alexis) was well off economically, having held a small government job, and, though a bastard by birth, was well liked by his wife's people and had been permitted to take their name. He asked De Sartine for direction on how to proceed. This was an exceptional case, but everywhere the mixed couples seem to have faced no hostile public.

It so happened that the French Revolution of 1789-1795 brought an end to slavery, and the war with England after 1793 virtually stopped Negro immigration to France. Hence the problem of miscegenation was settled in a manner different from that originally planned, but that needs no discussion here.

---

[23] See Archives Nationales, Colonies, F¹B3 and F¹B4; Archives Nationales, Z¹D138; Archives de la Gironde, C 3669; and Archives de Bouches-du-Rhône, C 4621, C 4622.

For service in carrying out the terms of the Act of 1777 *dépôts de noirs*, or prison camps, were set up in the port cities of Dunkerque, Le Havre, Saint-Malo, Brest, Nantes, La Rochelle, Bordeaux, and Marseilles. For the most part they occupied a portion of the prisons of these places. The government gave much thought to their establishment. It specified that the Negroes must be kept apart from the criminals, the sexes must be separated, the quarters should be habitable, and the Negroes permitted daily to walk in the court. Masters who so desired might arrange with the prison concierge for an extra allowance of food to be given their Negroes. One boy of ten, evidently a favorite of his master, was thus placed on a ration costing 7½ livres per day, whereas the ration for the others was from 1 to 2 livres. In general the depots do not appear to have been crowded, but the procurator of the Admiralty at Le Havre protested at crowded conditions there in 1783-1784 and was able to arrange for more commodious quarters at the General Hospital. The largest number of Negroes in any one depot in 1777-1778 was at Nantes, where at one time there were six women and eight men.[24]

The plans of the officials in 1777, however, despite the careful thought given them, were to meet failure almost from the outset. Fate intervened to block them. War broke out with Britain shortly afterward, as France went to the aid of the revolting American Colonies, and for six years (1778-1783) commerce between France and her colonies was brought virtually to an end, and during this period few if any Negroes were sent home or brought to France. A small number had been returned to the colonies in early 1778;[25] after that the government accorded masters an extension of time in which

[24] Many papers on the establishment of the depots are in Archives Nationales, Colonies, F¹B3. See also Archives de la Ville du Havre, Fonds Marine, letters between De Castries and Mistral in 1783-1784; Archives de la Gironde, 8 J 422, portefeuille on "Traite des nègres: Colonies, 1714-1830"; and Peytraud, *L'esclavage aux Antilles françaises*, pp. 394-95.

[25] "Avis du Comité de Législation sur les deux questions . . . ," Archives Nationales, Colonies, F¹B4; Vignols, *Les esclaves coloniaux en France*, p. 5. On the slaves returned in 1778, see "Etat des noirs . . . rembarqués au Port de Nantes pendant le mois de mars," Archives Nationales, Colonies, F¹B3.

to return their slaves to the colonies. The expense of upkeep for these slaves in the depots must have been considerable, but there was no avoiding it.

On the restoration of peace in 1783, the Council of State ordered a renewal of the police certificates *(cartouches)* given the Negroes for identification purposes. Designed originally for Paris alone, they were extended to other cities.[26]

Scores of Negroes were arrested in the period 1777-1789 and placed in the part depots for transportation to the colonies. Most were slaves, including several runaways. Some were arrested on request of their owners; others were found to be undeclared or unregistered. One was arrested on demand of his former master after the latter had given him freedom.[27] Another was arrested through error after he had been properly registered.[28] Some arrested claimed to be free. A Negress named Henriette Lucille, belonging to a Madame Paquot, claimed freedom in 1780 on the ground that slavery did not exist in France. She also claimed mistreatment. The Countess de Bethune espoused her cause and eventually obtained freedom for her through the King's interference, after an earlier decision that she must be returned to the colonies. She had been brought to France to care for the small children of her mistress. The case was a *cause célèbre* and ran for some time. It revealed that a powerful friend could sometimes get a Negro liberty.[29]

Throughout the eighteenth century the question continued

[26] "Arrêt du conseil d'état du Roi . . . du 23 mars 1783," Archives de la Charente-Inférieure, B 5592.

[27] This concerned Louis Collet, a mulatto, who had married a white woman. The intendant, reporting on the case, said that several children had been born to them out of wedlock, and his marriage to her was probably the best step for him to have taken. De Castries thereupon directed that he be left in France. Letters of De la Tour to De Castries, 31 Dec. 1790, 24 Jan. and 11 April 1781; and letter of De Castries to De la Tour, 17 May 1781. Archives des Bouches-du-Rhône, C 4621.

[28] This concerned one Narcisse, at Nantes, in 1776. De Caradeux to the Procureur du Roy de l'Amirauté de Nantes, 4 March 1778, Archives Nationales, Colonies, $F^1B3$.

[29] Several papers on the case are to be found in Archives Nationales, Colonies, $F^1B1$.

to be raised as to whether slavery could exist in France. Since slavery was forbidden there, was not every slave at once a freedman on entering French soil? Many argued that this was the case, and a number of lawsuits on the matter came up during the century, with the slave often the winner. In general, however, it was held that the slave imported on French soil remained a slave, provided that the technicalities of the law had been complied with. Hence slavery did exist in France, despite the law and with the approval of the law. For the law could be cited for defense of both the conflicting positions.

In one case a mulatto named Philippe Orphée was arrested and imprisoned at Carentan in 1781. He had come to France before the Declaration of August 9, 1777, and was recognized as free. The case was referred to De Castries, Minister of the Marine, who wrote back that the man must be set free and the expense of his detention be paid by the state. In that day the jailer had to be paid before a prisoner would be freed; De Castries ordered that the jailer be paid thirty livres.[30]

Few apparently were the Negroes arrested found at large; scores were ordered returned to the colonies, and after 1783 these were rather faithfully sent back. Nevertheless, there still continued some carelessness on the part of owners and officials, as an instance will illustrate. In 1788 the Admiralty at Versailles became greatly concerned over the whereabouts of two Negro nurses, Marie Rose and Françoise, who had disembarked at La Rochelle on August 20, 1786, and on whom it had no further reports. What had happened to these two Negresses, inquired the Minister La Luzerne. The officials at La Rochelle did not know, nor did they know the whereabouts of their owner, the Comte de Maulevrier. La Luzerne rather exasperatedly informed them that Maulevrier was in Paris, rue de la Planche. Thereupon the Admiralty officers at La Rochelle wrote him and asked him the same question—what had happened to the two Negresses—and directed him to

[30] De Castries to Mistral, 9 Sept. 1781, Archives de la Ville du Havre, Fonds Marine.

return them at once to La Rochelle. In response they received a letter saying that there were two Comtes de Maulevrier, and that they had written to the wrong one. The Comte replying said that he did not know where the other Comte could be found. So they were as much in mystery as before. The officials at La Rochelle wrote the Minister that the Negresses had never been placed in the depot at La Rochelle, and they knew nothing whatever of them; and as for the Comte they were seeking, "perhaps he has returned to the colonies with the two Negresses." La Luzerne, evidently disgusted, sent them 100 blank forms for use in the future in reporting the arrivals and departures of Negroes, and let the matter drop. That was in June, 1789. Perhaps this little incident reveals much about the French indifference to the Negro problem of that day.[31]

The government had feared that the restriction of the importation of Negroes might be evaded by ship captains and owners. Accordingly it inserted a clause in the Declaration of August 9, 1777, strictly prohibiting evasion; and an ordinance of February 23, 1778, directed ship officials afresh to refrain from bringing any Negro or mulatto to France who was not properly authorized. The preamble stated that some captains had been letting Negroes disembark in French ports without official permission. Every future violation would bring a fine of 300 livres and loss of employment for three months.[32] This enactment came after an episode in which a Negress named Marguerite had been dropped ten leagues out at sea from Nantes by her ship and put aboard a lighter. The Negress later came ashore, where she was arrested and placed in the depot. Full details were reported to the Admiralty at Versailles.[33] Thereafter for several months the Admiralty office at Nantes sent a representative to board all incoming vessels ten leagues at sea and check them for Negroes that might be found

---

[31] The letters on this case are in Archives de la Charente-Inférieure, B 5592.
[32] Besson, "La police des noirs," 444.
[33] Dupé to Chardon, Archives Nationales, Colonies, F¹B3.

either as passengers or crew. It was rare for a Negro to be found as a sailor in the eighteenth century, especially on French vessels, and it is still rare today. Nevertheless, two Negroes entering Nantes in March, 1778, were reported as members of a ship's crew, and it was claimed that they had made several crossings as such.[34] As is commonly known, smuggling both on land and sea was a recognized sport among Frenchmen of the eighteenth century. When an owner offered to pay handsomely for getting his Negro into France, why not take the risk? No doubt there were captains who did. On the whole, though, despite some ludicrous incidents and cases of appalling carelessness, a close check on the movements of Negroes during the last ten or twelve years before the Revolution appears to have been observed.

It will be recalled that one of the grounds specified for the Declaration of August 9, 1777, was the charge that the Negroes were debasing morality and encouraging crime. To what extent was this true? Let it be said that the scant records possibly do not reveal the full story, certainly in the matter of morality, which is difficult to measure. At Nantes were several instances of Negresses who declared their pregnancy out of wedlock. The father was named in each case, and if the Negress was a slave, the name of her master was given. One French girl pregnant by a Negro was also named. The number of instances in which Negresses were involved, nevertheless, was minute in comparison to the hundreds in which French girls were involved.[35] From these records it appears that French morals were already debased, and that the Negroes were not contributing more than their share. In the Admiralty reports later in the century one finds many references to illegitimate children, but not more than one might expect from people in a servile class forbidden to marry. No doubt there was much promiscuity among them, and perhaps black females offered

34 Archives Nationales, Colonies, F¹B3.
35 "Declarations de grossesse, 1733-1742," Archives de la Ville de Nantes, GG 748; Ville de Nantes, *Inventaire sommaire des archives antérieures à 1790,* GG 747, 748, 750, 754, 756.

their easy virtue to French males for low charges and found a thriving business. The police records seem to say little on the matter however.

As for crime, the Negroes appear to have had a better record than the French. Only here and there is a Negro criminal mentioned. One who set afire some bedding in the hospital for the galleys at Toulon has already been cited. In 1718 a Negro was hanged for running amuck on the streets of Saint-Cloud and stabbing a shoemaker without provocation.[36] A Negro hired to administer a beating to the poet Roy has been mentioned. Two Negroes, George and Charlotte, were charged in 1788 with giving the police of Le Havre a great deal of trouble and were sent back to Santo Domingo.[37] In 1789 a Negro was arrested for trying to sell a jeweler a cross of Saint-Louis, which he declared his master was tired of since it was no longer fashionable to wear one.[38] The most atrocious crime charged to a Negro in France during the century, so far as known, was a case of attempted poisoning at Brest by the Negro Jean Mor. The case attracted much attention at the time and deserves more than bare mention.

Jean Mor, a twenty-year-old slave from Martinique, had come to France with his master, a naval officer named Le Nort stationed at Brest, and served him as cook. Many times he asked his master to grant him freedom, without avail. Hearing that it was wretched for a slave who returned to the colonies from France, he determined to escape that condition by poisoning his master, an idea which he later declared was suggested to him by Louis Rodin, a free mulatto whom he had met in the naval hospital at Brest. There Rodin was treated for venereal disease; Mor, for a sore foot. Rodin allegedly suggested that Mor use a poison from Africa and the West Indies called *lianne* or *piment de bois*, and gave him eighteen

[36] Mathorez, *Les étrangers en France*, I, 399.

[37] La Luzerne to Mistral, 11 July and 7 Nov. 1788, Archives de la Ville du Havre, Fonds Marine.

[38] Edmond Seligman, *La justice en France pendant la Révolution* (Paris, 1901), p. 229.

grains of it. The grains resembled the seed of muscat grapes, being hard, smooth, and yellowish in color. On three evenings in January, 1764, Mor employed this poison in the dressing for roast chicken that he served his master. The master seems to have been especially fond of chicken! On the first two occasions the master became sick but not seriously, and Mor confessed later to despair that the poison would not work and so asked Rodin for advice. Rodin, so Mor reported, advised him thereupon to crush several of the grains before he put them in the chicken dressing. In this fashion the poison was tried on January 17, the evening of the third attempt. On this occasion the lieutenant had two friends as guests, a Madame Plusquellec, who owned the home where Le Nort and Mor lived, and her father, a surgeon named Fouet. Shortly after the meal all were taken violently ill, and fearing that some form of poisoning had occurred, they resorted heavily to the use of tea, milk, and other drinks, which perhaps proved their salvation. On the morning of January 20 the Negro, who had taken his leave, returned to see what had happened to his master. Finding him in bed, he asked for some money to pay the postage on some letters that he alleged had come. His ruse succeeded and he obtained six livres, but he did not return with the mail. Thereupon De Nort arose and went in search of the Negro, whom he found in a cafe. Taking him home, he threatened to kill him if he did not own up to what he had done. Mor made a full confession before De Nort and others. De Nort then had him imprisoned. He likewise tried to force Rodin to confess his part, but without success. Rodin denied everything; yet he, too, was imprisoned.

Since Rodin was a servant of the Chevalier de Grasse, a naval officer resident in Paris, De Nort wrote him of the affair. He also notified Choiseul, Minister of the Marine. The latter wrote back asking for a careful examination of the affair and for a just trial.

The case was tried before judges in Brest in April. A physician and two surgeons testified that it was a case of poisoning.

On April 14 Mor was condemned to be hanged and strangled after being subjected to torture to ascertain his own guilt and the guilt of others. For he had changed his early confession to a denial of guilt. As for Rodin, he was to be subjected to torture also, inasmuch as he continued to deny all knowledge or complicity in the poisoning.

Mor appealed, and the case was taken to the Parlement of Rennes. On May 7, as a preliminary to the trial, Mor underwent torture before three officials who plied him with questions and recorded his answers. The elaborate report still exists. Mor was suspended, it appears, over a fire, and nine times was lowered close to the flames, as he repeatedly showed reluctance to talk. But he slowly and piecemeal confessed everything, restating all that he previously had confessed to his master. Rodin was then brought in, confronted with Mor's confession implicating him, and asked if guilty. His vigorous denial satisfied the judges, who proceeded to eliminate the use of torture. The next day the two men were ordered returned to Brest, separately, and imprisoned. Mor was ordered executed by strangling and burning on the marketplace at Brest on May 28, and whatever he possessed (a pathetic note) was to be confiscated to the crown. He also was condemned to make *amende honorable* at night in one of the churches, with a two-pound candle in his hand, clothed in a nightshirt and wearing a large placard on which was written "POISONER," and he was to ask forgiveness and mercy from God and the King. His ashes were to be scattered to the winds.

Burning was the common punishment in France for poisoners prior to the Revolution, and Mor was not discriminated against because of his race or social condition. Recently there had been an outbreak of poisoning of slaves and slaveowners, by slaves, in Santo Domingo. There seems to be no doubt that Mor was guilty, even though admitting that evidence extracted through force and torture is open to question. Mor was called an "imbecile" at one time by Rodin, and it is clear that he was stupid. Rodin was clever, and his escape no doubt was due to denials, for Mor's accusation that he had planned the matter probably was true. It was a pathetic affair, and it is ironical that it occurred in the very year that Beccaria's little treatise condemning torture was written. In the margin of one of the documents on the trial it is written that the "spices" (monetary gift to the judges in the trial before parlement) were 150 livres. Who paid this, the Negro slave or his owner, whom the state would recompense 1,500 livres for his slave?[39]

Such is the most atrocious crime of which a Negro in France was convicted during the century. Could it have been the factor that gave the Choiseul government the idea that the Negroes were dangerous to French society? Hardly so, for the idea was already expressed by it in 1762 and 1763. Could it have been important in instigating the legislation of 1777-1778? Far from likely, for it is not alluded to in any of the documents of the time or in the writings of literary men. It appears to have had local interest entirely.

It may be concluded therefore that the Negroes and mulattoes were not sufficiently numerous, sufficiently immoral, or sufficiently guilty of crime to be a hazard to French society in the period before the Revolution of 1789. Perhaps if no Revolution had occurred and colonists had continued to flock to France with their slaves after 1793, the story might have been different. But the Revolution, for various reasons to be discussed, reduced the influx of Negroes. After the Revolutionary and Napoleonic wars and the reopening of sea commerce in 1815, masters once again were to trek from the colonies to France with their slaves, but not in quite the same numbers. Never again until the twentieth century, and more particularly after World War II, were Negroes and mulattoes to come to France in significant numbers. Accordingly, the Negro problem of the 1770's and 1780's was actually something of a tempest in a teapot.

[39] The papers for this trial are found in Archives Départementales, Finistère, B 2188. The matter, strangely, is not mentioned in Maurice Bernard's *La municipalité de Brest de 1750 à 1790* (Paris, 1915), nor in Arthur Le Moyne de la Borderie's *Histoire de Brètagne* . . . (Rennes, 1914, 6 v.).

FOUR      LIBERATION AND
POLITICS

*THE FRENCH* Revolution came as
a boon to the Negro, whether slave or free. It espoused the
rights of the common man; it proclaimed liberty, equality, and
fraternity; from an early date it declared all men equal before
the courts. Slavery could not exist long when these broadly
stated principles set forth in the Declaration of the Rights of
Man of August, 1789, were carried to their logical conclusion.
In May, 1791, all free colored men, whether in France or the
colonies, were accorded full legal rights, and in February,
1794, the slaves in all French colonies were emancipated and
made citizens. This did not come without a struggle, and
some Negroes and mulattoes stationed in France had a small
part as actors in the movement.

All revolutions have causes, and those of the French Revolution are well known. For the Negro or mulatto, even though
he was in France, there was the recollection of the infamous
Code Noir, first drawn up in 1685 by the government of Louis
XIV and subsequently modified by legal enactments and
regulations of the French government affecting the colonies.
Thus in the 1767 edition of the Code Noir, a small work in
duodecimo, can be found numerous royal ordinances, orders
of the Council of State, royal letters patent, and edicts published in the eighteenth century regulating the slave trade and
the life of slaves in the colonies. Among them were the Edict
of 1716 and the Declarations of 1738 and 1762 mentioned

earlier. The legislation was designed not only to set forth the demands and limitations placed on the slave, and even the free Negro or mulatto, but also to protect the slave and the free colored man against mistreatment from the whites. Even with all the legal protection given him, life for the slave was arduous, monotonous, and cruel. For the free Negro or mulatto, it was somewhat better. He might own land and slaves, and he might become wealthy (and some did). But he might never enjoy the social, professional, or legal position of the white race. He could enter no profession; the *maréchaussée* and militia were open to him, but in them he could hold no position of rank; and he could never raise his hand in violence against a white. If the peasant of France felt aggrieved against his lord and against the state for unfair conditions, the Negro and mulatto of the colonies had vastly more of which to complain. It is no wonder that discontent had long been rife in the colonies, and that runaway slaves, designated *marrons*, were numbered by the hundreds and often lived in bands in the swamps or mountain recesses beyond the zone of recovery.[1]

For the free Negro or mulatto residing in France, life was incomparably better, even though he might have to live in squalid quarters. At least he was treated by most persons without social discrimination, and before the law he had equal rights. Even for the slaves that could follow their masters and mistresses into France the change was a boon. The situation was bad only for those confined in the *dépôts des noirs*, where after 1777 most of the slaves coming to France were placed.

It is therefore not to be wondered at that all Negroes and mulattoes, both in France and in the colonies, were ardently in favor of the Revolution. A very large number, too, were to fight in its behalf. Although not directly a concern of this study, the colonial aspects of the Revolution, it is noted, are extremely interesting and complicated—the Revolution in some of the colonies being more violent than in France itself.

[1] Copies of the Code Noir are rare. Its terms are more accessible in *Recueil général des anciennes lois françaises*, XIX, 494-504.

It is of interest here that the free mulattoes of Santo Domingo, as early as 1784, five years before the Revolution, sent one of their number, Julien Raimond, to France to see if something could not be done to better their lot.[2] It appears that he himself was the organizer of the group, and that he freely offered to go on the mission. An octoroon whose father had gone out from Buanes-sur-Bahan, near Saint-Sever, France, and had married a quadroon, Julien had been born free and rich, for his father at his death in 1772 had left a fortune estimated at 322,000 livres, including 37 slaves. Julien was but one of the heirs, for there were twelve children, but two "easy" marriages, the second in 1782 to a very wealthy mulattress, had made him a man of fortune. That fortune was destined to be spent on the enterprise begun in 1784.[3] Raimond was one of about five hundred free Negroes and mulattoes from Santo Domingo who had fought with the French army in the American Revolution, and perhaps it was from the Americans that he contracted the spirit of revolt.

Two of his sisters had earlier come to France for an education, had married well, and were living there at this time. He settled in Angoumois for a time near one of them, later moving to La Rochelle and Angoulême. Not until the Revolution was he a resident of Paris. The Comte de Jarnac, a military acquaintance, took an interest in his enterprise and gave him some aid up to 1789. So, too, did De Bellecombe, former governor of Santo Domingo, who in late 1785 or early 1786 introduced him to the Marquis de Castries, Minister of the Marine. Raimond told De Castries of his mission and later sent him three memoirs setting forth the grievances of the mulattoes in the colonies and their demand for betterment of condition. De Castries expressed interest and promised an investigation, and proceeded to forward the memoirs to La Luzerne and De Marbois, administrators of the colony, who in

---

[2] The name is often written Raymond, but Julien himself wrote it Raimond.

[3] On Raimond's parentage and wealth, see Debien, "Les travaux d'histoire sur Saint-Domingue," 465-66; Luc Nemours, "Julien Raimond, le chef des gens de couleur et sa famille," ed. by Georges Lefebvre, *Annales historiques de la Révolution française*, année 23 (1951), 257-62.

turn were not unfriendly to the suggestions.[4] Raimond himself believed that some improvement might result. Correspondence reposing in the Archives Nationales indicates that De Castries was sincerely interested, but he did not remain long in office and no reform resulted.[5]

Reform was in the air at this time in France, but whether it could have been made substantial enough to have satisfied the free mulattoes is doubtful. They wanted equality with the whites, social as well as professional and civil, and subsequent events were to demonstrate that the white colonists were not ready to accept them as equals. Beyond the presentation of these memoirs, Raimond appears to have done little for his cause prior to the outbreak of the Revolution. He was not even a member of the Amis des Noirs, noted organization founded in 1788 by Brissot in behalf of terminating slavery and the slave trade, until after the Revolution had begun. Indeed, Raimond was little interested in Negroes or slavery or the slave trade; he was fundamentally interested in his own group solely, the free mulattoes.

Raimond's mission to France was not exactly a novelty. For two decades Court de Gebelin had been in Paris as a representative of the French Protestants to the government, and Pereire had long served as representative of the Jews.[6] Neither of them had any official position, but both took occasion to intercede and protest to the government whenever they found it expedient. That the mulattoes of Santo Domingo had ever heard of them, however, is most unlikely. By accident they tried the same method.

[4] Nemours, "Julien Raimond," 261-62; Debien, "Gens de couleur libres et colons de Saint-Domingue," 217-19; J. Raimond, *Réclamations addressées à l'Assemblée Nationale, par les personnes de couleur, propriétaires & cultivateurs de la colonie françoise de Saint-Domingue* (n.p. [1790]), p. 5n.

[5] Several letters between officials relative to these memoirs by Julien are to be found in a dossier marked "St. Domingue, Décisions 1719-1722," in Archives Nationales, Colonies, C⁹C4.

[6] Jack Alden Clarke, "A Protestant Philosophe at the Constituent Assembly," *The Historian*, XX (May, 1958), 293; Ernest La Rochelle, *Jacob Rodrigues Pereire, premier instituteur des sourds-muets en France: sa vie et ses travaux* (Paris, 1882), p. 150.

The Amis des Noirs, which came into existence in 1788, was a powerful group that included some members of the high aristocracy and even the King himself. The membership fees were high, being two louis (approximately $9.00), and the money was largely spent on the publication of pamphlets. When the Revolution came, a large group of free mulattoes like Raimond came under its wing and engaged actively in propaganda that would promote their cause. It was this organization that coordinated all the efforts to get remedial legislation for Negroes and mulattoes in the colonies, as well as to abolish the infamous slave trade that had now come in for censure by all humanitarians.

*[margin handwriting: radical association N.D.p.p]*

The aggressive policies of the Amis des Noirs alarmed the colonists resident in France at the outset of the Revolution, and in defense they organized a counter group called the Club Massiac, after the Hôtel de Massiac, where they had their headquarters. Until forced out of existence after the King's removal from office in August, 1792, the Club Massiac bitterly opposed the Amis des Noirs and in every way possible struggled to maintain white supremacy and slavery in the colonies.[7] A tug of war went on in France between these groups, at least during the first years of the Revolution.

With the outbreak of the Revolution the planters scored a victory by getting a group of their delegates accepted as members of the National Assembly. The free mulattoes of Paris protested this action without success, trying to get a panel of their own deputies as part of the colonial representation and insisting that in Santo Domingo the free mulattoes were as numerous as the whites.[8]

The colonists also acted to bring about if possible a cessation

---

[7] The best study of this group is G. Debien's *Les colons de Saint-Domingue et la Révolution: Essai sur le Club Massiac (août 1789–août 1792)* (Paris, 1953).

[8] Their letter to the National Assembly, dated 23 Nov. 1789, may be found in *Archives parlementaires de 1787 à 1860*, ed. by J. Madival *et al.*, sér. 1 (Paris, 1862-1913), X, 329-33. It was read to the Assembly on 28 Nov. 1789. Among those signing it were Raimond, Ogé, Du Souchet de Saint-Réal, Honoré de Saint-Albert, and Fleury.

of movement between France and the colonies on the part of all Negroes and mulattoes, free or slave; they endeavored to enlist in their support the chambers of commerce of the various French seaports, which in turn were to bring pressure on the Admiralty to permit no Negroes or mulattoes to leave the country. They also put pressure on the colonial governments to permit no sailing of Negroes, nor to admit any returning from France.[9] The idea was to prevent news of Revolutionary happenings like the fall of the Bastille from being carried back to the colonies, where only a spark was needed to set off an insurrection. In preventing Negroes from going to France, they would only be employing a double check to prevent communication. The Negroes and mulattoes in France were regarded as leaders and incendiaries who must be isolated and kept there.

Such was the design of the colonists, but seemingly they experienced only temporary success. In April, 1790, even De Marbois, intendant of Santo Domingo, apparently failed in his attempt to take back to the colony with him a young servant of mixed blood that he had brought to France. The Admiralty explained that the action came from the shipowners, not from the government.[10] Several mulattoes were refused sailing privileges from Bordeaux in the summer of 1790; then they applied and were refused at Le Havre. Thereupon they complained to the National Assembly at Paris. The Committee of Reports of this body in turn communicated with La Luzerne, Minister of the Marine, demanding an explanation. The committee stated that all French citizens had the right to come and go as they pleased, and that no fetters should be placed on travel. It considered that Mistral, port intendant at Le Havre, had exceeded his powers. La Luzerne forwarded to Mistral a copy of the letter and suggested that in the future

[9] Much correspondence on this matter is found in the départemental archives for the years 1789-1790.

[10] Minister of the Marine to De Marbois, 23 April 1790. Archives Nationales, Colonies, F$^3$ 150.

all parties be allowed sailing privileges, save in cases where the police recommended otherwise in writing.[11] Thenceforth Negroes and mulattoes wishing to sail from France had no trouble.

In this affair something was to be said for each side. On the one hand, there existed no legislation to deprive the Negroes and mulattoes of their rights. On the other, some were incendiaries working to promote insurrection in the colonies. This we know better than did the government officials of 1790. One alleged incendiary, a girl named Agathé Audebert, was returned to France from Santo Domingo, where she had fallen under suspicion, and the Chamber of Commerce at Bordeaux received a request that she be prevented from returning.[12] A case more significant concerned the sailing of Vincent Ogé *jeune*, a free quadroon, for Santo Domingo in the early summer of 1790, and his shipment of munitions. Could Ogé have been deterred, a serious insurrection would have been avoided and perhaps the subsequent history of the Revolution in that colony mitigated. Actually, Ogé did not sail from a French port, but from England. Knowing that the French port officials were on guard to prevent him from sailing, he decided to avoid the risk. Before embarking, he had a conference with the Abbé Grégoire, chief proponent of the men of color in the National Assembly, and the Abbé advised him strongly not to go.[13] But Ogé was an impetuous hothead. His intention was to go to Santo Domingo and see to the enforcement of a law enacted in Paris on March 28, 1790, which he considered granted civil rights to the free mulattoes; and if force was needed, he was prepared for insurrection. En route home he

[11] Entry for 19 Aug. 1790, Minutes of the Chamber of Commerce of Bordeaux, Archives de la Gironde, C 4259; Comité des Rapports to La Luzerne, 7 Aug. 1790, and La Luzerne to Mistral, 9 Aug. 1790, Archives de la Ville du Havre, PR, F² 12. La Luzerne earlier had approved Mistral's policy in this matter; see letter by him of 10 March 1790, *ibid.*, F² 10.

[12] Archives de la Gironde, C 4259, p. 57.

[13] *Mémoires de Grégoire, ancien évêque de Blois* . . . (Paris, 1837, 2 v.), I, 396.

visited the United States and obtained a shipment of arms, which was smuggled in.[14] It is needless to relate here the story of his insurrection, his eventual capture, and his brutal execution at the wheel. The incident inflamed the colony as nothing hitherto had done, and both there and in France it incited the Negroes and mulattoes to more determined efforts toward freedom and equality. The insurrection had been carefully planned in Paris by Ogé and certain confederate mulattoes. Ogé had bought arms in Le Havre, but they were not shipped for some reason.[15]

It is of interest that Ogé had been educated in France and that prior to this episode he had published a seven-page tract demanding for the mulattoes a part in the political deliberations in Paris affecting the colonies. The brochure is the impulsive demand of a young man for liberty, which he insisted was for all persons and worth risking one's life for. He asserted that he would gladly risk his. He mentioned that he was facing a court trial in Paris, but wondered whether he should let that stand in the way. The tract has a vein of fanaticism.[16]

Before leaving for Santo Domingo, Ogé in January, 1790, ran up a bill of 10,000 livres for porcelain at the Royal Manufacture of Porcelains in Paris, and escaped to the colonies without paying it by posing as a merchant.[17] Possibly he used this porcelain in some manner to get funds for munitions; possibly, too, it was this matter to which he referred in his brochure as occasioning a court trial.

---

[14] Raimond in his pamphlet entitled *Réponse aux considérations de M. Moreau, dit Saint-Méry* . . . (Paris, 1791), pp. 28-44, has much to say of this expedition and exonerates Ogé of planning insurrection, but the evidence otherwise is strong.

[15] See Debien, *Les colons de Saint-Domingue*, pp. 211, 222, 223, 226, 350. With Ogé were executed twenty-two others, and seventeen were sent to the galleys.

[16] It is entitled *Motion faite par M. Vincent Ogé jeune à l'Assemblée des colons, habitans de St.-Domingue, à l'Hôtel de Massiac, Place des Victoires* (n.p., n.d.).

[17] Report by Dangivillier, dated Paris, 20 Feb. 1791, and statement by the Manufacture des Porcelains du Roy of 15 Feb. 1791, in Archives Nationales, Colonies (Fonds Moreau de St.-Méry), F³ 150.

Ogé was not the only mulatto in France at this time trying to obtain ammunition for his fellows in the colonies. Another was Bonnard, aide to André Rigaud, himself an ambitious mulatto in Santo Domingo destined to give much trouble in the years ahead and to rise to the rank of general. Rigaud had sent Bonnard to France. There he purchased fifty kegs of powder, which were secreted in fifty barrels of rice and shipped from Marseilles to Santo Domingo. All might have gone well for the shipment had not a sailor revealed the matter to the Admiralty at Cayes. Investigation was made, and the arms were confiscated.[18] However, as the report stated, the mulattoes in Santo Domingo were not to be deprived of guns and powder; the United States was only too glad to take advantage of this opportunity to increase its commerce, even to the point of smuggling.

Ogé had considered that Article 4 of the Act of March 28, 1790, granted civil rights to the free mulattoes, but there was obscurity in the language. The matter was cleared up by a definite grant of civil rights by the National Assembly on May 15, 1791. In the colonies news of this decree was received as a catastrophe by the whites, who endeavored in every way to avoid its enforcement; but in France it had little significance. There the free mulattoes were already treated as citizens; nevertheless, they took enormous interest in the matter, for it was the thing they most desired, the thing for which they had been working, had organized, written pamphlets, made untold visits to gain the support of politicians, and on several occasions sent delegations with petitions to the National Assembly. To most of their activities we have only fleeting references in letters, pamphlets, and memoirs of the period. The pamphlets and petitions still remain in print, although of interest today only to the antiquarian.

[18] This information is found in a report on André Rigaud, evidently in 1802 or 1803, entitled "Précis de la conduite d'André Rigaud, chef de la révolte des gens de couleur et instigateur de la guerre civile actuelle," Archives Nationales, Colonies, C⁹B40.

Despite their dust, these pamphlets reveal much of historical significance. They number perhaps a score, written and published in 1789 and the 1790's. Virtually all were written by free mulattoes; only two or three were by Negroes. They reveal a group of writers, mostly young men, burning with hatred for the discriminations they had experienced in the colonies and aflame with enthusiasm for the keywords of the Revolution which they considered would bring them a new heaven and a new earth. It is not without interest that most of them wrote rather well, and one wonders if they acquired this training from tutors, since schools for them did not exist in the colonies. Some, but not all, had been sent to France for an education. They were natural sons, for the most part, recognized by their fathers, who supplied them liberally with money.

The greatest number of pamphlets were by Raimond. First and last he published eight or ten. He literally rushed into print, eager like the common run of eighteenth-century pamphleteers to pitch into a quarrel. He charged his opponents with falsehood, ignorance, bigotry, and malice, and himself he set forth always as correctly informed, unbiased, eager to report the truth, and a champion of the Revolution. In himself was all virtue; in his opponents, the colonists, only evil. Had he been in the chair of St. Peter, Raimond would have admitted to heaven no colonists, whether of planter class or the little whites—they were all too wicked. Possibly he would have admitted the slaves, to serve his class. For the remarkable thing about Raimond, and indeed most of the mulattoes, was their class interest. They were concerned only with the mulattoes—the free mulattoes—and not with the Negroes. Only in one or two of Raimond's later pamphlets is any espousal whatever of the cause of the slave. No, Raimond was a planter and a slaveowner as haughty and proud in his fashion as any white. He and the other free mulattoes considered themselves on a par with the whites, economically and in merit, and demanded political, professional, and social equality also. They wanted the whites to receive them as equals, not only in France but also in the colonies.

Raimond wrote as if he had dipped his pen in vitriol. He was caustic and sarcastic. Never a spark of humor from him or any other mulatto writer of this period! Like the other French revolutionaries, they were deadly serious. Raimond went about his self-appointed task as if commissioned by God. John Wesley showed no more zeal than this man. Despite the fact that his brochures were published, for the most part by the friendly press of Brissot or others maintained by the Amis des Noirs, he reported that he had paid for their publication. He paid for his cabs to make calls daily on politicians and others who could aid his cause. And he saw his fortune slowly ebb away, as he spent it gladly in the cause so dear to his heart. In the history of the French Revolution, no other mulatto or Negro had so gallant a role.

It is hard to evaluate Raimond's influence for the reason that it is not known to what extent his brochures were read. Although he wrote with verve and fire, his writings did not reach a second or third edition. Possibly the number of readers was limited largely to the Amis des Noirs and others especially interested in colonial matters. Up to his day he was perhaps the most remarkable mulatto that had set foot on French soil.

Raimond's reading had not been wide. Almost the only book of significance that he cited in footnotes was Hilliard d'Auberteuil's *Considérations sur Saint-Domingue*, a two-volume study published in 1776-1777 sharply criticizing conditions in Santo Domingo and advocating reforms. In turn it was bitterly attacked by the planters and banned from circulation; some years later Hilliard was mysteriously killed. For information on recent events on the island Raimond relied on letters from one of his brothers at Aquin and other collaborators.

The degree to which he devoted himself to his cause can be gauged from the fact that when he went to France, he had a revenue of 55,000 livres a year from his estates in Santo

Domingo, and yet by 1790 he had spent half of his fortune
and sold his silverware and his wife's jewels, all for his cause.[19]
His enemies at Paris, not knowing this, charged him with
exploiting the mulattoes back in the colony. The charge,
expressed in a pamphlet, drew Raimond's sharp reply and a
report of the heavy expenditures he had incurred.[20] He partly
laid himself open to such a charge by grandiosely offering to
the National Assembly in 1790 the freewill gift of 6,000,000
livres from his fellow men in Santo Domingo. Its theatrical
value was enormous, and no doubt it had its part in wringing
political concessions from the Assembly. It was an adroit
political move. Only an infinitesimal part of the sum was ever
paid, but no one gave attention to that. The offer was big and
it oozed patriotism and the Revolutionary sentiment. It was
natural, however, that his enemies, less risky in their offers,
should be astounded at the money at his disposal and bring
charges of personal aggrandizement.[21]

Another clever move by Raimond came in 1792, after the
declaration of war against Austria and Prussia. The French
had met with reverses and consternation prevailed. Blame was
laid on the aristocrats. At this stirring time, with French
borders invaded, Raimond offered to the National Assembly
the service of a brigade of mulattoes, provided that the
Assembly would permit their organization. This, again, was
a theatrical offer, designed for political effect. For there was

[19] See A. Brette, "Les gens de couleur libres et leurs députés en 1789," La
Révolution Française, XXIX (1895), 402 n1; Debien, Les colons de Saint-
Domingue, pp. 37-39, 161, et passim; Mercer Cook, Five French Negro
Authors (Washington [1943]), chapter on Raimond.

[20] See his Correspondance de Julien Raimond, avec ses frères, de Saint-
Domingue, et les pièces qui lui ont été adressés par eux (Paris, an II), pp.
iii-vi, 2-3.

[21] In a Première lettre, écrite dans la partie de l'Ouest (Paris, 1791), he
criticizes the mulattoes in the colony for their failure to pay the promised sum,
and calls on them anew to pay it and to send an additional 1,398,000 livres to
present as gifts to those in the Assembly who had written or spoken in behalf
of the men of color. Among those whom he would make gifts were Brissot,
Grégoire, Pétion, Clavière, Robespierre, and Lucas (p. 5). Here again (p. 3)
he details his own expenditures over the past seven years in behalf of his cause.

nothing to prevent any free Negro or mulatto in France from enlisting in the army. For decades many had so served. There was this qualification; if granted the privilege of organizing as a unit, they might have their own officers. The privilege was granted, and the mulattoes once more were identified with the Revolution. In more ways than one it was a colorful unit, and more will be told about it in the next chapter.[22] Raimond was a clever propagandist, theatrical, generous, vocal. He stressed the errors of his adversaries and the righteousness of his own cause.

After civil rights were granted the free mulattoes in the colonies by the Act of May 15, 1791, Raimond might have been expected to retire in silence. On the contrary, several pamphlets emerged afterward. In the first place, the National Assembly, in response to shrieks from the colonists, virtually shelved the act by its Decree of September 24, 1791, which put all legislation affecting the inner life of the colonies in the hands of the colonial assemblies. Enforcement of the matter was thus postponed until the arrival of the commissioners Sonthonax, Polverel, and Ailhaud in 1793. The first two quickly assumed control and by a concatenation of circumstances freed the slaves, forced out the whites, and established Jacobin government in the island. Raimond continued to express his sentiments on the race question in the colony, but he became increasingly concerned in the island's politics. Eventually he came to break with Sonthonax, whom originally he had looked upon as a savior. Under the Directory he was sent as member of a commission to investigate conditions in Santo Domingo, but there he cut a sorry figure. He thought that the people on the island should be grateful for what he had done in France in their behalf; but the leaders of the various groups were interested in their own ambitions and paid him little regard.

[22] Raimond's petition to the National Assembly, 7 Sept. 1792, and his own offer of 500 livres toward equipment of the "Legion" to be organized, is republished in his Correspondance, pp. 114-15.

One of Raimond's finest acts of his entire career was to adopt a little mulatto girl, who had been abandoned by her father, and to bring her to France with him and his wife in 1784.[23] Though without doubt Raimond was the most vocal and the most capable of the colored pamphleteers in France who endeavored to influence opinion at this time, there were others who deserve fleeting mention. None save Ogé wrote in the early years of the Revolution; they were active only after 1793, and most of them after 1795. Though residing in France, their minds and hearts, like the Hebrew harps, were hung on the willows of Babylon: their concern was in the colonies and with petty politics. The earliest though not the most capable of these later tractarians was Janvier Littée (or Littey), a mulatto deputy elected from Martinique to the National Convention September 19, 1792. His sole brochure was written in reply to an abusive attack by a white from Martinique, P. J. Leborne, who had charged him with being a turncoat, deserting his own race and aiding the colonists. Leborne charged that, despite the decree of emancipation, Littée's mother was still a slave in Martinique (October, 1794) and so were his relatives on Saint-Lucie.[24] Littée's reply vindicated his failure to support a petition that Leborne and some mulattoes in Paris ardently supported. He charged that the men who had gone to present it before the Convention had lived in Paris for twenty or thirty years and were out of touch with the needs in the colonies. He labeled Leborne in turn an intriguer, traitor, robber, and murderer who had escaped execution only "through the protection of Governor Laborie" (of Saint-Lucie), a collaborator with Sonthonax, Polverel, and Robespierre.[25] It

23 *Correspondance*, p. vii n1.
24 Leborne's pamphlet was entitled *P. J. Leborne, ci-devant commissaire de la marine aux Isles du Vent de l'Amérique, à Janvier Littée, homme de couleur député de la Martinique* . . . (Paris [1794]).
25 *Résponse de Janvier Littey, homme de couleur de la Martinique, et député à la Convention Nationale, à P. J. Leborne* (Paris, an III), pp. 1-7. The pamphlet was published in October, 1794, and the petition referred to was presented on 5 vendémiaire.

would appear that Littée had the distinction of being the first mulatto ever elected to a French legislative body.

Another minor pamphleteer was Pierre La Chapelle, a mulatto born in Santo Domingo who had come to France at the age of three and later had served sixteen years in the army. Though charged by a fellow mulatto with being a royalist, he had endeavored to avoid a factional stand during the Revolution and in consequence was chosen, along with J. A. Garrigou, to go as commissioner from the city of Cayes in Santo Domingo on a special mission to the French Directory in 1795, namely to denounce the chaos into which the colony had fallen. The two men went to Paris and there published a 78-page pamphlet depicting the sad state of the colony and criticizing those they considered responsible. The pamphlet was written in Portsmouth, England, where they had been detained en route to France, evidently as prisoners of war.[26]

One of those severely criticized for his part in events in the colony was Pierre Pinchinat, a mulatto. Elected a deputy to the Legislative Corps of the Directory, Pinchinat replied to his two accusers and others with a 171-page blast which may be designated by its first word, *Réponse*. It is a wearisome account of the stormy politics that had rocked the island. He had been charged by his adversaries with having been responsible in 1792 for sending 300 Negroes to France; he insisted that it was only 200. He charged that through the machinations of his opponents he had been imprisoned at Cherbourg for four months while en route to Paris. And of more interest, he stated that the Legislative Corps had refused to let him and Chanlatte, a Negro, take their seats as representatives from the colony.[27] A second pamphlet he devoted more particularly to Sonthonax, with whom he had broken; in this he called himself "deputy to the Legislative Corps, not admitted." This brochure

[26] Their pamphlet was entitled *Comte rendu des événements survenus dans le département du sud de St.-Domingue, les dix fructidor et jours suivans de l'an IV* ([Paris, an IV]).

[27] *Réponse de Pinchinat, député de Saint-Domingue . . .* (Paris, n.d.), pp. iii-iv, 16, 163.

was briefer and better written than the former. It, too, was taken up with recent political happenings in Santo Domingo. That he could employ strong language was shown in his accusation that Sonthonax had displayed toward Rigaud (Pinchinat's hero) malice, villainy, and imbecility.[28]

Last but not least in interest among the pamphleteers was the Negro general Martial Besse, who published at Paris two brochures in the year VI (1797-1798). Both were answers to the charges made against him by the former governor and commandant of Santo Domingo, Hughes Montbrun. Montbrun had published some accusations in a journal entitled the *Pacificateur*, which had just the opposite effect from pacifying Besse. The latter rushed into print. He alleged that Montbrun did not know of his presence in France, but stated that he had been there a year. He denied responsibility for the fall of Port-au-Prince to the British, retorting that it had fallen through the desertion and treachery of Montbrun.[29]

The short pamphlet was seasoned with sharp adjectives, and Montbrun was goaded like a bull. He hastened into print with a defense and more charges, and Besse in turn felt obliged to write a second pamphlet. He charged that Montbrun had issued "a violent diatribe" against him. This time he had to defend himself against the accusation not only that he had been responsible for military defeat, but also that his conduct of the army had been marked by corruption and scandal. This he did to his own satisfaction and countercharged Montbrun with the most shameful corruption and inefficiency.[30] Like the other pamphleteers, Besse resorted to invective and countercharge as defense, and insisted upon the purity of his own motives and conduct.

These pamphlets as a whole are wearisome reading, but they

[28] *Santhonax réfuté par lui-même* . . . (Paris [an VII]), p. 46. Pinchinat refers to the fact that he grew up in France.

[29] *Appel à l'opinion publique, par Martial Besse, général de brigade, employé à St.-Domingue* (Paris, an VI), pp. 15.

[30] *Deuxième appel à l'opinion publique, par Martial Besse, général de brigade* (Paris, an VI), pp. 31.

hold some interest. Above all, they reveal that after the departure of the colonists (1793), the islands, notably Santo Domingo, had become prey to internal factions of Negroes and mulattoes, and that these groups came to hate each other with as much venom as formerly they had displayed in print toward the whites. Formerly it was the whites who were the villains, now it was the opposing political faction of mulattoes or Negroes. If liberty and equality had come to the islands, fraternity had not; and France got the backwash of it all.

Reference has been made to the Atlantic crossings during the 1790's by Raimond, Besse, Pinchinat, and others. To what degree were crossings possible for Negroes and mulattoes? No restriction by the government at Paris was imposed at any time. There was some restriction in 1789-1790 by the colony of Santo Domingo, and perhaps by other colonies. In France an effort was made by the colonists and the chambers of commerce of certain port cities to close these ports to emigrating Negroes and mulattoes, and to prevail upon fellow colonists to leave their slaves for the time being in the *dépôts des noirs.* Success was faint. It appears to have made the mulattoes in France more determined than ever to return to wave the flag of insurrection. Prior to the war with England in 1793, the Atlantic crossings did not lessen to a great extent. Proof of this can be found in the shipping figures for the period.

In 1789 the sum of 153,000 livres was deposited with the government of Santo Domingo as guaranty for the return of 102 slaves, at the rate of 1,500 livres a slave. This implies that 102 slaves sailed that year with their masters from a single colony. Also that year, 68 slaves were returned from France to Santo Domingo, and deposits of 98,500 were returned to their owners.[31] Figures for subsequent years were not available, possibly due to the carelessness of the colonial intendants succeeding Barbé de Marbois; but Admiralty records show that in 1790 eleven Negroes and mulattoes arrived in the port

---

[31] See itemized financial report, part VII, "Etat des caisses des consignations pour passage d'esclaves," Archives Nationales, Colonies, C⁹B40.

of Nantes, and in 1791 eighteen.[32] Among the latter were two sons of African chiefs, come to France apparently for an education. Both had sailed to the West Indies and thence to France.[33] On one of the ships was a stowaway, Tomain, a Portuguese Negro slave who had boarded it somewhere en route. Several stowaways are mentioned in the late eighteenth-century records.

For 1792 there were forty-two arrivals of Negroes and mulattoes at Nantes. Not all were slaves. One was Fangou, son of a chieftain of Angola, traveling at the expense of the French government. Among the stowaways on this vessel were five slaves from Santo Domingo—three Negresses, a mulattress, and a Negro. Several of the group were natives of Africa. These arrived at Nantes alone, but they reveal that in the early 1790's sailings did continue for the Negroes and mulattoes.

Le Havre had something of the same story. A port with fewer arrivals and departures than Nantes, it had fourteen Negro and mulatto entrants in 1791, ten in 1792. Eight or ten other domestics are listed, either whites or freedmen. In this era, however, it was customary to mention any evidence of color.[34]

Both Nantes and Le Havre suffered a great diminution of Atlantic crossings during the years 1793-1801. At Nantes only twenty-seven ships arrived in 1793, with only three Negroes aboard, all little boys, one of them a free eight-year-old from Africa. Similarly during 1794 the arrivals and sailings were few. Many Negroes and mulattoes left Santo Domingo for Norfolk and New York, apparently accompanying their émigré masters and mistresses. Le Hardy sailing from Santo Domingo in June carried twenty Negroes and mulattoes, most of whom disembarked in American ports; only four continued to Brest,

[32] "Passagers débarqués en France, Nantes, 1790-1817," Archives Nationales, Colonies, F5B24.
[33] Many French vessels, especially the négriers or slave ships, made the triangular sailings—France, Africa, West Indies.
[34] "Passagers débarqués en France, Le Havre, 1791-1820," Archives Nationales, Colonies, F5B12.

including a Negro deputy to the National Convention named George and his aide-de-camp.[35] The records show only four Negro arrivals for the city of Nantes in 1794, four at Paimboeuf, and four at Brest. No doubt there were others, but transatlantic travel for the French had dwindled to a trickle, and the ships that did attempt the crossing came in convoy. From 1795 to 1800 no vessels are listed as coming from the West Indies to Nantes. The crossings made in this period, as those by Besse, Pinchinat, and Raimond, possibly were made via New York, where a change of vessels was effected. Certainly some travelers used that route. During these years several French Negroes and mulattoes fell into British hands, some at sea.

During the Thermidorian Reaction in late 1794 a large number of Negroes and mulattoes in Guadeloupe were taken by *muscadins* (colonial reactionaries) and the British and placed aboard British vessels headed for Britain. En route the mulattoes on two of the transports seized control and steered to Rochefort, where they asked that the ships be declared prizes of war. How many were involved in the action is not indicated; a committee of five mulattoes made the demand.[36]

This virtual cessation in sea traffic that prevailed during the war years 1793-1801 was to continue when war with Britain was resumed in early 1803, to last until 1815. The sailings were extremely few, and Negro and mulatto crossings shrank nearly to nothing, save for the period of the Leclerc Expedition in 1801-1802, a brief interlude of peace.[37]

While the chief factor responsible for this diminution of travel for Negroes and mulattoes was of course the British blockade, a secondary factor of importance was the emancipation of slaves in the colonies by the National Convention

[35] These last two are also listed as arriving on *Les Deux Josephines, ibid.,* F5B24.
[36] *Pétition à la Convention Nationale par les patriotes, citoyens de couleur, déportés par les Anglais et débarqués à Rochefort, après s'être rendus maîtres des transports no. 34 et 42 par le 41me dégré de latitude nord* (Paris, 1794?), pp. 19.
[37] A few Negroes and mulattoes for this period are listed in Archives Nationales, Colonies, F5B24.

through the Decree of February 4, 1794. That incident, though it affected the colonies primarily, also in a lesser degree affected France also. A war measure, much as was Lincoln's emancipation of the slaves in the United States in 1863, the decree was brought about fundamentally by the colons resisting the Jacobin government of France and making an alliance with France's enemy Great Britain. It was precipitated by the arrival of three deputies from Santo Domingo to the National Convention, one of them being a mulatto and another a Negro.[38] On February 2 they applied for seating in the Convention; on February 4 they were admitted, and one of them was asked to report on conditions in the colony, a topic of great interest and solicitude. He made an eloquent report, denouncing the perfidy of the planters and portraying in glowing terms the loyalty to France on the part of the Negroes and mulattoes. It was reported that Sonthonax, the counterpart to Robespierre in the colony, already had granted the slaves freedom. Danton, Levasseur, and Lacroix, the president of the hall, spoke in favor of freeing the slaves. A Negro deputation was received at the same time, one member of it being an aged woman, an ex-slave allegedly 101 years old. She was presented to the president of the Convention, who gave her the accolade on each cheek. In the excitement it was proposed that slavery be abolished on the spot, without referring the action (as customary) to a committee for study and report. Lacroix himself was a protagonist of this view. He put the question to a vote. It was unanimous. Frenzied excitement followed. So quickly was slavery abolished in the French colonies.[39]

[38] The mulatto was Jean Baptiste Mills, born in Jamaica, and the Negro (formerly a slave), Mars (Jean Baptiste) Belley. C. L. R. James, *The Black Jacobins* (New York, n.d.), pp. 112-13; *Dictionnaire de biographie française*, ed. by Prevost and D'Amat, V, 1355; *Grande Encyclopèdie*.

[39] *Réimpression de l'ancien Moniteur*, XIX, 387-95; *Mercure français, historique, politique et littéraire*, 1794, pp. 292, 297-300. Professor Lefebvre thinks that another motive for the French action in emancipating the slaves was to provoke insurrection in the British colonies. See Georges Lefebvre, *La Révolution française* (new ed., Paris, 1951), p. 635.

In France the action must have opened the doors to freedom for any slaves still in the *dépôts des noirs,* save for those held because of legal infractions. It also entitled them to remain in France as citizens. In the colonies the effect was varied. In Santo Domingo freedom had already been granted on August 29, 1793, as a revolutionary measure. In Martinique, which fell to the British in March, 1794, the conquerors refused to recognize the decree. And in the eastern colonies of Ile-de-France and Ile Bourbon (Réunion) it was not enforced. Only in Guadeloupe and in French Guiana, accordingly, did the Decree of February 4 have real effect.[40]

The Negro deputation that was admitted to the floor of the National Convention on February 4 was the last and most successful of several that had been received by the various legislative bodies at Paris since 1789. The Negroes were not alone in this mode of petition, but they used it effectively for their various requests. Raimond had been the spokesman, if not the instigator, of one or two of their earliest visits. On one of the last visits, in June, 1793, a deputation had been permitted to file across the floor with a large banner. Among their number was an aged woman, reputedly 114 years old (perhaps the same woman who later attended the meeting of February 4, 1794), supported by two men. All deputies arose out of respect to her, and the president kissed her cheeks.[41] This mode of propaganda evidently had its effect.

Mention has been made of a mulatto who was elected deputy from Martinique to the National Convention in 1792 .In subsequent years several others were elected to it and other bodies. Since they were the first Negro deputies in France, some notes on them may hold interest. A man named Carstaing was elected from a constituency in France itself, in December, 1793, in replacement of a deputy who had been executed. During the Reign of Terror, he married the Comtesse de Beauharnais, sister-in-law of General Beauharnais, Josephine's

<hr>

[40] Trayer, *Etude historique sur la condition légale,* p. 100.
[41] *Archives parlementaires de 1787 à 1860,* sér. 1, LXVI, 57.

first husband. He was a widower with four children, she a divorcee with one.[42] Later he was a deputy to the Council of the Five Hundred and a deputy to the Legislative Corps under the Consulate.

Both Jean Baptiste Mills and Mars Belley likewise served as deputy to the National Convention and to the legislative bodies of the Directory, Mills sitting in the Council of Ancients, Belley in the Council of the Five Hundred. Born on the island of Gorée, near the present Dakar, Belley had gone far.[43] He later was shot in Santo Domingo after the Leclerc Expedition. Two other Negroes were elected from Santo Domingo as deputies to the Legislative Corps during the year V (1796-1797), but they were not permitted to take their seats.[44] They were Pinchinat, the pamphleteer already mentioned, and Antoine Chanlatte, a brigadier general who later served in various campaigns in Europe before his death at Paris in 1816. Finally there was Etienne Victor Mentor, Negro deputy to the Council of the Five Hundred from Santo Domingo, who was expelled from the Legislative Corps and from Paris after Napoleon's coup d'état of 18 Brumaire.[45] It is interesting that so many Negroes were elected to French legislative bodies in the 1790's, and the fact that they did not distinguish themselves as deputies is not to their discredit.

In smaller roles many had taken some part in French politics during the Revolutionary years. Two mulattresses were members of the fraternel Jacobin Society at Paris in 1791 and were expelled because of their tendency to violent action.[46] The

[42] Walter Geer, Napoleon and his Family: the Story of a Corsican Clan, I (New York, 1927), 70; J. F. E. R. Robinet, Dictionnaire historique et biographique de la Révolution et de l'Empire, 1789-1815 (Paris [1899], 2 v.), I, 344-45.

[43] Robinet, Dictionnaire historique, I, 148, II, 563.

[44] Pinchinat, Réponse, p. 16; Robinet, Dictionnaire historique, I, 375.

[45] Robinet, Dictionnaire historique, II, 552; Grégoire, De la littérature des nègres, pp. 101-102. Grégoire relates an exploit in which Mentor had taken possession of a British boat on which he was being carried prisoner to England and brought it into the harbor at Brest. He speaks of his "brilliant qualities."

[46] Isabelle Bourdin, Les sociétés à Paris pendant la Révolution (Paris, 1937), pp. 37-38, 275n, 278.

Abbé Grégoire tells of a Negro administrator in the department of Gard in southeastern France in 1791 who was much "esteemed."[47] In 1792 a deputation of four was sent to Paris by the free mulattoes "to solicit a revocation of the disastrous decree of 24 September of the year previous."[48] Zamore, an East Indian Negro, who had been reared by Madame du Barry and was a witness against her at her trial in early December, 1794, was employed at the time of the trial by the Committee of Public Safety at Versailles. He was thus considered a good Jacobin.[49] Finally, there was Delorme, a mulatto whose Jacobin zeal led to his arrest and execution by the guillotine in Paris, following an attempted coup of May 20, 1795.[50] These are but just a few of the many Negroes and mulattoes who eagerly pressed forward to have a part in the promotion of the Revolution. Often they appear to have been hotheaded, indiscreet, rushing to extremes. No doubt, however, many were sober, and some even indifferent.

This chapter had been restricted to the matters of emancipation and politics. Much was happening in the social, educational, military, and other milieus of interest to the reader. Happily, we know more of the Negro and mulatto for the Revolutionary period because more printed and manuscript material concerning them is available for this era. This, in turn, was due in part to the fact that more Negroes were getting education and training, in one way or another, and a far larger number were free from the shackles of slavery than formerly. The Negro was making an advance, and rightly he recognized the Revolution as an opportunity to be seized.

47 *Lettres aux citoyens de couleur et nègres libres de Saint-Domingue et des autres isles françaises de l'Amérique* (Paris [1791]), p. 8.
48 Raimond, *Correspondance*, p. 71 n2.
49 Archives Nationales, W 100.
50 The matter is sarcastically related in a brochure, entitled *L'African Gambari, à Toussaint l'Ouvertoure africain, et général de brigade* (Paris, n.d.), pp. 1, 3. Gambari suggests that perhaps Delorme would not have been executed had he been from Santo Domingo, since mulattoes and Negroes from that colony were treated in France as privileged persons by the revolutionaries.

FIVE     WEARING THE UNIFORM

*R*ECORDS OF Negroes serving in
the French army are found dating back to the late 1600's.
Moreau de Saint-Méry tells of a Captain Vincent Ollivier, a
freedman from Santo Domingo, being buried on the island in
1780 at the age of about 120. When young he had accompanied
his master as a slave to the siege of Cartagena in 1697.
Later captured at sea, he was taken prisoner and carried to
France, where because of his tall stature he was presented to
Louis XIV. Fond of the military life, he enlisted in the
French army and served under Villars in the War of the
Spanish Succession. Afterward returning to Santo Domingo,
he was appointed captain general of all the Negro militia in
the region of Le Cap. He was commonly known as Captain
Vincent, and was received and treated on equal terms with
the whites, even sitting as a guest at the table of the governor
general, the Comte d'Argout. He was highly regarded by
everyone. Louis XIV presented him a helmet and a sword,
which he always wore. Ollivier had a part in enrolling men
for the expedition against Savannah in the late 1770's. With
his great height, his black skin, and his white hair he made
a very impressive appearance. Because of his services, the
colonial officials gave him a 600-livre pension in 1776.[1]

[1] Moreau de Saint-Méry, *Description* . . . *de la partie française de l'Ile de
Saint-Domingue,* new ed. by Blanche Maurel and Etienne Taillemite (Paris,
1958, 3 v.), I, 229.

The great French Marshal Maurice de Saxe, of German origin, was reportedly the first French leader to recognize the Negro's fighting qualities. During the War of the Austrian Succession he formed a brigade of Negroes, Arabians, and East Indians as part of a foreign legion. The Negroes came from Madagascar, Guinea, Senegal, the Congo, and from the western colonies of Santo Domingo and Guiana. Their leader, Jean Hitton, claimed to be the son of an African chieftain and was given the rank of *sous-brigadier*. All were of the Moslem faith.[2] The Marshal took a personal interest in the formation of the Saxe Volunteers, as the unit came to be called. It was recruited in France of Negroes who found themselves there in one capacity or another. Seven were from the prison of Orleans, the reason for their detention not being given.[3] Two others were engaged by recruiting agents of the Marshal at Bordeaux and held there in prison by the intendant Tourny until the Marshal could be notified and their acceptance declared. They asserted under oath that they were former slaves, one to a merchant named Quin, the other to a ship captain named Roze, that they had been in France several years, and that they had been liberated by their masters. Certification of these claims was sent the Marshal, but the Negroes had never been registered in France by their masters and doubt existed about their status. Saxe, anxious to obtain the men for his unit, wrote asking the Minister of War D'Argenson to issue an order for their conduct to him by a person he would designate. D'Argenson, however, questioned their claim to liberation and referred the matter to Maurepas, Minister of the Marine. Apparently Saxe got his two Negroes, but this case shows the care taken to enlist only freedmen, lest legal complications develop. It is of interest that one of the Negroes in this affair was nineteen, the other sixteen, and

[2] Eugène Fieffé, *Histoire des troupes étrangères au service de France depuis leur origine jusqu'à nos jours* . . . (Paris, 1854, 2 v.), I, 280-81; Mathorez, *Les étrangers en France*, I, 185, 403.

[3] Barentin to Maurepas, 11 Nov. 1747, Archives Nationales, Fonds de la Marine, B[3] 461, f 202.

both wished to enlist for life.[4] It is possible that the seven Negroes from Orleans cited earlier were not necessarily charged with lawbreaking, but like these last two were merely held in prison while order for their transfer came. The two cases give us some small insight into their mode of enlistment.

Organized only late in the war, the regiment of which the Saxe Volunteers was a part nevertheless distinguished itself in one of the battles of 1748. It was the last regiment returned to France from Flanders, and for a time it was stationed at Saint-Denis. Saxe himself retired to Chambord after the peace of Aix-la-Chapelle and requested permission to keep this regiment on war footing at Chambord. The request was granted, and until he died, November 30, 1750, the regiment was stationed at Chambord. Saxe is reported to have granted his soldiers the privilege of taking either Negro or French wives.[5] Whether it would have been possible at that time to have found in France a sufficiently large number of free Negro women, however, is doubtful.

At Chambord the regiment regularly went through its drill exercises, and one day each year, November 28, was set apart for the visit of the King, his family, and his court to witness them. The parade ground was the plain of Sablons, and Marshal de Saxe himself, wearing the uniform of the regiment, directed the exercises in person.[6]

When the Marshal died, his body was embalmed and kept at the Château de Chambord until January 8, 1751, when it was taken to Strasbourg for burial. The cortege was accompanied by an escort of one hundred dragoons of this regiment. Such was the slowness of transportation and such also the pomp of funerals of that period for distinguished persons that a month was required to reach Strasbourg, a distance of perhaps 300 to 350 miles.[7]

[4] Ibid., B³ 460, ff 83-88.
[5] Mathorez, Les étrangers en France, I, 403.
[6] Mes rêveries: ouvrage posthume de Maurice, Comte de Saxe, Duc de Courlande et de Semigalle, maréchal général des armées de sa Majesté très-chrétienne (Amsterdam et Leipzig, 1756, 2 v.), I, cxix-xx.
[7] Ibid., cxxiii-xxv.

Saxe in his will had expressed the wish that after his death this regiment might be placed under the command of his nephew. This was not done; it was broken up and its men "dispersed to other units."[8] Many became kettledrummers. Occasionally thereafter a Negro soldier was mentioned in police reports up to the Revolution, notably in the registration in 1777 required of all Negroes and mulattoes resident in France.

Among the number of soldiers and former soldiers designated in the 1777 registration was a 66-year-old Negro, Davijon, a retired kettledrummer of the Royal German Regiment of Alsace. A native of the Gold Coast of Africa, he had come to France in 1743. A second retired kettledrummer was Pierre Hector, thirty-six years old, from Saint-Pierre, Martinque. He had served twelve years in the French cavalry, and later six years in the infantry. At the moment of registration he was living at Paris with a white wife he had married in Poitou. A third was a mulatto thirty-seven years old, named Joseph Aubin, from Santo Domingo. He had been brought to France in 1742 by his father, but on his father's death the heirs had taken him to Martinique and sold him to a lawyer named Dahon. In 1759 Dahon returned with him to France, and died fifteen days later, granting him freedom by his will because of his faithful service. Afterward, Aubin served two stretches in the army, one of eight years as dragoon in the Regiment of La Rochefoucauld, and another in the Irish Regiment of Dillon. He had discharges from 1771 and 1775 to verify his claims. At the time of registration in 1777 he was living at Dunkerque, a servant and tableboy at the prison. Guilty of registering late, he had been placed in prison and lacked the money to pay his way out.[9]

References to these soldiers were not restricted to the

[8] Fieffé, *Histoire des troupes étrangères,* I, 281; Mathorez, *Les étrangers en France,* I, 185, 403.

[9] Archives Nationales, Colonies, F$^1$B4; *ibid.,* Z$^1$D138, f 39; *ibid.,* Colonies, F$^1$B3, "Extrait des registres du greffe de l'amirauté de Dunkerque" and a letter from Coppeus, 27 Nov. 1777.

registration of 1777, however. In 1763 an escaped Negro slave named Pompée was recognized in a company of soldiers at Le Havre by his master, a former military officer in Santo Domingo, and immediately this officer made requisition for his return to the colony. A letter from the Duc de Choiseul, Minister of the Marine, in August, 1763, directed the port intendant at Le Havre to place the Negro in prison for detention and to return him to Santo Domingo at the expense of his master, De Warrener.[10] This is but one of a number of cases of runaway slaves enlisting in the French army. No doubt many recruiting officers were lax and ready to believe any statement a Negro might make concerning his status, and probably most of them escaped detection afterward. Army life was almost certainly preferable to slavery, even to the easygoing slave status that existed in France. The Negro in this instance was unfortunate in having a master who was an army officer. Even then, however, he had gone three years in service without detection.

Another case of detection no doubt carried more cruel consequences. In 1779 the Duc de Lauzun had formed in Senegal six companies of Negro troops, but they proved insubordinate. In 1781 a lieutenant Moreau was murdered. One of those convicted for the deed by court-martial was Joseph Roques. He was sentenced "to have his wrist cut and to be broken alive," but he escaped and came to France and enlisted in a colonial auxiliary battalion. At Lorient in 1786 a sergeant major recognized him, and he was returned to Senegal for trial. What happened to him is not reported, but one can well surmise.[11]

Later, in 1791, a company of Negro troops from Guadeloupe and Santo Domingo was transported to France, and thence to

[10] Choiseul to Mistral, 29 Aug. 1763, Archives de la Ville du Havre, Fonds Marine, Nègres et Esclaves, 1763-76.
[11] Claude Faure, "La garnison européene du Sénégal et le récruitement des premières troupes noires (1779-1858)," *Revue de l'histoire des colonies françaises*, année 8 (1920), 9.

Senegal.[12] Their residence in France appears to have been brief.

The French Revolution with its war abroad and at home brought greater opportunity for military service on the part of the Negroes. It should not be overlooked that five hundred free Negroes and mulattoes from the West Indies are reported to have served in the French army that aided in the American Revolution. But these soldiers were not taken to France. Repeatedly under the Old Regime the colonials had warned the French government against the enlistment and training of Negro troops, lest dire consequences result in the colonies, where the whites were vastly outnumbered.[13] Possibly this did act as a deterrent to Negro enlistment before the Revolution.

After August, 1789, it became the rage to organize National Guard units in all French towns and cities for preservation of law and order. One might think that the free Negroes and mulattoes in France who shared the revolutionary zeal would have rushed forward to join. At Paris, under Lafayette's inspiration, some did, but no doubt most of them were deterred by the requirement that the guardsmen provide their own uniform and arms, and by the additional fact that they were not paid. The National Guards of 1789 and immediately succeeding years were from the "easy classes," and this excluded most of the Negroes and mulattoes.[14] The few like Ogé and Raimond who were comfortably fixed could have joined, but their primary interest was in the colonies and not in maintenance of current conditions. The National Guards were rather too conservative for them.

The situation was quite different after the outbreak of war in the spring of 1792. The first phase of the Revolution was completed and vast reforms had occurred. Among them was the recognition of civil and professional rights to the free Negroes in the colonies. It was therefore not surprising that

[12] Ibid., p. 11.
[13] Fieffé, Histoire des troupes étrangères, I, 281.
[14] Lefebvre, La Révolution française, p. 150.

in September, 1792, shortly before Valmy, with Verdun taken and Paris expected to fall to the Prussian and Austrian forces, a group of Negro citizens at Paris offered to form a military unit to serve the country. Raimond was chosen to make this offer. "Even as all Frenchmen," he said, "we burn to fly to the frontiers." He commented that they were small in number, but he predicted that a unit if formed would soon grow. He regretted that age prevented him personally from serving (he was now forty-eight); moreover, he stated that he was in France on another mission. Nevertheless, he offered to contribute the sum of 500 livres yearly toward equipping the unit and to give a "similar sum" as prize to a member of the unit whom the Assembly might judge worthy of it.[15] The president of the Assembly replied similarly in *beau geste* and the Assembly accepted the offer. In consequence, there was organized at Lille on September 15 the notorious "Black Legion," consisting of one hundred Negroes from the American colonies. It was a cavalry unit with the official designation of "Free Cavalry Legion of Americans and the South," but it also went by other designations, such as "Legion of the Americans," "Hussars of Santo Domingo," "The National Legion of the South," the "Legion Saint-Georges," and the "Legion of the Men of Color."

The organizer and leader of the Black Legion was an accomplished mulatto by the name of Joseph de Boulogne, Chevalier de Saint-Georges. Born in Guadeloupe in 1745, very early he had been brought to France by his father, a farmer-general, and given excellent training in the arts and accomplishments of the leisured class of society. Placed in pension in the home of a famous swordsman of the day, La Boissière, he was drilled in fencing, dancing, and swimming. He became in time one of the best fencers in France, and is reported to have fenced with

---

[15] *Adresse des citoyens de couleur résidans à l'Assemblée Nationale, suivie de la réponse de M. le Président, du 7 septembre 1992* [1792], *l'an 4e de la liberté, et le premier de l'égalité; imprimées et envoyés aux 83 départemens & aux armées par ordre de l'Assemblée* (Paris [1792]), p. 3; also *Réimpression de l'ancien Moniteur*, XIII, 643.

the famous swordsman the Chevalier d'Eon de Beaumont. He was thus perhaps the first Negro athlete of modern times. He also studied music under prominent teachers, Jean Marie Leclair and Gossec, and became sufficiently skilled in the violin to be "considered in 1776 for membership in the Royal Academy of Music." Later he published several musical works. He maintained his interest in music, and in 1791-1792 he conducted some concerts at Lille that attracted attention. He thus appears to have been the first Negro musician in Europe. These accomplishments made him very popular socially. In addition, he was for a time prior to the Revolution employed as a secret agent of the Duc d'Orleans, who sent him on missions to Belgium and England. The nature of these missions has never been known.[16] Such was the man placed in charge of the unit. Almost certainly he was the most broadly trained man in the group, and he should have had an auspicious future.

Second in command was Alexandre Dumas, also a mulatto and natural son of an aristocratic father, the Marquis de La Pailleterie, who brought the boy when young to Bordeaux from Santo Domingo and gave him educational advantages. Younger than Saint-Georges, he was thirty at the time of the organization of the Black Legion, but he had had much experience in the army, which he had entered at the age of twelve. It was perhaps natural that trouble should develop between the two men, as soon it did, the cause being some expenditures by Saint-Georges that Dumas called rash. Friendship between the two was soon restored, but Saint-Georges was charged by others of graft and misuse of funds, placed in prison, and dismissed from his command. After a year of imprisonment he was restored to his rank, with friends aiding in reestablishing his honor. But it was only for a period, and he shortly retired to private life, dying in 1799 at Paris in obscurity and poverty.

[16] Louis Jacob, "Saint-Georges et la 'Legion Noire' de Lille en 1793," *Revue du Nord*, XXXIII (1951), 6-17; Grégoire, *De la littérature des Nègres*, pp. 98-99; Fleming and Pryde, *Distinguished Negroes Abroad*, pp. 63-68.

Not so with Dumas, who was to rise to the rank of general, distinguish himself for extraordinary bravery, serve with the French army in several countries, including Italy and Egypt, and leave after him a son and grandson who were to become literary men of renown in the nineteenth century. In August, 1792, Dumas had distinguished himself in action at Maulde, Belgium, where he captured thirteen prisoners. Almost immediately after this incident he was named lieutenant colonel of the Black Legion. His attachment to that unit was therefore not the result of enlistment but of transfer.[17]

The Black Legion was at once made a part of the Thirteenth Infantry Regiment, with Saint-Georges as brigade commander and Dumas as second in command. At the outset the regiment was composed of 800 foot soldiers and 200 cavalry, as specified by the decree of the Legislative Assembly of September 8, 1792, but on December 6 another decree ordered that the entire body be composed of cavalry. In late 1792 the legion was stationed at Amiens, but in January, 1793, it was transferred to Laon, and in February to Lille, where it became a part of the Army of the North, facing the Austrians. In March the legion was ordered to Brest, to be shipped for service in the colonies. But the orders did not come through at once, and it was moved about still more. One detachment was sent to Rouen, and then to Nantes; another was sent first to Paris, then to Nantes, then to Brest. In September the legion was ordered again to Brest, and all but the First American Company of Negroes were sent to the West Indies. This last company was still in France in April, 1794, when the Minister of War ordered it anew to Brest for shipment to Santo Domingo. The men of this company objected to going to that colony, however, and sent some of their number to Paris to protest, with the result that the order was changed and they were sent to the Vendée instead.[18]

[17] André Maurois, Les trois Dumas (Paris, 1957), pp. 13, 29; Nouvelle biographie générale, XV, 163-64.
[18] P. Descaves, Historique du 13me régiment de chasseurs et des chasseurs à cheval de la garde . . . (Béziers, 1891), pp. 1-18.

The legion saw little, if any, service against the enemy. It was afflicted with low morale, and there were many desertions. The representatives in mission sent out by the government as inspectors charged it with anarchy. There were also malversations in connection with which Saint-Georges was suspect, and he was never able completely to clear himself. Though released from prison on 9 thermidor and given his old rank of brigade commander, he was not actually given the command. Even this restoration was of short duration, for he was again removed in late October, 1795, and despite desperate efforts he was unable to get reinstated a second time. In his petition to the War Department he spoke of his burning zeal and his willingness to shed every drop of his blood for the republic, all to no avail.[19]

In addition to the criticism of the legion's bad morale by M. Jacob, there is the criticism of its record at Nantes during the Reign of Terror by Professor Gaston Martin. At Nantes the legion was used as an execution squad in early 1794 to shoot aristocrats, a job which the troops performed with relish and brutality. Any victims not killed by their bullets they dispatched with the bayonet. But they disdained to bury their victims, either leaving them unburied or placed in very shallow graves, which were disturbed by wandering dogs. The result was a terrible stench in that suburb of the city and the outbreak of cholera. The citizens thereupon had to take sanitary measures themselves that negligence of the Negro hussars had necessitated. It was this menace to health resulting from the shootings that caused some to favor the executions by drowning. Professor Martin caustically charges that the hussars left "a detestable reputation" at Nantes for their part in the Terror.[20]

From this point the Black Legion fell into obscurity. It continued to constitute a fragment of the Thirteenth Cavalry

[19] Jacob, "Saint-Georges et la 'Legion Noire,'" pp. 12-17.

[20] Martin, *Négriers et bois d'ébène*, p. 110; Gaston Martin, *Carrier et sa mission à Nantes* (Paris, 1924), pp. 279, 336-37.

Regiment and took part in many campaigns—that on the Sambre and Meuse in 1797, that in Italy in 1799-1800, that on the Rhine and Danube in 1805, that in Prussia in 1806, that in Spain in 1810-1813, that in Germany in 1813, and that in France in 1814; but the historian of this regiment does not mention the Negroes in connection with them. We are not told whether the unit was left intact or broken up and transferred. No mention is made of any gift by Raimond in recognition of a gallant action by a member of the band, although he remained in France until the late 1790's and despite the fact that some gallant actions did occur. In particular, Alexandre Dumas distinguished himself at Brixen in 1796 in Napoleon's First Italian Campaign. There he held a narrow bridge single-handed against a large number of Austrians, using his saber to kill many. This was the most famous of his several daring exploits and won from Napoleon the sobriquet of "Horatius Coclès of the Tyrol." But Dumas was no longer in the Black Legion, having been promoted to the rank of general in September, 1793, and placed in charge of the Army of the Eastern Pyrenees, and during the next two years he moved about several times.[21]

After the two draft laws of 1793, the second of which took for the army all able-bodied unmarried men between the ages of eighteen and twenty-five, Negroes and mulattoes in France were drafted like other young men of their age, and occasionally Negro units were formed. The article in *Nouvelle biographie générale* on Dumas refers to his "black division" in the Tyrol during Napoleon's First Italian Campaign. The *Moniteur,* moreover, tells of a company of Negro and mulatto soldiers on the Island of Aix, near Rochefort, being formed in June, 1798.[22] This company consisted of 120 Negroes captured in the West Indies by the British but released. Finding themselves in France, they organized their unit with Negro and mulatto officers—Marin Pèdre captain, Varin lieutenant, Alain *aîné*

[21] *Nouvelle biographie générale,* XV, 163-64; Maurois, *Les trois Dumas,* pp. 16-18.
[22] *Réimpression de l'ancien Moniteur,* XXIX, 285.

second lieutenant, Yauyau sergeant major, and Morel quartermaster sergeant. In 1799 the company was sent to Senegal and there had a part in repelling a British attack in January, 1801.[23]

Many Negro and mulatto prisoners of war were brought to France from England in the 1790's. They had been captured in the West Indies or on the high seas, transferred to English prison camps, and exchanged or released as having no value to the English. In May, 1795, a neutral Swedish ship brought to Le Havre a contingent of 568 French prisoners of war, including many designated as Negroes and mulattoes, sent "not [as] the result of an exchange." The Committee of Public Safety was wary of the gift, lest they might be getting a Trojan horse, and advised officials at Le Havre "to interrogate the prisoners very closely on their conduct and motives, and to submit them to the most severe police formality."[24] Similarly in October and November, 1797, several hundred prisoners of war were returned to France from British prisons, many being designated as Negroes and mulattoes. A letter of October 18 told of 560 such prisoners arriving at Le Havre aboard three vessels, and another letter reported a new landing at Le Havre on November 16. Among the 57 prisoners from this last vessel were twelve Negroes and nineteen mulattoes. The *Emilie* which brought them had embarked in May with them for New York, but two days out at sea had been captured by the British. Afterward the British permitted them to go to Dunkerque, and thence they were returned to Le Havre.[25] No doubt there were similar shipments to other ports.

During the period of the Consulate three Negro companies were organized in France, composed of Negroes and mulattoes released from British prisons following the Treaty of Amiens and given the designation of "Battalion of Black Pioneers."

---

[23] Faure, "La garnison européene du Sénégal," 11-12.

[24] Comité de Salut Public to the Commission, 25 floréal an III, Archives de la Ville du Havre, PR, section I², 114-126, carton 6.

[25] Letter of 18 vendémiaire an VI and "Liste des déportés des colonies . . . ," *ibid.*, carton 30.

Their leader was Joseph Damingue, called "Hercule," a Negro who had distinguished himself in Italy and Egypt. In 1806 the unit was used as an auxiliary in engineering, working at projects under the direction of engineering officers.[26]

Hercule had a remarkable career. Born in Cuba, he was brought to Bordeaux by his father and became a drummer boy in the army prior to the Revolution. During the Revolution he changed first to the infantry, then to the cavalry. He later claimed to have been in charge of a Negro battalion destined for an attack on Ireland during the time of the Convention, but none was made. Later he was a sergeant in Napoleon's First Italian Campaign, during which his most famous exploit occurred. At Arcola, at Napoleon's direction, he made a cavalry charge with twenty-five men on the rear of an Austrian infantry column, blowing bugles and causing a diversion. Napoleon considered it significant in the winning of the battle and handsomely recognized the fact, not only with a large monetary sum, but also with a saber and afterward with one of a hundred sabers which he gave in recognition of the bravest deeds performed by his men. Hercule accompanied Napoleon to Egypt, fought well in the battles of the campaign, and was one of the limited number whom Napoleon brought back with him to France. Put in charge of the Black Pioneers, he became disgusted with them and asked to be removed from their command. This Napoleon did, and continued his salary. Seemingly he remained in the army throughout the period of Napoleonic rule, and afterward married an Italian girl by whom he had two children. He is said to have scorned the Negroes of Santo Domingo and to have entertained a grudge against Napoleon for failure to make him a marshal.[27] His military career somewhat rivaled that of Dumas.

[26] Fieffé, *Histoire des troupes étrangères*, II, 54-55. Fieffé gives an illustration of the uniform of these Pioneers, facing p. 54. Shortly afterward the Pioneers became the Royal African. "Troupes coloniales: les contingents créoles," *Revue de Paris*, V (Aug., 1913), 25-26.

[27] Frédéric Masson, *Cavaliers de Napoléon* (ed. def., Paris, [1920]), pp. pp. 328-31.

While in Egypt, Kléber is reported to have bought a large number of slaves imported from Ethiopia and enrolled them in his Twenty-First Half-Brigade of Light Infantry. These made satisfactory soldiers after brief training. Kléber's army, as well known, was later surrendered to the British, and whether these Negroes afterward saw service in France is not recorded.[28]

No subsequent Negro company, however, attracted the attention of historians like that of the "Legion of the Americans" of Saint-Georges. Nor has any other Negro soldier in France during that era attracted the same attention as Alexandre Dumas, although several Negro generals from Santo Domingo came to France during the 1790's and early 1800's, among them Besse, Pétion, Rigaud, and Dessalines. Most of these came on visits, but their military commissions were recognized in France and some of them were given assignments. Dumas accompanied Napoleon to Egypt and acquitted himself well with his cavalry corps in the Battle of the Pyramids; but before long he manifested disloyalty to Napoleon, some hot words passed, and shortly Dumas sailed for home aboard a freighter. The vessel sought safety from a storm in enemy territory, and Dumas was seized and imprisoned at Brindisi until April, 1801, when he was exchanged as the result of an armistice. During his imprisonment he suffered poisoning, maliciously intended, so he held, and never again did he enjoy his former splendid health or strength. Nor did he enjoy the good will of Napoleon, as might be concluded. To all purposes, this ended his military career. Neither the army physician Desgenettes nor the famous surgeon Corsivart was able to restore his health. He got steadily worse and died in 1806, at his home in Villers-Cotterets.[29] Thus died a French soldier whose reputation has become legendary, and who continued to live in his son and grandson, the first of a dynasty termed by André Maurois "The Three Dumases."

28 Fieffé, *Histoire des troupes étrangères*, II, 49.
29 Maurois, *Les trois Dumas*, pp. 23-32; J. Lucas-Dubreton, *The Fourth Musketeer: The Life of Alexandre Dumas* (New York, 1928), p. 5.

France herself contributed to the Revolutionary and Napoleonic armies a remarkable Negro surgeon, François Fournier de Pescay (1771-1833). Born in Bordeaux of parents from Santo Domingo, he studied medicine in his native city. Entering the army in 1792, he found himself a surgeon and saw service during the next several years with army units in various areas. About 1796 he founded a medical school at Brussels, where he himself taught pathology until 1806, when he moved to Paris and once again took a position with the army. For a time he served as personal physician to Ferdinand VII of Spain, who pensioned him. In 1814 he was made secretary to the Council of Health for French armies, and after taking the throne, Louis XVIII conferred on him the Cross of the Legion of Honor. He was sent on a diplomatic mission to Santo Domingo (now become Haiti) which was unsuccessful, but while there he had a part in the establishment of the first lycée on the island. He wrote a number of treatises on medical subjects, one on tetanus being recognized in 1802 by the Society of Medicine of Paris; also he wrote a biographical sketch of his father. Fournier was without doubt a man of merit.[30]

While these things were taking place in the 1790's and the Napoleonic period, the government was sponsoring within France the education of some select military orphans and colonials. In the 1770's an Irishman named Pawlet had founded in France a school for the orphans of military men, and around 1786 another had been created by the Duc de la Rochefoucauld-Liancourt. The latter institution during the Revolution was taken over by the state, and by a decree of June 1, 1795, it was stipulated that among those to whom it would be open in the future would be the sons of colonists who were victims of the Revolution. The students selected would be sent to the institution at government expense. Within the next year students from Santo Domingo, white and black, applied and were received. Among them were the son and stepson of Toussaint

[30] *Biographie universelle, Supplément,* ed. by Michaud, LXIV, 385-86.

Louverture, Isaac and Placide, aged about fifteen, who landed at Rochefort with five others, presumably whites, in August, 1796. Already by April, 1796, however, there were several Negro boys enrolled at the Ecole Liancourt, as a letter from the Minister of the Interior stated.[31] Several other Negro students were received in time, interesting for the fact that most of them were the sons of prominent fathers, all military men it would appear but not "victims of the Revolution," nor were these boys orphans. They were the sons of the Negro leaders who were running Santo Domingo at this era. In addition to the son and stepson of Toussaint Louverture, there was the son of General Rigaud, second to Toussaint in importance in the island; Lacroix, the son of a prominent Negro farmer; and Fernand Christophe, the son of the prominent Negro general, later king of the island. In addition, the Negro boy from Senegal, Jean Amilcar, was awarded a scholarship to this institution.[32]

This was not a military institution. At the outset protest was made to an effort of the War Department to gain control of it. The protest asserted that it was not a military school but one whose curriculum embraced the liberal and mechanical arts, the sciences, and agriculture. The school was situated in the country, so that the boys might engage in farming, but if they wished, they might apprentice themselves at certain trades.[33] It is interesting that none of the Negroes appears to have apprenticed himself, but rather restricted his attention to the liberal studies. Of them all, young Rigaud was the one who applied himself most. He was at the institution for several years, and his name is always inserted on the list of men who had attended the school. For some reason, the names of the other boys were soon dropped from the rolls.

31 Decree of 3 vendémiaire an 4 and letter of 3 floréal an 4, Archives Nationales, F17 6745; Ferdinand-Dreyfus, *Un philanthrope d'autrefois: La Rochefoucauld-Liancourt, 1747-1827* (Paris, 1903), pp. 36-40, 371-73.

32 Archives Nationales, F17 6744, 6745; "Extrait de delibérations, 9 prairial an 4," Archives Nationales, F17 1144.

33 "Rapport présenté au ministre de l'intérieur," 21 pluviôse an IV, Archives Nationales, F17 6745.

There was almost certainly a political motive in the scholarships to colonials at this school—to bind the colonies close to France. Before the Revolution the Chevalier de Boufflers, governor of Senegal, had much the same idea. He wanted to send several Negro students to France to learn trades and European ways which they would later bring back to Senegal.

The Ecole Liancourt suffered from lack of funds and from outbreaks of sickness, and in 1800 it was moved from Liancourt to Compiègne, and after 1806 to Châlons. Napoleon visited the school at least twice, and was not favorably impressed with its work. On its records the Negro students are seldom so designated, and it is difficult to know how many they were. After the expedition of Leclerc and its debacle in 1802, no more Negro students came to France for study during the Napoleonic period.

By June, 1800, young Rigaud had negotiated a transfer from Liancourt to another state-supported school where better conditions prevailed, the Institution Nationale des Colonies.[34] This latter school, set up in February, 1797, was the old Collège de la Marche at Paris under a new name and under government patronage. Under the direction of Coisnon, a capable former professor of the University of Paris who showed great devotion and initiative, the institution for some years did better than the Ecole Liancourt. The government designed it for colonials whose parents had suffered from the Revolution, and grants of 500 and 600 francs per year were made to the students admitted. Some Negro boys were among them, but these were all sent home and the school closed in October, 1802, at the time of the Leclerc expedition. Coisnon, who in 1806 reported this in a letter to Josephine, referred to the fact that he too had gone on that expedition, accompanying the son and stepson of Toussaint, who, like Rigaud, had transferred to this institution. He had attempted to keep the institution going with private funds, and besought her to permit its reestablishment under

[34] Roume to André Rigaud, 19 messidor an 8, *ibid.*, Colonies, CC9B2.

the name of Collège Josephine.[35] The appeal struck a deaf ear. This closed the door of opportunity to young Negro colonials to study in France for the period of Napoleon.

The expedition of Leclerc had yet other effects on Negroes resident in France. A number of Negro and mulatto military men were in France on the eve of that expedition, having been forced out of Santo Domingo by the rivalry between Generals Rigaud and Toussaint. Rigaud, Pétion, Villate, and a considerable number of mulatto leaders had fled to France for safety in 1800 or 1801, and remained there until late 1801, when they accompanied Leclerc in his endeavor to bring about a change of government on the island.[36] The expedition was significant also for the fact that several score Negro prisoners were returned to France as a result of it. They included Toussaint and his family, and many of his generals, aides, and attendants.

It is needless to relate here the details of the expedition, save to explain why it was undertaken and why those arrested were taken to France. Since 1796 Toussaint Louverture had emerged as the outstanding Negro general, indeed the dictator, of the turbulent colony of Santo Domingo, where in 1743 he had been born a slave. Conditions in the colony appeared to be better under his rule than they had been since the outbreak of the Revolution. Peace was restored between the warring factions, and agriculture and commerce appeared on the mend. Unfortunately, Toussaint incurred the ire of the French government by his actions in three respects. First, he negotiated with the British and made them friends and allies while France, the mother country, was still at war with Britain, and he refused to heed French warnings that this tie with Britain must cease. Secondly, he promulgated a constitution for the island without consulting the French, or even notifying them of it. Toussaint was recognized as the military leader in the island, but not as the political leader, who was a Frenchman

---

[35] Coisnon to Josephine, about 1806, and "Rapport du 24 pluviôse an 13 . . . ," *ibid.*, F[17] 6765.
[36] Article on Pétion in *Biographie universelle*, XXXIII, 474-77.

sent out from Paris. Notice of the new constitution was brought to the attention of the French government by a letter smuggled out to it from a French official in the colony. Thirdly, Toussaint became exasperated with the French political leader Roume, who bore the designation of Particular Agent. He had Roume and his family arrested and taken to a lonely mountain near Dondon, in the interior of the colony, and held incommunicado for several months. There the prisoners were kept in a thatched cottage, under military guard, and deprived of medical care and everything except the bare necessities of life.

Roume thought that it was destined that he die under these privations. But a Negress named Sanite Moka who had access to the Roumes acted as a secret intermediary and carried some notes crudely written by Roume with charcoal to the French Secretary General Blanchard, a young man of merit and ingenuity. Blanchard in turn informed his government by letter, sending it, evidently by way of the United States, through a secret and trusted agent.[37] The letter reached Paris, as did also another that followed it. Blanchard moreover got in touch with the American Consul General Henry Stevens, who succeeded in obtaining some betterment in conditions for Roume, and eventually in gaining from Toussaint permission for the Roumes to return to France. A letter from Roume to Stevens, written from Dondon before the release, also found its way to the French government.[38] Eventually Roume and family were allowed to return to France, via New York and Philadelphia, where he spent several months recuperating in health. He was accompanied by two faithful servants, Sanite Moka and Manuel, whom the Toussaint government had permitted him to take along.

While in Philadelphia, Roume drew up a twenty-four-page

[37] Blanchard to the Minister of the Marine and the Colonies, 8 nivôse an 9, Archives Nationales, Colonies, CC⁹B2. This carton contains the official correspondence relative to the Toussaint-Leclerc Affair. In his second letter, of 15 thermidor an 9, *ibid.*, Blanchard describes the notes from Roume as "petits chiffons de papier" on which were "demandes écrites avec du charbon." This letter was smuggled out of Santo Domingo by a citizen named Sauvage.

[38] Letter of 19 messidor an 9, *ibid.*

report of his arrest and imprisonment for the French govern-ment.[39] He also wrote a memorandum of twenty-five pages, giving the government his confidential impression of Tous-saint's various subordinates and their parts in the Revolution in the island. In addition, he wrote from Philadelphia two letters to Leclerc congratulating him on his appointment as general-in-chief of the planned expedition to Santo Domingo and giving him an estimate of Toussaint and several dozen of his subordinates, those trustworthy and those to be distrusted. By this time he had become bitter toward Toussaint, whom he painted as treacherous, cruel, and crafty.[40]

In view of these things, it can readily be seen why Napoleon sent Leclerc and his army to Santo Domingo in December, 1801, with 35,000 men to discipline Toussaint and restore French control. With the expedition he sent Isaac and Placide, the son and stepson of Toussaint, accompanied by their precep-tor, Coisnon, who carried a letter and verbal greetings to Toussaint. Prior to their departure Napoleon gave the boys an interview, inquired which was Isaac, and gave him personal greetings and a letter to his father, whom he called "a great man."[41] The next day the boys were given a splendid meal with the Minister of the Marine, Leclerc, Bougainville, Bénezech, and others. Almost immediately afterward they set out for Brest and sailed with the fleet. Arriving in Santo Domingo, they and Coisnon set out at once on horseback to meet Tous-saint and their mother. Coisnon delivered the letter. Toussaint replied that while Napoleon wrote in soft words, his actions, through Leclerc's army, were a declaration of war.[42]

In the meanwhile, Leclerc landed troops at two or three points on the island with slight opposition. He issued the proclamation which Napoleon had given him and sent terms

[39] Report to the Minister of the Marine and the Colonies, 2 nivôse an 10, ibid.
[40] Report of 11 frimaire an 10 and letters of 28 ventôse an 10, ibid.
[41] M. J. R. Marboutin, "Notes historiques sur l'expédition de Leclerc à Saint-Domingue et sur la famille Louverture," Revue de l'Agenais, année 42 (1915), 199-201.
[42] Ibid., 202-204.

for Toussaint to accept. Toussaint played for time and gave only partial acceptance. Distrust led to trickery and treachery, each side being guilty. All the Negro leaders surrendered or were captured by mid-June, including Toussaint himself, with little fighting having occurred, and it appeared that the expedition was achieving its goal with great success.[43]

Not until after these leaders had been shipped as prisoners to France or to Guiana did revolt in the island became general. The incident precipitating this wholesale uprising was the reestablishment of slavery on the island of Guadeloupe. News of this action, which reached Santo Domingo in early September, had the same effect as gasoline on a fire. Thenceforth the revolt got steadily worse, as did also the epidemic of yellow fever, the latter being the real cause of the island's loss. Napoleon and his minister Decrès shamefully neglected Leclerc, but other factors were mainly responsible for the collapse of the expedition, the most important being the resumption of war between France and Britain in 1803. Even so, some remnants of Leclerc's men on the island did not surrender until 1809.[44]

Since the reestablishment of slavery on Guadeloupe was so important a factor in the failure of Leclerc's expedition, it might be asked if Napoleon planned to restore slavery on Santo Domingo. It can hardly be doubted that he did, for on May 20, 1802, a consular order (that is, by Napoleon himself) had once more legalized slavery under the same laws that had formerly governed it.[45] It seems that the colonists of Guadeloupe had anticipated Napoleon's order to Richepanse and restored slavery there. Whether Napoleon had discussed the matter with Leclerc before he sailed is not known. No pronouncement on the subject either by Napoleon or Leclerc was

[43] For details of the expedition, see *Lettres du Général Leclerc* . . . , ed. by Paul Roussier (Paris, 1937). On the arrest of Toussaint, see *ibid.*, pp. 169-71.

[44] Jean Savant, *Recueil des sources pour servir à l'histoire de la tentative de réconquête de Saint-Domingue* (Paris, 1956), p. 77. The last forces to surrender were those of General Barquier.

[45] Trayer, *Etude historique sur la condition légale*, p. 100; J. B. Duvergier, *Collection complète des lois* (2nd ed., Paris, 1834-1906), XIII, 446.

made. Yet it is almost certain that the matter was discussed and decision made.

Napoleon did call upon Leclerc to rid the island of its "gilded Africans" (its Negro leaders), saying "there will not remain anything more to wish."[46] This Leclerc did. He shipped them out in wholesale lots in June, 1802. On June 6 he wrote one of the ministers, "I send out today fifty on the *Muiron*," which was ordered to take them to Corsica. He wrote that he was sending twenty to Cayenne, calling them "assiduous scoundrels of Toussaint." Toussaint and his family he was sending back to France, he reported in a letter of June 11 to the First Consul, aboard *Le Héros*, bound to Brest.[47]

*Le Héros* was but one of eighteen or nineteen vessels that sailed back as a fleet to Brest, the *Muiron* with them, although that ship was to proceed on to Corsica and Toulon. Aboard these vessels, apart from those of the *Muiron*, were several score Negroes and mulattoes as prisoners or hostages. *Le Héros* carried Toussaint, his wife, his sons Isaac and Saint-Jean, and his stepson Placide; the *Conquérant*, Augustin Rigaud, his wife, a relative of his wife, and two servants; the *Rhinocéros*, General of Brigade André Rigaud (who had sailed with Leclerc in December), his wife, and two sons; and the *Foudroyant*, eleven Negro boys, aged sixteen to eighteen, all born in Santo Domingo of leading Negro families and delivered over by agents of Toussaint. The youths were hostages, and were recommended for training as seamen. In addition to these Negroes and mulattoes from Santo Domingo, two vessels in the fleet carried Negroes and mulattoes that had been giving trouble in Guadeloupe. The *Fourgeux* bore twenty-five Negro officers, with their wives, children (in at least one case), and servants; the *Rédoubtable*, three. All aboard the *Foudroyant* were in irons, and a Negro sergeant aboard the *Union* likewise was in chains. Most of these were disembarked at Brest and were to be imprisoned. A list of fifty-nine Negro and mulatto officers

---

[46] *Lettres du Général Leclerc*, p. 305.
[47] *Ibid.*, pp. 162, 170, 171.

was sent along. They were designated as criminals "guilty of great crime, such as the slaying of whites," and were said to be "almost all Congo or Orado by nation." It was recommended that they be sent to the hulks or galleys. The records are confusing about the total of the Negroes and mulattoes returned to Brest, but aside from those on the *Muiron*, they numbered between fifty and a hundred. It is interesting that one does not find the name of Dessalines or of Christophe on the list. Not all the ringleaders of trouble in Santo Domingo, accordingly, were returned; but the greater number of them were. Why were so many vessels employed in returning them? Was it not to make absolutely certain that no mishap occur and these leaders escape?[48] Certainly Leclerc must have felt that in the return of this fleet and its prisoners he had the insurrection stamped out, and that he could devote his efforts thenceforth to reestablishment of peace and reforms.

Toussaint and his family were separated before going on board *Le Héros* and in fact never learned of their mutual presence on it. Separation was also followed thenceforth. Toussaint, kept incommunicado, was taken under heavy guard across France to Fort Jouy, near Besançon on the Swiss frontier. This was in accordance with recommendations of Leclerc, who urged that he be imprisoned in the interior of the country where escape would be impossible.[49] No doubt the Minister of Justice in sending him to Jouy had in mind Toussaint's imprisonment of Roume. There was much similarity in the two imprisonments. Jouy was in the Alps, cold, isolated, and supposedly escapeproof. Yet two Vendean leaders placed there did manage to escape. The Minister of War ordered that Toussaint be adequately clothed and fed, but Toussaint's biographer and admirer, Colonel Nemours, denies that these instructions were followed, saying that he was fed but once a day, inadequately clothed for the severe cold of the Alps,

---

[48] The names of boats returning to Brest and their passenger lists are found in Archives Nationales, Colonies, F5B30. Not all the boats carried prisoners.
[49] *Lettres du Général Leclerc*, pp. 173, 183.

allowed an insufficient amount of fuel during the winter, and not permitted to write letters or communicate with anyone save his servant Marc Plaisir, who was there with him for a while. Colonel Nemours attributed his early death in April, 1803, to the rigorous weather and deprivation of the necessities of life.[50] The manner in which he died has done much to give Toussaint the halo of a martyr, and he is commonly regarded as perhaps the most famous member of the Negro race. He was intelligent, brave, resourceful, and strove to be fair; at the same time he was deceitful and cruel. His cruelty showed itself not only in the treatment of Roume but also in the brutal execution of his nephew, Hyacinthe Moyse (or Moïse), in December, 1801, for supposed treachery and bad administration, by having him attached to a cannon and blown to pieces.[51] Those who make him a martyr and the greatest of the Negroes have much to which they must close their eyes.

As already indicated, Toussaint's family were sent elsewhere. Madame Louverture, her sons Isaac and Saint-Jean, two nieces, and some servants were sent to Bayonne; Placide, natural son of Madame Louverture, to Belle-Isle. In 1803 Madame Louverture and her sons by Toussaint were allowed to go to Agen, and pensioned. They were ordered, however, not to leave the bounds of the département of Lod-et-Garonne. Saint-Jean died at Agen in 1805, and his mother in 1816. Isaac and Placide each married, Isaac his cousin Louise Chancy, and Placide a girl named Josephine Lacaze, evidently white. On the marriage register Placide wrote his name as Louverture (instead of Clerc), and this led to a quarrel and court trial, as Isaac protested his right to use the name Louverture. The court decided in Isaac's favor. The matter was appealed by Placide, and two years later a second court decided in like manner. This incident broke up their warm friendship.[52] In 1817 Isaac obtained permission to move to Bordeaux, where he spent the

---

[50] *Histoire de la captivité et de la mort de Toussaint-Louverture* (Paris, 1929), pp. 13-16, 30, 52-53, 59, 185.
[51] The details are given in *Nouvelle biographie générale*, XXVI, 830-32.
[52] Marboutin, "Notes historiques," 80-86.

remainder of his life, living under relaxed police oversight but forbidden to leave France. He died in 1850. While still at Agen, around 1815, he wrote a manuscript account of the Leclerc expedition and of the Louverture family's removal to France, sending it in 1819 to a French writer, Metrol, at Paris. The latter published it, and many details concerning the family's history are derived from this account.[53]

Two other prisoners incarcerated at Jouy at the same time as Toussaint, Generals André Rigaud and Martial Besse, did not succumb to the cold. Nor did two other Negroes, Jean and Zamor Kina, originally from Santo Domingo, who were arrested in Paris in July, 1802. They had served in the British army, and were arrested as suspects and placed for a time at the Temple. Then the Minister of Justice ordered them sent to Jouy, where they occupied the cell immediately beneath that of Toussaint. A sentinel was placed before their door. Reportedly they, too, were poorly cared for, but they survived until 1804, when they were offered release on condition that they would serve in Italy with some battalions of Negro troops. They accepted the offer, and Jean Kina's wife and baby who lived nearby in the village were ordered to accompany them.[54] The offer came in response to a petition from the two Kinas for release that they might ply their trade of carpenter in French seaports. This the French did not want, but the army offer followed. It is interesting to speculate on what might have been Toussaint's reputation, and what the history of Santo Domingo, had he survived the rigors of Jouy. Like Nelson, the great British sea captain, however, he died at a glorious moment, perhaps as he might have wished it.

So much for the story of Negroes and mulattoes whose role in the military in one fashion or another brought them on French soil, some to serve, some seeking a place of refuge, some as prisoners. Several hundred, it would appear, donned

[53] *Ibid.*, 80. Colonel Nemours (*Histoire de . . . Toussaint-Louverture*, p. 154) places Isaac's death in 1854.

[54] Marboutin, "Notes historiques," 380; Nemours, *Histoire de . . . Toussaint-Louverture*, pp. 59, 96-101, 103-105, 262.

the uniform and fought under the French banner in Europe. Perhaps two or three hundred others were brought to France at one time or another as military prisoners. For those that served, it marked the dawn of a new era, in that the Revolution had brought freedom and all could now enlist, whereas previously only the freemen could do so, and in that the standard of life in the army, though rigorous, was certainly better than that which most Negroes had known hitherto in the garrets or the slum districts of French cities. The door of opportunity was open for Negroes to rise to high rank in the army, even to that of general. But with opportunity came also factionalism, and bitterness displayed itself not only between white and Negro, but also between Negro and mulatto. It was a stormy period, the passions of which have not subsided even at the present.

# SIX     SOCIAL ASPECTS OF THE REVOLUTION

*M*UCH ALLUSION to social conditions has been made in previous chapters, but it has been brought in incidentally and other phases have not been mentioned—how the Negroes of the era lived, how the Revolution aided or blocked them in their ambitions, what employment they found, what were their virtues and their vices, what were their relations to their former owners. Certainly freedom proved a mixed blessing. Friends of the Negro like the Abbé Grégoire and Lafayette feared such a move as was taken by the National Convention on February 4, 1794, in granting emancipation and citizenship to all slaves in one fell swoop. The British in 1833, apparently profiting from the French experience, provided for gradual emancipation. Unfortunately, references to social conditions in the contemporary records are limited, although flashes of light are thrown on one aspect after another in the stories of individual Negroes who for one reason or another are mentioned in the police or Admiralty records or elsewhere.

Certainly the Negroes shared in the excitement of the times, and all save a few devoted servants who remained in the service of their masters and gave little thought to what was happening joined with the *sans-culottes*. The slack police enforcement made it easier for slaves to run away from their masters than formerly. A merchant from Martinique who found himself in Paris in 1791 complained to the police that a Negress for whom he had paid 3,000 livres had deserted him.

He felt helpless. Evidently she had served him or his family as a nurse, for only in such a capacity could he have brought her into France.[1] No doubt there were many masters in the same position. On the other hand, an occasional master freed his slave. One slaveowner, General Dugommier, in charge of the army in the East Pyrenees, made a trip to Paris to grant freedom to a twenty-five-year-old slave that he had brought from Guadeloupe early in the Revolution.[2] Why he had been allowed to bring him into France is not explained. Evidently some laxness prevailed.

Some Negroes found themselves in trouble with the police. One such was a Negro servant of a man named De Combe, charged with theft or malversation after his master had left him in Paris in charge of his apartment. Another, named Bengala, in the employ of the Duc d'Orleans, was found in fraudulent possession of a banknote for 10,000 livres belonging to the Duc de Biron.[3] It is doubtful, however, if there was any increase of thievery by Negroes during the Revolution.

In July, 1792, a Negro in Paris named Jacques Indou was ordered arrested and confined in the Conciergerie for having attempted to cut a turnkey with a knife at the detention depot at Saint-Denis.[4] What further elapsed is not related. Another Negro, named Edouard, formerly a servant of the Duc d'Orleans, was arrested, imprisoned, and executed on the same day in early May, 1794. He had become a captain in the transport service, and was stationed with the Northern Army. The arrest was ordered by the Committee of Public Security, and so, too, his death warrant; but the ground of complaint is not given.[5] On that we can only speculate, but it was at the height of the Terror, when suspects of every type were sent on the slightest grounds to the guillotine.

[1] *Répertoire général des sources manuscrites de l'histoire de Paris pendant la Révolution française,* ed. by Alexandre Tuetey (Paris, 1890-1914, 11 v.), II, 184, no. 1743.
[2] J. Adher, "Les colons réfugiés d'Amérique pendant la Révolution," *Bulletin de la Société de Géographie de Toulouse,* année XXXIV (Toulouse, 1915), 164.
[3] *Répertoire général,* II, 154, no. 1451, and 205, no. 1931.
[4] *Ibid.,* VI, 81, no. 711.       [5] *Ibid.,* XI, 532, no. 2028.

3# 114 THE NEGRO IN FRANCE

One smart mulattress thought to blackmail her owner, a military man from Santo Domingo named Grouchet. Only seventeen years of age, she circulated the word that she was the natural daughter of Grouchet by a free Negress. She tried to obtain from him a settlement of 20,000 livres for living expenses, and even brought in to act as arbiters two persons who no doubt were confederates. But Grouchet parried this act, showing proof that she was merely a slave.[6]

Prostitution had engulfed some Negresses and mulattresses prior to the Revolution, and it continued to do so during it. One sufficiently known to find mention in print was the mulattress Bersi, who in the period of the Revolution was one of a dozen fashionable prostitutes with handsome quarters on the second floor of a building facing the Gardens of the Palais Royal. These women had expensive furniture, set a fine table, attended theaters and the opera—in short, played a grand role, to the extent of 50,000 livres in expenses a year. Like the fashionable ladies of the period whose style they aped, they were accompanied each by a small Negro boy who performed minor services. Their best patrons, reportedly, were foreigners, who were willing to pay heavily.[7]

There was also the quadroon Madame Hamelin, one of a "bevy of frail and lovely ladies" organized by Madame Tallien, herself a noted beauty of the period. Palmistry and parlor games were a feature of this salon, though evidently not the chief attraction. This group included also Josephine Beauharnais, and it is related that Napoleon visited this salon and was there introduced to Josephine by Madame Tallien. Yet it is difficult to harmonize this story with that of Bourrienne, who relates the shock Junot produced some years later when he uncovered to Napoleon the story of Josephine's past.[8]

[6] *Ibid.*, V, 318, no. 3088.

[7] Edmond and Jules de Goncourt, *Histoire de la société française pendant la Révolution* (Paris, n.d.), p. 225.

[8] F. M. Kircheisen, *Napoleon*, tr. by Henry St. Lawrence (New York, 1932), p. 65; L. A. F. Bourrienne, *Memoirs of Napoleon Bonaparte*, ed. by R. W. Phipps (rev. ed., New York, n.d.), I, 170-72.

Many Negroes were in prisons during this era, in fact many more than in the preceding decade when planters arriving from the colonies had to maintain so many in the *dépôts des noirs* during their sojourn in France. This increase was due to political and military developments. Thus, for some reason, a large number of mulattoes expelled from Santo Domingo found themselves in French prisons in 1796. The deputy Bourdon reported to the Legislative Corps in that year that more than forty were "illegally detained" at Rochefort and Bayonne. Sonthonax, who had been sent several years previously by the Legislative Assembly as one of three commissioners to rule Santo Domingo and who had made himself a despot there, was blamed as responsible. Bourdon asserted that Sonthonax had reduced the mulatto population of the island from 25,000 to 15,000, and forecast that soon he would likewise reduce that of the Negroes.[9]

About this same time three Negroes deported from Santo Domingo and Guadeloupe arrived at Le Havre, brought to France from England aboard the French ship *L'Amiable Céleste*. Two years previously the British had captured Guadeloupe and made many prisoners there, white and Negro. Evidently these were of that number.[10] Throughout the 1790's one reads of Negro and mulatto military prisoners.

More shocking was an occurrence in February, 1798, at Nantes, where thirty Negroes from the Indian Ocean occupied a building that was formerly a refinery. The owner of the building brought complaint to the city officials, evidently being unable to evict them. He accused them of making themselves a nuisance in the neighborhood, asserting that they slept on straw and sat about all day and night smoking cigars. They were thus a fire hazard. They either urinated on the floor or dropped urine on it, so that it emitted a fetid odor, and they were charged with being filthy in their persons. The

---

[9] *Réimpression de l'ancien Moniteur*, XXVIII, 481.

[10] "Bureau des Armemens et Classes," dated Le Havre, 10 thermidor an 5, and letter by Hozutener Hugo, 8 fructidor an 3, Archives de la Ville du Havre, PR, section I², 114-126, carton 30.

owner hoped for alleviation of the situation. What was done is not reported, although the police did take notice at least to the extent of recording the story.[11]

At Bordeaux more Negroes were to be found at the time of the Revolution than anywhere else, says M. Debien. He comments that in that city much bad feeling between the races developed in consequence of the recognition of equal rights in the colonies for free mulattoes and the abolition of the slave trade. Early in the Revolution, household servants and lackeys in Bordeaux called a meeting to petition for the abolition of wearing livery, for an increase in wages, and for sending back to the colonies the Negro servants, whom they looked upon as unfair competitors. Police broke up their meeting, however, and arrested fifty-two.[12] During the period of the Convention a street came to be designated Chemin de Terre-Nègre, no doubt from the fact that Negroes there were numerous. It was in a very poor section. Previously called Rue Mirabeau, its name was changed after Mirabeau's secret dealings with the court became known.[13]

If Negroes were eager to demand their "rights" and to share in the excitement of the Revolution, many also were loyal to their masters and mistresses. An incident illustrating this occurred near Lyons in 1791. A certain Guillin was attacked by a band of National Guards and peasants at his country home, but thanks to the aid of his Negro servant, he was able to fight them off for five hours, when he was killed. A Paris royalist newspaper carried an unbelievable story about cannibalism in respect to the body. Alas, it did not report whether the Negro escaped or even give his name.[14]

Another story appertains to a Negro faithful to a friend of

[11] Report by police commissioner Jean Augustin Brussetié, 8 ventôse an 6, Archives de la Ville de Nantes, I², Police générale, 147, carton 34, dossier 1.

[12] Debien, Les colons de Saint-Dominique, pp. 106-107.

[13] Marguerite Castel, "La formation topographique de quartier Saint-Seurin," Revue historique de Bordeaux et du département de la Gironde, XV (Bordeaux, 1922), 310.

[14] Journal de la cour et de la ville, July 8, 11, 13, 1791.

his former mistress. Theodore was a turnkey during the Reign of Terror at the Prison du Plessis in Paris. Among a group of aristocrats brought as prisoners to Paris was a certain Madame de Vassy. She recognized Theodore, and obtaining the opportunity to speak to him alone, she called him by name, identified herself, and gave him some money. This had its mellowing influence, and he thereafter rendered her a series of favors in accommodations, which she has described in her prison memoir.[15]

A new feature of the Revolution was the participation of Negroes in the ceremonial occasions that came into being. This in turn happened because the Negroes had become a small bloc in politics and their support was solicited. Thus in Paris in April, 1792, a fete was arranged for greeting the mutineers of Nancy (some Swiss soldiers who had defied their superiors in 1790), who had been sentenced to the galleys and afterward released. Members of several groups, such as "Conquerors of the Bastille," were to take part. One of the representatives so selected was a Negro, chosen as a foreigner and a supporter of the Revolution.[16] Later came a "Feast of the Negroes" at Grenoble, and a similar "Feast of the Affranchisement of the Men of Color" at Le Havre. At Le Havre an elaborate ceremony, commemorating the emancipation of slaves by the National Assembly on February 4, 1794, was planned and carried out, a leading feature of which was a military parade with various groups of citizens represented, including a large group of Negroes.[17] It would seem that other cities, too, joined in celebrating the abolition of slavery. The Jacobins realized that they had much in common with the Negro and needed his aid. These gestures of friendship were so many bids for support. More than one cynic of the

[15] Albert Savine, Les geôles de province sous le Terreur (récits de prisonniers) (Paris [1911]), pp. 46-53.
[16] J. M. Thompson, The French Revolution (4th ed., New York, 1950), p. 264.
[17] Inventaire sommaire . . . Isère, L 145; Archives de la Ville du Havre, PR, K, carton 3, liasse 45.

period charged that a Negro from Santo Domingo could ask about what he would in France and get it.

If Negroes were courted with public honors, however, they had by no means emerged from difficulties, and especially economic need. The larger number of Negroes were still in the role of domestic servants. Many were on the relief rolls, and some found themselves in prison or vagabond concentration camps. Government relief was made available to them, even as to white refugees from the colonies, by laws of September 18 and December 27, 1794.[18] One applicant was a Negress named Marie Louise, a deportee from Santo Domingo after the burning of Cap Français and now for two years a resident of Le Havre. She reported that she had married a year previously, and that her husband, also a Negro, had been called on business to New England, leaving her without resources. She remarked that her failure to make application earlier was due to the fact that she had not known of this aid. We are not told whether she was successful; probably she was.[19]

Two recipients of this form of aid at Le Havre were a Madame Rocheblave and her mulatto servant, Marie Aimée Magdalene, but much time and correspondence had been required before they were successful. Certain details had to be cleared up, and the French clerical officials were not famous for speed. Both the recipients were refugees from the burned Le Cap. At first their application was turned down by local officials, on the ground that they had lived in France for seven years and were not refugees or deportees. Later, however, their names appeared on the account sheet of recipients, showing that they did receive, at least for a while, the sum of 50 francs each a month.[20]

The sums varied with the individual. On the same relief rolls at Le Havre, two Negro men received 75 francs each per

[18] Letter of 9 ventôse an 4, Archives des Bouches du Rhône, L 1247.
[19] Petition of 26 germinal an 4, and certificate of good citizenship attached, Archives du Havre, PR, section I², 114-26, carton 30.
[20] *Ibid.*

month, another 50, and a Negress 15.[21] The same variation is
seen on the relief rolls at Marseilles. One Negro received a
total of 712 francs for nine and a half months, another 622
francs for eight months and nine days, and yet another only
415 francs for eight months and nine days. The last sum, in
fact, was paid to two boys of thirteen and to a twenty-six-
year-old Negress, all for the same period of eight months nine
days. Youths did not receive as much as adults, nor women
as much as men. Apparently they were not expected to eat
as much. Most of the recipients were young Negroes.[22] The
Revolution was not a period when work was difficult to find,
and it is surprising to read of young recipients in need of
relief.

Possibly there were some, especially in the ports, who did
not care to employ Negroes. This seems suggested by certain
letters that passed between officials in Le Havre at the time
of the arrival of a large contingent of Negro prisoners of war
on the Swedish vessel, cited earlier. One letter thus begins,
"Some complaints have been brought to us against the men
of color that you have announced to us." The fear appertained
to the distribution of these Negroes over the district. It is
clear that they were undesirables. It will be recalled that
prior to the Revolution many planters had brought Negroes
to Le Havre, and many were still resident there. More were
not wanted.[23]

One of those who fell into distress during the period of the
Consulate was a mulatto with a career of much interest. His
name was François Poithier. His uncle had brought him to
France in 1760, at the age of four, and for many years he had
studied painting at Loches. Early in the Revolution his uncle
left France, and Poithier was compelled to earn his living.
But his painting brought him small returns. After a while he

[21] *Ibid.*, carton 31.

[22] "Secours publics. Réfugiés corses et égyptiens et colons . . . , an V, 4
cahiers." Archives des Bouches du Rhône, L 328, cahier 1.

[23] Letters of 27 floréal and 19 prairial an 3, Archives de la Ville du Havre,
PR, section I², 114-26, carton 30.

left Loches for Nantes, and served for a period in the navy. Then he made a second unfortunate try at painting, afterward enlisting in the army. He served in Italy in 1801, and was captured by the Austrians. Poithier was not troubled in the slightest. He proceeded to enlist in the Austrian army and serve until the time of the Treaty of Amiens, and then deserted. Wandering on foot through France in 1803, he was arrested as a vagabond and suspect, and taken to the town of Pontarlier, near Fort Jouy, where Toussaint was then prisoner. Poithier was ill at the time and so was taken to the local hospital, where he was treated for a long time.[24] The most remarkable feature of this story was Poithier's ability to find a way out of every difficulty and keep going. He had resourcefulness. The account of the two Kinas as told by Colonel Nemours reveals somewhat the same difficulties encountered by them, and their checkered success and failure. Such an experience appears to have happened to many a Negro in France in this period. The Revolution bettered their condition very little in some ways, but it brought them adventure and an opportunity to see more of the big world.

More successful than Poithier in his aspiration to become an artist was the mulatto Guillaume Guillon (1760-1832), who later took the name of Lethière. The son of a baron in Guadeloupe, he early showed promise as a painter but the father at first refused to let him train for a profession of which he did not think highly. Later, however, his opinion changed, and he sent the boy to Paris to be taught by Doyen. In the 1784 competition in painting, Lethière won second prize, and thanks to the support of the Comte de Montmorin, he was sent to Rome for further training. After four years in Rome, he returned to Paris. It was in 1795 that his reputation began, with his notable painting, the *Mort de Virginie*, later placed in the Louvre. He came to the attention and good graces of Lucien Bonaparte, who was appointed ambassador to Spain and who took along with him Lethière to purchase Spanish

24 Nemours, *Histoire de . . . Toussaint-Louverture*, pp. 69-71.

paintings and form a collection. Thanks also to Lucien, he was made director of the French Academy of Painting at Rome (1807), after a brawl in a café on the rue Saint-Honoré in Paris in which Lethière killed and wounded several officers and was forced to flee. The incident forced the closing of his workshop in Paris and the dispersion of his pupils, but in a sense it brought him a promotion. Later, in 1815, he was elected to the Institut de France, but because of Lethière's known republican views, Louis XVIII for a time refused to confirm the election. The King, however, soon altered his attitude, and Lethière was received in the Institut. In 1819 he was made professor at the Ecole des Beaux-Arts, where he drew many pupils, some of whom later became celebrated painters. Not a great painter but one who had risen to the top in honors and public esteem, Lethière died in Paris in 1832. The list of his many paintings reveals that nearly all were on classical subjects, but that others were on matters of French history.[25]

Genius also showed itself in another mulatto who visited Paris in the revolutionary period. In 1799 a public concert was given there by the ten-year-old reputed musical prodigy George Augustus Polgreen Bridgetower, who had been born in Poland, the son of an African father and a European mother. His performance was attended by the elite in music and it received praise. He was afterward invited for further performances in various salons in the city. His early indication of future greatness, however, was not borne out. He long remained a protege of George IV of Britain, but died in 1860 "in comparative poverty and obscurity."[26]

Some of the more outstanding Negroes and mulattoes received invitations into the salons or drawing rooms of

[25] Pierre Larousse, *Grand dictionnaire universel du XIXe siècle*, X (Paris, 1873), 416. Some slight differences in detail are found in the sketch in *Nouvelle biographie générale*, XXX, 1011-12. Lethière is likened to General Alexandre Dumas by S. Linstant, *Essai sur les moyens d'extirper les préjudgés des blancs contre la couleur des Africains et des sang-mêlés* ([Paris], 1841), p. 155.

[26] J. A. Rogers, *World's Great Men of Color* (New York, 1947, 2 v.), II, 358-62.

the time. Raimond listed among his expenses in representing his fellow mulattoes the item of cab fare for his many visits to the homes of politicians in his efforts to sway legislation. Thomas Clarkson, the English antislavery writer, is reported to have been delighted, when visiting France in 1790, to find Lafayette at table with two Negro National Guard officers from Santo Domingo as his guests.[27] Times were beginning to change for the Negro, even if few were to benefit. One reads with interest in the ship records of 1798-1799 the listing of Mills, former deputy to the National Convention, his wife, and two daughters, among some passengers going back to Santo Domingo at government expense.[28] But though these developments favoring the Negro were welcomed in many circles, they were met with sarcasm or even bitterness in others. The celebration for the Negroes at Grenoble on March 21, 1795, already mentioned, ended in the destruction of one citizen's house, for which he later sought reimbursement by the government.[29]

From the above sidelights it is seen that for the Negro in France at this era, life was varied, perhaps more so than previously, and thus it was destined to continue. The motto of the Revolution was "Liberty, Equality, and Fraternity," but many of the Negroes, in common with the peasants and workers of France as a whole, remained poor, ignorant, handicapped, and troubled. For some the Revolution brought better things. A few basked in military and political glory; all were backslapped, so to speak, by the Jacobin politicians, and no doubt felt very important as citizens; only a few, like the prostitute Bersi, had a good income and money to "throw around." There were some who shrugged their shoulders at these baubles and remained with their former masters and

[27] *Mémoires, correspondance et manuscrits du Général Lafayette, publiés par sa famille* (Paris, 1837-38, 6 v.), II, 290-91.
[28] Minute of 3 germinal an 7, by the Bureau des Colonies, Archives Nationales, Colonies, F5B112, dossier marked "Passagers allant aux colonies, an 7 (1798-1799)."
[29] *Inventaire sommaire . . . Isère*, II, 274, L 145.

mistresses, even going on the relief roles with them, and some possibly to prison with them. Some were imprudent; others thought that the way of crime was the best road to take. Many landed in the hands of the police, yet probably no more than formerly. Due to the mania of the revolutionaries for written reports, for newspapers and pamphlets, more complete records came to be left. Thus we are enabled to get a slightly better picture of the times than previously.

# SEVEN     UNDER SLAVERY AGAIN

*THE NAPOLEONIC* order of May
20, 1802, restoring slavery as of 1789 in the French colonies
had less significance before the Congress of Vienna than
afterward. As for Santo Domingo, it was never put into effect,
for after Rochambeau surrendered there the next year, the
island was lost to France. In the Indian Ocean colonies the
emancipation decree of 1794 had never gone into effect, and
thus the Napoleonic order merely legalized a state already
existing. The Caribbean colonies, save for Santo Domingo,
did remain under French rule, however, until conquered by
the British colony by colony from 1803 to 1810. The British,
reluctant to see the fever for emancipation strike their own
Caribbean islands, left slavery in practice in the captured
French possessions. Thus, only after the Congress of Vienna
was the French authority definitely felt in its possessions.[1]

Within France itself the order seems to have had little
importance. There is no evidence of former slaves being
returned to their owners, or of Negroes and mulattoes on any
large scale being returned to the colonies in the interval of
peace (1802-1803), as specified by another order of July 2,
1802. This second order prohibited any foreigner to bring a
Negro or mulatto into France, and it similarly forbade any
Negro or mulatto to enter France without special authorization
from the Minister of the Marine and the Colonies. Violators

[1] *Cambridge Modern History*, IX, 240.

would be arrested, detained, and deported.[2] A few arrests were made, but the renewal of war in 1803 eliminated the problem. It is obvious that the government was disturbed by the presence of the Negroes. It regarded them as responsible for the confusion that had reigned in the Caribbean colonies since 1789, and it wished to restore order and economy to these colonies. It considered them moreover as troublemakers in France itself, as may be deduced from a number of police reports made in Paris in the period 1800-1803. One of these reports, in 1800, stated that the Negroes were hostile to the government, and charged some with making indiscreet remarks. Another report, of March, 1802, observed that for some time Negroes had been riding in elegant carriages, and that some of them employed white servants, thus causing complaint. A later report of that same year expressed alarm at the number of Negroes resident in Paris and at the prospect of blood mixture. A report of 1803 told of police raiding the headquarters of a band of Negroes.[3]

To head off potential trouble from the Negro and mulatto residents of France, it was decided to keep them under observation, much as the government of the Old Regime had done. In 1800 a census of Negroes in French maritime ports was made, perhaps as a part of the general census taken at that time, the first in France. The Admiralty wanted a complete count of Negroes and mulattoes living in the maritime cities since the outbreak of the Revolution, and a similar report was ordered made on the first of each month thereafter. In these reports were to be given the name, age, sex, occupation, and other data concerning the Negroes, so that the government might keep informed of their movements. At Nantes, where records of the matter still exist, a dozen or more reports were sent, one for each section or ward of the city. Two or three dozen Negroes were reported, scattered in several areas.

2 Duvergier, *Collection complète des lois*, XIII, 485.
3 F. A. Aulard, *Paris sous le Consulat* (Paris, 1903-09, 4 v.), I, 341, II, 789-90, III, 349, 393, 731-32, IV, 547.

Some had intermarried with the whites, had families, and were desirous of intermingling with the French. Usually in these mixed marriages the husband was Negro, the wife white; but occasionally the reverse occurred. At Nantes was an example of this in the marriage of a Negress named Adelaide to a white husband named Turpin, a cannoneer. The report indicates that the Negroes were gainfully employed at various trades.[4]

In 1807 another census was made in the maritime cities. For Nantes forty or forty-five persons were listed, about half of them being mulattoes. The majority were adults. Some were soldiers or former soldiers. Information sought concerned the name, age, trade, place of birth, local address, home ownership, marriage status, and number of children.[5] The prefect of Finistère was careless about submitting his report and in consequence received a reprimand. Réal, the police official in Paris, informed him that he was the only prefect who had failed to comply, and demanded an explanation. The information had been requested by July, and five months had since elapsed. The prefect hastened to report that his apparent negligence was due to the fact that he had not completed the gathering of his information. According to Réal, the census was required by the law of July 2, 1802, which specified that every Negro or mulatto, other than those serving in the French army or navy, who arrived at a seaport was to be put in a depot and sent to the colonies as soon as possible. Negroes and mulattoes of foreign crews, if found on French soil, were likewise to be reported and placed in the depots. The census of 1807 was primarily for the maritime cities, and designed to check on the arrivals of Negroes, whether from the colonies or elsewhere.[6]

In the meanwhile, all persons employing Negroes or mulattoes were ordered to report them to the police and make a

[4] "Gens de couleur," Archives de la Ville de Nantes, I², Police générale, 147, carton 34, dossier 1.
[5] "Etats des hommes de couleur, 1807," ibid.
[6] Archives du Finistère, Police générale et administrative, Surveillance des étrangers et Israélites, 1800-1848, série M, letter of 30 July 1807.

declaration for them, as prior to the Revolution. This declaration was to be attested by two residents. The Negroes thus declared would be given identity cards, which they must keep and be prepared to show when demanded. They were especially needed when moving from one area to another. Here, once again, was a return to the state of things existing prior to 1789.[7]

Rumor went in Paris in 1802 that two rich Negro merchants from Senegal had arrived in the city, having come at the expense of the French government, and apprehension arose that the slave trade would be revived. This actually occurred, and the traffic continued until 1814, when renounced by Napoleon shortly before the Congress of Vienna.[8]

One reads much less of Negroes during the period of Napoleon than during the Revolution, partly because they no longer figured in French politics, and partly too no doubt because most of the able-bodied were in the army. Only occasionally did Negroes figure in the records, and some of these because of police troubles. The police in Marseilles in 1806-1807 experienced a great deal of trouble from some Egyptian Negresses who were among a large body of Egyptian and Algerian refugees in the city. The police commissioner arrested five on one occasion and imprisoned them briefly for rowdiness and public disturbance. The commissioner wrote to the mayor charging that they were habitually drunk and made themselves a public nuisance, by dancing, fighting, and receiving soldiers, apparently for immoral purposes. Some in the neighborhood complained, but when the arrests were made, the mayor received a letter in their behalf, asking for their release on the ground that they did not know the law, and stating that one of the women, Victoire, was to vaccinate his (the writer's) child. The mayor hit the rowdy women with a feather, so to speak, by giving them an admonition and releasing them. Four months later there was an arrival of seventy-four additional refugees, including some more Egyptian Negresses. Whereupon the prefect Thibaudeau wrote

[7] Aulard, *Paris sous le Consulat*, III, 349.          [8] *Ibid.*, 467.

asking the mayor to watch these women more closely. All
were bad, but the Negresses were "the worst of all." Still later,
in February, 1807, a further complaint was made against them,
this time by a citizen named Pierre Barthélemy. Writing to
the general commissioner, Permon, he charged that "a turbulent
Negress" named Bembé, an Egyptian refugee, along with two
other Negresses, had attempted to enter his home the previous evening to visit a Negro servant in his employ. When
Barthélemy and his wife refused them entrance, Bembé, who
had a reputation for immorality, made a public scene by the
use of foul language that decency would not permit him to
repeat, and by seizing him by the collar, so that all the French
and Egyptians in the neighborhod ran up to see what was
happening. It was necessary for him to summon the police to
get her away. These episodes are reported by a careful
historian in a special study of lawlessness in Marseilles during
the period 1806-1820.[9]

There were a few other instances. In 1808 an Admiral
Williams, accompanied by his mulatto servant Arondo Pedro,
wished to go to Brest, and had to obtain a permit from police
official Réal before setting out. In 1812 another mulatto was
in France without permission, and the Minister of the Police
at Paris ordered the prefect at Nantes to arrest him. The
arrested man had the name of Diégo Correa.[10]

Runaways still figured in the police records. Among several
such who are cited in the archives at Nantes was a Negro boy
named Narcisse, whose master had brought him to France
and had given him an education, and now, in 1807-1808,
posted money for his return passage to the Ile-de-France.
Knowing of his master's plans, Narcisse fled, sought work as a
domestic, and was still at large several months later when his

[9] Paul Gaffarel, "Un épisode de la Terreur Blanche," *La Révolution Française*,
XLIX (1905), 326-30.
[10] Note of 16 June 1808, Archives du Finistère, série M, Police générale et
administrative, Surveillance des étrangers et Israélites, 1800-1848; and letter of
4 Sept. 1813, Archives de la Ville de Nantes, I², Police générale, 147, carton
34, dossier 1.

boat was ready to sail.[11] Another fugitive slave belonging to a Spanish prisoner of war in France was arrested in Nantes in 1814 and returned to his master.[12] These incidents reveal that under Napoleon the ties of slaves to their masters were still respected in France, as under the Old Regime. Slave hunts in fact continued after the fall of Napoleon, showing that wherever any trace of slavery was found, *marronage* or flight also existed.

The same spirit of paternalism as under the Old Regime was found to exist, if only for a short time. Evidence of this can be seen in an interesting baptismal ceremony for a Negro servant of Madame de Staël which occurred at Chaumont in 1810. Acting as godparents for this twenty-two-year-old native of Africa, the Vicomte Mathieu and Madame Récamier accompanied him to the font and as his sponsors promised to give him religious and moral instruction as required by their role. It appears a bit odd that Madame de Staël, a Protestant, would see her Negro servant baptized into the Catholic faith, but on the one hand she was no stickler for sharp religious distinctions and on the other there were reasons for his being a Catholic, as were the other Negroes in France. Not apparently until very recent times, perhaps since 1900, has any Negro in France been a Protestant, at least if he came from French possessions.[13]

That the slave was not always embittered at his lot may be seen in the fact that two slaves on the Ile Bourbon (later Réunion) were offered freedom and refused it. One of them accompanied his master to France in 1817, eight years afterward.[14]

At the Congress of Vienna, Great Britain became the champion of emancipation and of abolition of the slave trade. Pro-

[11] *Ibid.*                                [12] *Ibid.*
[13] Maurice Le Vaillant, *Une amitié amoreuse: lettres et documents inédits* (Paris, 1956), p. 221. The author is indebted for notice of this incident to Madame L. Braibant.
[14] Comte C. Mareschal de Biève, "Etudes sur l'Ile Bourbon à l'époque révolutionnaire," *Revue de l'histoire des colonies françaises,* année 5 (1917), 183, 185.

fessor Gaston Martin thinks that she was motivated by a desire to prevent French restoration of commerce in the colonies.[15] She was successful in getting all the major nations there represented to agree to the abolition of the slave trade, but the date for each nation was left to its own decision. Recognizing that smuggling of slaves might continue indefinitely, due to the great profits involved, Britain sought both then and later at various conferences to set up an international inspection control. Finally in the 1820's, in a series of private agreements, all save France agreed to the right of search of their vessels if suspected. Only in 1831 did France consent to such action, and then with qualifications. Even afterward some disputes were to occur. Despite this agreement the trade did not completely disappear, and in parts of French Equatorial Africa it was still practiced to some extend in the early years of the twentieth century.[16]

Even before the Congress of Vienna, Napoleon, by a decree of March 29, 1815, had abolished the slave trade for France, and legally it was not reestablished, but practically it was.

For a brief time following the Congress of Vienna the French government was too occupied with other matters to give much attention to the movements of Negroes and mulattoes, and to the enforcement of the law of 1802 restricting them. But in 1817 it focused its attention on the matter once again, under the direction of Molé, Minister of the Marine, and ordered the enforcement of nearly all the articles of the Declaration of August 9, 1777,[17] closing French ports to the entry of Negroes and mulattoes and prescribing measures for the return of any that accompanied their owners as servants on the voyage

[15] L'abolition de l'esclavage (27 avril 1848) (Paris, 1948), p. 8.

[16] An excellent account of this matter will be found in M. L. F. Sarrieu's doctoral study, La traite des nègres et le droit de visite au cours du XIXe siècle, dans les rapports de la France et de l'Angleterre (Paris, 1910), pp. 23-25, 99-100, et passim. See also James Bandinel, Some Account of the Trade in Slaves from Africa, as connected with Europe and America (London, 1842), pp. 169-72, and Gaston Martin, Histoire de l'esclavage dans les colonies françaises (Paris, 1948), pp. 251 ff.

[17] Articles 1-2, 4-8, and 12.

to France. It ordered reestablished *dépôts des noirs* in the most active ports to take care of such slaves.[18]

This statute affected only slaves and not free Negroes, who might gain special permission to enter France. To prevent confusion on the matter, a circular was sent out in 1818 by the Admiralty stipulating that freemen might enter and leave France at will, without providing caution money for their return, provided that they followed the regulations covering travel.[19] This distinction had its effect, and in consequence an ever-increasing number of free servants, Negro and white, accompanied their masters in the period 1815-1848, as may be seen in the multitudinous lists of *voyageurs* in the Archives Nationales.

The Atlantic crossing which was rarely attempted during the period of the Napoleonic wars was open once again after the coming of peace. But in 1815 there were few who made it. In 1816 the number greatly increased, and thereafter it continued large, though the total number never again approached that of the last years of the Old Regime. More Negroes came in other capacities than slave, however. Soldiers, stowaways, servants, and free Negroes traveling independently became more numerous, reflecting an increase in liberty and in economic status. From the Ile-de-Bourbon in 1815-1816 four stowaways came to France. All were slaves, and were held in prison awaiting direction from their owners or from the governor of the island. Their masters, of course, had to pay their expenses.[20] Among several hundred soldiers taken from France to Senegal in the summer of 1816 were a dozen or more Negroes and men of color. The designations of "noir," "mulâtre," and "homme de couleur" were still used. With the

18 Molé to the administrators of the colonies, 17 Oct. 1817, in *Annales maritimes et coloniales, partie officielle*, ed. by M. Bajot, année 1817, part 1 (Paris, 1817), 385-86.

19 Minister of the Marine to the Commissaire principal at Nantes, Archives de la Ville de Nantes, I², Police générale, 147, carton 34, dossier 1.

20 Cases of Jean Augustus, Ambroise Choisy, Jean Baptiste Monfort, and Edouard. Archives Nationales, Colonies, F⁵ B111. Two other stowaways in 1815 landed at Brest. *Ibid.*, F⁵B30.

regiment or battalion, oddly enough, went a Negress, Murie Zaïde, wife of Corporal Nicolas, evidently white, since his color was not specified.[21] It is interesting to observe that at this period, as under the Old Regime, Negroes were integrated in the ranks with white soldiers. During the French Revolution and under Napoleon there had been a number of segregated units.

In 1817 twelve Negroes or mulattoes were among the voyagers coming to France from Guadeloupe; in 1818, twenty-two. Of the latter number several were slaves. Caution money for their return had been advanced, and they were sent to depots. Several of the twenty-two, however, were traveling independently. Of those, most were mulattoes, for in general the mulattoes were in better financial circumstances. Of the twelve in 1817, nine were servants, three independent passengers.[22] These figures were for Negroes traveling between France and a single colony, and that not the largest. If therefore the number from Guadeloupe in 1818 was twenty-two, the total number coming from all French colonies might have approached a hundred. Unhappily, the shipping lists do not record the total number of voyagers for any year, for census figures on ocean travel were not kept.

That the numbers of Negro travelers after 1815 remained smaller than before 1793 may be illustrated by the fact that in 1791 fourteen Negroes and mulattoes came to Le Havre (out of a total of 240 persons making the crossing), and ten in 1792 (out of 288 persons), whereas in 1816 there were only four (out of 192 travelers), in 1817 only five (out of 300), and in 1820 only five (out of 310).[23] The decline was perceptible, and the number of white servants accompanying masters and mistresses was larger. Eight or ten such were listed in 1820, and the number seems in keeping with that of other years.

Consider the number of Negroes that went to France from Martinique in the 1820's. Martinique was larger than Guade-

21 Archives Nationales, Colonies, F⁵B9.                    22 Ibid., F⁵B32.
23 "Passagers debarqués en France, Le Havre, 1791-1820," ibid., F⁵B12.

loupe, and after Santo Domingo, the most important of France's Caribbean possessions. In 1820 there were twenty-one entrants; in 1822, twelve; in 1823, seventeen; in 1824, eleven; and in 1825, eleven. In general they were about evenly divided in numbers as to male and female, and Negro and mulatto. Many of the females were free mulattresses. Of the seventeen entrants in 1823, fourteen were females, and of these all but one were of mixed blood. Ten were free. The three males were all mulattoes, and two of them were free. This percentage of females did not hold true for other years, however. In 1822, only six out of twelve entrants were females; in 1824, five out of eleven; and in 1825, six out of eleven. All eleven entrants for 1824 were designated as free persons, and nine of the eleven for 1825. The status for the other two entrants for 1825 is not indicated. Here again the figures are not in line with those of earlier years. For in 1822 seven out of twelve entrants were slaves, and in 1823 five out of seventeen. Yet these figures reveal to us markedly the tendency of the times. Travelers from the colonies very clearly wished to avoid the restrictions imposed upon slaves, aside from the caution money involved, and found it preferable to bring servants, Negro and white, whereby they could escape these nettling requirements. Their preference was for female servants, possibly because they were more docile, possibly because they were needed to serve madame or the children. Mulattresses seem to have been preferred over Negresses, possibly because they had been associated more with the whites and accordingly had more social graces.[24]

It is not clear why the number of Negro entrants varied considerably from year to year, but it did so for all the colonies. Martinique, for example, had eighteen entering French ports in 1826, six in 1827, seven in 1828, and twenty in 1829. Occasionally other servants are designated by a single name,

---

[24] *Ibid.*, F⁵B36. The caution money for the slave Pierre Gabriel of Martinique in 1820 was 1,000 francs, deposited with the colonial treasury. *Ibid.*, F⁵B111.

without reference to color. It had not yet come to be the practice to omit mention of color, however, and it is to be assumed that these were whites. Only in the 1840's did this custom get under way.[25]

As time passed, there was a tendency to see on the ship lists more and more free Negroes and mulattoes traveling in independent fashion. Some, especially women, were accompanied by children. Nevertheless, the majority of the travelers continued to be in the servant class.

It is of interest that though one observes on the passenger lists the names of many paupers in this period who were being returned from the colonies to France at the expense of the government, virtually no Negroes or mulattoes are included as such. A law of March 31, 1831, provided that French subjects abroad who ran out of funds might obtain passage home at government expense. Thereafter for several decades many took advantage of it, as the passenger lists reveal. In 1865 the Minister of the Marine and the Colonies complained in a letter that the law had been much abused, commenting that recently the sons of two high government officials had tried to obtain passage home on it, although not entitled to its benefits.[26] One might expect to find an occasional Negro on the list who traveled in this manner, but of course most of the Negroes were colonials and would accordingly not come under the scope of the law. Yet one instance has been recorded, although it antedated the 1831 law. In 1819 a Negress named Eurtaud, born in Dijon, was returned from the Ile-de-Bourbon to Nantes because she was a "bad character" (mauvais sujet) and without funds (sans moyens d'existence). Since she was employed at that time as a domestic servant, it would seem that the economic aspect weighed less than the other. At any rate, she was returned to France at government expense.[27]

It is also worthy of observation that while numerous colonial youths traveled to France for study during this period, as seen on the passenger lists, one looks in vain for mention of

[25] Ibid., F5B36.          [26] Ibid., F5B115.          [27] Ibid., F5B111.

Negroes and mulattoes among them. That some of the latter did go is attested by the fact that in 1834 four young men of mixed blood from various colonies were graduated in medicine from the University of Paris.[28] Possibly the names of such students appear on the ship lists but their color is omitted. This practice that developed increasingly in the nineteenth century and that has continued in the twentieth has made it very difficult for researchers to track the steps of Negroes in the records. Another interesting omission in these post-1815 records is the virtual absence of African princes coming to Paris, although one named Papel, "Negro prince from Bany," came to Nantes in 1816 or 1817.[29] Possibly the legal ending of the slave trade explains this cessation.

No longer were slaves brought to France to learn a trade and be instructed in the principles of the Christian religion. Not once does this expression appear on nineteenth-century ship lists. It is odd and even ironical that in the Age of Reason so much concern about religion should have been expressed, and that in the Age of Romanticism, supposedly more consonant with religion, so little.

Guadeloupe and Senegal had a law by which convicts were sent to France, but in only one or two instances was this done. In 1796 Senegal sent to Rochefort two convicts, one a Negro named Henry Frichant, the other a native Spaniard.[30] Neither were many Negroes sent back to the colonies as undesirables. A Madame Monlieu wrote the police at Nantes in 1818 accusing her husband's slave Charles of vagabondage and asking that he be sent back to Martinique. Her husband was willing to pay the slave's expenses, but the slave did not want to go. The real issue here, of course, was not vagabondage. By way of reflection, how did it happen that this slave had been carried into France when the law pointedly forbade it? The many

[28] Cook, *Five French Negro Authors*, p. 47.
[29] He is listed as arriving on *La Sénégalese* on 15 Jan. 1816, and also as arriving on *La Belle* on 28 Oct. 1817. *Ibid.*, F5B24.
[30] *Ibid.*, F5B9; *Annales maritimes et coloniales*, série 3, année 29, LXXXIV (Paris, 1844), 1274-76.

similar cases that mark the records since 1777 indicate that
French officials were often willing to wink at legal enforcement.[31]

Racial discrimination has been manifested so seldom in
France that a writer is provoked to designate those instances
where it has occurred. In the period 1817-1825 an incident
took place in Paris that inflamed the Negro who was involved,
and he wrote a hot letter of indignation to the *Constitutionnel,*
a journal edited by the Abbé Grégoire, but the Abbé evidently
decided that its publication would not help his cause. The
letter rests today in the papers of the Abbé Grégoire at the
Bibliothèque de l'Arsenal, according to Professor Mercer Cook.
A Haitian, in company with a young Frenchman, tried to enter
a casino at the Palais Royal and was excluded on the ground
of his color. So at least he was informed. That it happened
seems to be satisfactorily attested, but that it was most unusual
is also clear. It is the first known instance of exclusion from a
building or entertainment in France because of color.[32]

During the 1820's and 1830's France became the scene of
propaganda on the race issue in the colonies by several mulatto
agitators who were driven from the colonies. Several *causes
célèbres* that arose in the colonial courts were brought to the
French Court of Cassation through appeal. The defendants
in these trials were Bissette, Fabien *fils,* Louisy, Richard, and
Houat, free mulattoes, who had become involved in the racial
issue, were tried by colonial courts, convicted, and sentenced
—all to have these sentences modified or revoked through
appeal.

The most significant of these defendants was Cyril Charles
Auguste Bissette, who in some respects was a nineteenth-
century Raimond. A well-to-do mulatto born in Martinique
in 1795, he was a property owner who resented the subsidiary
role to which his class of men was relegated. In 1822 an

[31] Archives de la Ville de Nantes, I², Police générale, 147, carton 34, dossier
1.
[32] Mercer Cook, "Document: A Letter from a Haitian to the Abbé Gregoire,"
*Journal of Negro History,* XXXVIII (1953), 438-39.

uprising of Negroes and mulattoes took place in the island, after which twenty were executed. This brought a bitter denunciation of what had happened and of conditions on the island by Bissette and two fellow mulattoes, Fabien *fils* and Volny, who had the pamphlet published in Paris in 1823 under the pseudonym of Sieur Avila. Entitled *De la situation des gens de couleur libres aux Antilles* and disseminated in the island, it infuriated the colonists, who at last discovered the identity of the authors and brought them to court. Charged with writing and spreading sedition, they were banished from the island, but they appealed the decision and the verdict was changed by the Royal Tribunal of Martinique to one of life sentence in the galleys and branding with the letters GAL (for *galérian*). Again they appealed, this time to the supreme court of France, the Court of Cassation of Paris. They also published a 28-page pamphlet and addressed it to the Chamber of Peers, giving a history of the case and setting forth their inability to get their appeal brought before the Court of Cassation. They requested the legislature's aid in having the severe and unjust sentence broken. They denied the accusation of having fanned sedition, and pointed out a legal technicality which should have cleared them had it been observed.[33] The Court of Cassation heard the case in September, 1826, and referred it to the Court of Guadeloupe, which reduced the sentence to ten years' banishment from the island. This was about as severe a sentence as throwing a rabbit into a briar patch, for all three mulattoes went to Paris. There Bissette remained until 1858, save for one or two fleeting visits to Martinique when slavery had ended and he had acquired fame.

In Paris, Bissette like Raimond considered himself an agent of the mulattoes to the French people and published brochure after brochure as polemics denouncing colonial mistreatment.

---

[33] *A la Chambre des Pairs. Pétition additionnelle pour Bissette, Fabien fils et Volny, deposée le avril 1826* ([Paris, 1826]). Volny and Fabien *fils* were merchants.

He also contributed to several journals, *Le courrier français, La constitutionnel,* and *La tribune des départements.* In 1834 he founded the *Revue des colonies,* whose chief object was to advocate better conditions for the mulattoes and emancipation for the slaves. This review ran for several years and was the first literary journal given to the interests and culture of Negroes. Negro poetry and articles there found publication. To the white colonists it was a great source of annoyance.

It would be extraneous to give a detailed account of Bissette's several pamphlets; a few words to each should suffice. One of his earliest brochures was a three-page tract written by himself and Fabien pleading for a slave girl in Martinique named Adèle, who had been given a brutal scourging by court order for having sung the popular song *La Parisienne.* The brochure was merely a letter of protest which they sent to the King and later published.[34]

About the same time Bissette published a two-page, saucy reply to a white colonist who had expressed opposition to his plan for publishing a *Revue des colonies.* He served notice that he would write and publish what he pleased, whether it suited Langlois or not.[35] The next year he and Raimond, signing their names as "agents of the men of color of Martinique," assailed the governor of Martinique for his conduct in taking a census. The governor had ordered local officials to consider as free only those who could show papers to this effect. Bissette and Raimond were furious.[36] Like Julien, these men were more interested in what was occurring in the colonies than in France, although in this case it was Martinique, not Santo Domingo, which concerned them. Shortly afterward the two writers jointly published a twenty-four-page account of some recent racial clashes at Grand'Anse, Martinique.

[34] *Demande en grâce pour Adèle, jeune esclave de la Martinique, condamné à la peine du fouet pour avoir chanté la Parisienne* (Paris [1831]).

[35] *A mes compatriots* (Paris, 1831).

[36] *A la Chambre des Pairs. Plainte des manditaires des hommes de couleur de la Martinique contre M. le contre-Admiral Dupotet, gouverneur de cette colonie* (Paris, 1833).

The brochure is of interest as being the mulatto side of the story.[37]

After this, Bissette's brochures stopped for a time. When he resumed them, it was to attack his friends Arago and Schoelcher, the one an eminent scientist, the other the Assistant Minister of the Marine and the Colonies who more than any other person in France was to be responsible for the emancipation of the slaves in 1848. Bissette had been privileged to meet many eminent persons and count them among his friends and aides. Arago, Schoelcher, and Isambert, the famous jurist, all aided in the abolitionist movement. But in a pamphlet of 1846 Bissette sharply attacked both Arago and Schoelcher over some trifling differences of opinion and statement.[38] It was bad enough to attack two old friends in private, but to do so in print was worse. Bissette was too prone to rush into print.

Two final tracts of 1847 were concerned less with the mulattoes and more devoted to emancipation of the slaves than those previously. One was addressed to the French clergy, the other to French local officials. Bissette urged both to come out strongly for emancipation. Whereas some wanted gradual emancipation, with the children being freed first, he insisted on complete emancipation of all slaves at a single blow.[39] The appeal to the clergy was occasioned by a petition in favor of emancipation sent to the French government signed by three bishops and nine hundred clergy along with ten thousand other French citizens. Bissette, of course, was elated and hoped for wider expression on the matter from the clergy. The moment for emancipation, as events were to prove, was propitious, and its advocates realized it. Bissette was a religious man. He was also a man widely read; in fact, his reading was much wider than Raimond's. Like Raimond, he had a definite goal in life and was willing to subordinate all

[37] *Affaire de la Grand'Anse, Martinique. Au Roi, en son conseil* (Paris, 1834).

[38] *A M. Etienne Arago* (Paris, 1846).

[39] *Au clergé français* (Paris, 1847); *A MM. les membres des conseils généreux des départements* (Paris, 1847).

toward it. But his zeal in attaining that goal led him into polemics and carping criticism.[40]

His fellow victims of 1824, Fabien *fils* and Volny, collaborated with Bissette on certain tracts, as already mentioned. Fabien also published at least two tracts independently, one being a twenty-three page pamphlet in 1831 in behalf of the *patronés* of the colonies. The *patronés* he described as persons recognized as free although they had never legally been declared free. In Martinique alone he declared there were eight thousand such. He designated five distinct classes of them, and urged that all be accorded their liberty.[41] Fabien also published a brochure on the Louisy case, telling of the severe treatment of the *patroné* Louisy Adzée in Martinique for being in the company of some slaves who struck a white boy. His appeal was for support of French public opinion in the matter.[42] Fabien shows that he was well informed, intelligent, and evidently familiar with law. He and Volny did not acquire the reputation that Bissette did, and we know nothing of them save from these brochures.

Associated with these men was another West Indian mulatto, Mondesir Richard, who collaborated with Fabian *fils* and Bissette on a pamphlet at Paris in 1832.[43] He also published two pamphlets at Paris in 1831 pointing out the discrepancy in treatment accorded mulattoes in France and in the colonies, and making a plea for better treatment in the latter. Like the others, he was a resident of Paris but his heart was primarily in the colonies.

Shortly later another *cause célèbre* that was to affect France ultimately took place on Réunion (the former Ile-de-Bourbon), in the Indian Ocean. There in December, 1835, a mulatto music teacher named Louis T. Houat, later to acquire fame,

[40] The best account of Bissette is a chapter in Cook's *Five French Negro Authors*, pp. 38-71.

[41] *Patronés ou libres de savane. Réclamations en leur faveur . . .* (Paris, 1831).

[42] *Procès d'un patroné de la Martinique* (Paris, 1833).

[43] *Pétition à la Chambre des Députés relative à l'amélioration du sort des esclaves aux colonies.*

was arrested on the charge of plotting with twenty-eight others, some slaves, some free, to kill the whites on the island. All were thrown into prison, where they spent eight months awaiting trial. Houat furthermore was charged with carrying on a correspondence with abolitionists of France, and notably with those of the *Revue des colonies*. Some copies of this review were found in his room when he was arrested, and it was held, he claimed unjustly, that he was trying to inflame Negroes in the colony to demand liberation. The local court condemned him to deportation. News of the trial reached Paris, where Isambert succeeded in having the amnesty of May 8, 1837, to political offenders extended to cover him and others convicted in this affair. In consequence he should have been freed, but the officials on Réunion instead gave him and the others condemned seven years of banishment. Houat went to France, where he studied medicine and spent the rest of his days, save for some periods of travel in Italy, Germany, and Russia. He quickly became acquainted personally with Bissette, Isambert, and other abolitionists, and published an account of his trial, sending a copy to the Minister of the Marine. Even earlier he had smuggled a letter out of his prison on Réunion to Bissette, who had published it in the *Revue des colonies*.[44] All along Houat insisted that he was innocent of the charges against him on Réunion. In France he buried himself in other interests and was much less active a propagandist than Bissette or Fabien.

How many read the abolitionist tracts of these mulattoes and how great was their influence cannot be determined. Certainly they were few in comparison with those written by white emancipationists in Paris, who with speech and pen were actively promoting abolition, and under whose able leaders, like Isambert, Arago, De Tocqueville, and Schoelcher, the cause of emancipation moved rapidly to success in 1848.

Actually, this second abolitionist movement in France was

[44] *Revue des colonies*, III (1836-37), 117-22; L. T. Houat, *Un proscrit de l'Ile de Bourbon à Paris* (Paris, 1838), pp. 3-6.

but part of a worldwide movement that affected several European countries and the United States of America. The British emancipation of slaves in 1833, a measure carefully planned and equitably administered, with due consideration both to the slave and the slaveowner, exerted great influence on those countries that still remained slaveholding. A procession of other nations followed in the British train: Sweden, 1846; France and Denmark, 1848; Portugal, 1856; Holland, 1860; the United States, 1863.[45]

The action of emancipation on April 27, 1848, in France did not come as a lightning blow, but as a gradual process that had gained momentum since 1830. One of the preparatory steps had been the great number of manumissions. In the four colonies of Martinique, Guadeloupe, the Dominican territory, and Réunion, 22,137 former slaves had been freed before 1830, and 22,614 additional ones were freed between 1830 and 1848. Many of these purchased enfranchisement with their own earnings.[46] The larger number, however, were freed under clauses in the wills of their owners, for many masters so recompensed faithful service from their slaves.

Another step was an ordinance passed in 1836 rendering it easier for emancipated slaves to take surnames. This followed a report made to the King that year by Duperré, Minister of the Marine and the Colonies. This official pointed out that the great number of affranchisements in recent years had focused attention upon this crying need.[47]

Yet another action of 1836 operated in the same direction. A royal ordinance of April 29 stipulated that for the future any master wishing to bring a slave into France must make a "declaration of enfranchisement" for him before setting out

[45] Jean Perrigault, "Il y a cent ans. Nous mettions fin à l'esclavage, 1848-1948," Le revue maritime (1948), 415-16. In Brazil and certain Spanish possessions slavery continued much longer.

[46] Louis Lacroix, Les derniers négriers: derniers voyages de bois d'ébène, de coolies et de merles du Pacifique (Paris, 1952), p. 161.

[47] "Rapport au Roi concernant les noms et prénoms à donner, dans les colonies, aux esclaves appelés à la liberté," Annales maritimes et coloniales, année 21 (Paris, 1836, réimp. 1845), 514-17.

on the trip; and should he fail to make this declaration, the slave would be free anyway. Furthermore, it provided that all slaves at that moment in France were similarly to receive their liberty.[48]

In 1845 and 1846 two ordinances from Paris rendered more humane the discipline and regimen of the slaves in the colonies. For example, no other corporal punishment was permitted than the lash, and it might be administered only to male slaves and consist of not more than fifteen lashes. Each owner must keep a record of all chastisements, with full details. Food, clothing, hours, and other matters were to be more carefully regulated than in the past.[49]

These and other acts had pointed out very clearly the way toward complete emancipation, which came in early 1848 in the Revolution of that year. That many planters had foreseen it coming is revealed in the relatively small number of 248,560 slaves that remained; and that their owners had become somewhat reconciled to their loss is seen in the acquiescence with which they took it. Schoelcher, Assistant Minister of the Marine and the Colonies, was the dominant figure in the emancipation. The French government, following the pattern of the British, agreed to reimburse the slaveowners, and later in 1849 set apart 126,000,000 francs for the purpose.[50]

Abolition on this occasion, as in 1794, was due to the overthrow of royal power and the establishment of a republican government representing the middle and lower classes. The abolitionists had done a remarkable job of preparing public opinion for the step, so that the Schoelcher Commission, appointed early in 1848 to examine the matter, was able from its opening day to decide that slavery must go. It remained only to prepare the legal steps. The colonists realized that

[48] "Ordinance du Roi relative à l'affranchissement des esclaves aménés des colonies en France," ibid., 513-14.
[49] Laws of 18 July 1845 and 4 June 1846, Annales maritimes et coloniales, année 30 (Paris, 1845), 722-27, and année 31 (Paris, 1846), 621-24.
[50] Moniteur universel, 2 Feb. 1851, CXLIII, 347-48; J. Saintoyant, La colonisation française pendant la période napoléonienne (1799-1815) (Paris, 1931), p. 83; Perrigault, "Il y a cent ans," 425-26.

the die was cast and contented themselves with salvaging what they could in reimbursement.[51] They complained that they were not paid adequately and that reimbursement was almost wholly in government securities, but they realized that they had no alternative to acceptance.

The slaves were granted instant freedom, without the preliminaries set by the British Act of 1833; also they were granted citizenship. Thus all slaves, whatever their education or other qualities, were at once endowed with the right to vote and entitled to equal treatment before the law. Any fetters that hitherto prevented their coming to France, other than their empty purses, at once fell. They might now once again send deputies to the French government and have a hand in politics. The white man again had been kind, for all this came as a free gift. The whites had split, and those favorable to the Negro had come into power. This condition has lasted ever since.

[51] Martin, *L'abolition de l'esclavage*, pp. 56-63. Martin gives the same story with some additional details in his *Histoire de l'esclavage*.

# EIGHT     A NEW DAY IN POLITICS

*THE SECOND* French Republic brought a new opportunity for Negroes to participate in politics. Under the First Republic several had come to Paris and sat in the National Convention and the Legislative Corps or had called on the government to influence legislation. Brochures by Negro writers had been published, Negroes had participated as members in the Jacobin Society, and at least one was sent on a colonial mission. Something of the same experience was to renew itself in the days of the Second Republic, although there were to be some marked differences. There were to be fewer deputations and fewer pamphlets, but perhaps more Negro deputies, who were to take a more active role than the earlier representatives had done.

The Revolution of 1848, like that of 1789, found many Negroes and mulattoes resident in Paris. These became greatly excited, quite understandably, and in their enthusiasm a "deputation" of them called on the Provisional Government on March 9 to express "their sentiments of gratitude." For a few days earlier, on March 4, emancipation had been voted. They were cordially received, and Benjamin Crémieux, an ardent abolitionist, made a brief speech welcoming them on behalf of the government. Amid the enthusiasm of the occasion, one of the members of the delegation, a student from the Ecole Polytechnique, proposed to Crémieux that the government send Bissette to Martinique to carry the news proclaiming the republic, saying that it would be a fitting recognition of that man's sufferings for the cause of liberty. He called Bissette "a great martyr of liberty" and commented that on his shoulders he bore "the stigmata of infamy," left as a result of the branding in 1824. He hoped that Bissette might be sent back, and "on the same place where the hangman applied to him the mark of infamy on his shoulders, he himself proclaim the liberty of his brothers." Fitting remarks for that day of romanticism and sentiment! Crémieux responded in a few appropriate sentences. But the suggestion was not seriously taken.[1]

One of the seven members of the Schoelcher Commission, set up to study the matter of emancipation, was a mulatto from Martinique named François Auguste Perrinon (1812-1861), who had studied at Rouen, at Paris (in the Ecole Polytechnique), and at Metz. He had become a battalion commander in 1847 and had been made director of a foundry at Ruelle. Other Negroes in Paris were consulted by the commission, as were some planters, for their opinion on one or more matters, as the Schoelcher Report stated. The commission was solicitous as to what would happen economically in the colonies to the emancipated slaves. Both Negroes and planters believed that though the slaves might leave the fields temporarily, they would return to them.[2]

The constitution adopted in 1848 provided for a National Assembly of one house, to have a total of 750 members from France and the colonies. All males aged twenty-one or more were to enjoy the right to vote, with no educational or economic requirements. The vote moreover was to be secret. All men above twenty-one, indeed, were eligible to become electors, and all men aged twenty-five or more were eligible to hold political office. The representatives to the National

[1] *Moniteur universel*, 9 March 1848, CXXXI, 573.
[2] *Ibid.*, 3 May 1848, CXXXI, 927; Alfred Martineau and L. P. May, *Trois siècles d'histoire antillaise: Martinique et Guadeloupe de 1635 à nos jours* (Paris, 1935), p. 247; Cook, *Five French Negro Authors*, p. 54.

Assembly were elected for terms of three years, and might run for reelection.[3]

In the West Indies several Negroes ran for seats in the National Assembly, and some were elected. It was not necessary for a candidate to be resident in a constituency to run. Schoelcher, of Paris, was proposed and elected both in Martinique and Guadeloupe. He opted in favor of the former. He was not the only nonresident chosen, for Bissette, who had lived outside Martinique since 1826, also was elected, leading the ballot for three seats with 19,395 votes. Pory-Papy, also a mulatto, had 18,803 votes; and Schoelcher, 18,659 votes. Two alternates *(suppléants)* also were chosen, Mazuline, a Negro, having 18,046 votes, and France, 16,257. From Guadeloupe the deputies chosen were Perrinon, a mulatto long resident in France, 16,233 votes; Schoelcher, 16,038; and Charles Dain, 10,996. As alternates, Louisy Mathieu, a Negro, with 11,632 votes, and Wallon, with 11,582, were selected. Several other candidates had received a respectable showing, among them Bissette, who garnered there 5,349 votes. Louisy subsequently was named to take Schoelcher's place.[4]

The election in Guadeloupe was marked with abuses, and in consequence many protests were made to the National Assembly. These were turned over to its Thirteenth Bureau for examination. This body found that the charges were accurate, but decided to accept the results just the same, evidently considering that a new election would end in like fashion. Its report stated that after examining the figures, the frauds made little difference in the outcome. It lay the responsibility of the "tumults" to the "old colonists" and to "the citizens newly affranchised."[5]

Protests also developed for those elected from Martinique. The *Courrier de la Martinique* had charged in its columns that the election was fraudulent, and the matter came to be

---

[3] *Moniteur universel*, 31 August 1848, CXXXIII, 2239.
[4] *Ibid.*, 30 Sept. and 23 Oct. 1848, CXXXIII, 2641, 2951.
[5] *Ibid.*, 21 and 23 Oct. 1848, CXXXIII, 2916, 2951.

discussed on the floor of the Assembly. The charges chiefly concerned Bissette, who saw the storm clouds gathering and as early as October 5 wrote a letter to the president of the Assembly begging to decline service in view of the allegations. The letter was read to the Assembly, but it did not allay the storm, which broke later at the session of October 17, when the affair was much discussed. Some did not want to accept Bissette's resignation, thinking that he had no power to decline service when elected. Pory-Papy, without saying much on Bissette's case, spoke several times during the session and insisted that all had gone peacefully and honorably in the election. He did admit at one point that "a part of the colored population had taken part illegally in the election." The discussion was heated. Cloture was voted, then revoked. The election was finally validated, but Bissette was allowed to decline service because of "a personal incapacity." Some inquired into the nature of this disability, but an answer was dodged. Several charged that Bissette was running from the charge of fraud. Dupin de la Nièvre remarked, "He thus escapes the question of law." Even Crémieux, ardent abolitionist, joined in with the sarcastic remark, "To put himself in safety, he attacks others."[6] The president put to a vote the matter of acceptance of Bissette's request, and it passed.

The "personal incapacity" is explained by Mercer Cook as Bissette's bankruptcy. The law stipulated that a bankrupt person was ineligible to hold public office. Bissette had learned of it only after election, and his letter of resignation was motivated by a desire to avoid the unpleasant consequences, for he knew that adversaries would attack his election.[7] The vote of the Assembly saved him from public humiliation, and he had opportunity to repair his finances before the next election.[8]

Soon the Assembly had a chance to see what could be

6 *Ibid.*, 5 and 18 Oct. 1848, CXXXIII, 2721, 2878-81.
7 *Five French Negro Authors*, pp. 55-56.
8 How he filled his empty pockets by courting the whites in Martinique, and changing from a leftest to a rightest to do this, is set forth, *ibid.*, pp. 57-58.

expected of these Negroes. Their speeches were to be limited largely to matters colonial. Pory-Papy joined with Charles Dain and Victor Schoelcher on October 24 in proposing a constitutional amendment making all the laws of France applicable to the colonies "save for exceptions proper to each of them, which will be determined by law." In support of his action, Pory-Papy said that what provoked the amendment was Article 109, which would set up "individual laws" for Algeria and the French colonies. It appeared thus, he continued, that these were territories outside the limits of the constitution. This he and others wanted to correct. He made a fair speech, and it evidently had its part in the adoption of the amendment on November 4. While Louisy Mathieu and Mazuline were also sponsors of the amendment, they did not speak in its behalf.[9]

In February, 1849, it was proposed and carried that the number of deputies from Martinique and Guadeloupe be reduced from three to two for each. Dain, white representative from Guadeloupe, made a long speech urging the retention of the three for that colony, calling the matter "extremely grave." Pory-Papy refrained from speaking on it, but he did speak against a proposal to abolish the alternates from the colonies. He proposed having one from each colony, but his idea failed to carry, his opponent pointing out that even in the case of death to one of the deputies, another would be left to represent the colony.[10]

It remained for Louisy Mathieu to embroil himself in trouble on the floor of the Assembly by some untactful language. Louisy was a mulatto born in Guadeloupe in 1817 and had received little if any schooling. By the time of his marriage in 1840 he was comfortably wealthy. He seldom spoke before the august Assembly, and in his maiden speech on December 1, 1848, he made his *faux pas*. The debate that day was concerned with the colonial budget. Dain had spoken on money

[9] *Moniteur universel*, 24 Oct. and 5 Nov. 1848, CXXXIII, 2952, 3090-91.
[10] *Ibid.*, 1 March 1849, CXXXIV, 674.

needed for Negro schools and for inspection of the slave trade. Taking the opportunity offered by his colleague to digress from the question of the budget, Louisy defended universal suffrage, which he said some had criticized, saying that Negroes and mulattoes in the colonies valued it enormously, even though abysmally ignorant. He thanked the French for the emancipation of his race. After getting this good start, he unfortunately began discussing the relationship of the races in Guadeloupe. He mentioned the fear of the whites and the generosity of the Negroes, who, he remarked, had forgotten the past and held out the hand of friendship to the whites. But those white colonists who published a journal in which Negroes were called "some brutes, some savages," were *méchants* (reprobates). Use of the word *méchants* brought rebukes from the president of the Assembly and from a deputy named Lasteyre. When they had concluded, Louisy regained his feet and explained, "I did not have the intention to say that the colonists are reprobates, since in general I am able to assure you that I have the sympathies of all; I only wished to speak of the journal." Thereupon there were remarks of "Very well! Very well!" Thanks to a suggestion in the president's rebuke, he had recovered his balance.[11]

Whether or not this episode unnerved him, Louisy rarely spoke again in the Assembly. He is reported to have felt his lack of polish in a body of that sort. He contented himself in the Assembly with participation on a single committee, that of Algeria and the colonies, and usually voted with the extreme left. He opposed some of the steps of Louis Napoleon. In June, 1849, he returned to Guadeloupe and was elected municipal councilor for Pointe-à-Pitre, thus terminating his period as deputy.[12]

Mazuline was another alternate who had become a deputy in the Assembly—in this instance when Bissette declined to

[11] *Ibid.*, 2 Dec. 1848, CXXXIII, 3427.
[12] "Un constituant noir en 1848: Louisy Mathieu," *Revue de l'histoire des colonies françaises*, année 6 (1918), 118-200; Martineau and May, *Trois siècles d'histoire antillaise*, p. 242.

serve. Born of slave parents in Martinique in 1789, he had early followed his master, a naval officer, to France and afterward to the United States. Later he became a servant to another prominent French family and was taken back to France. This family took an interest in the education of his daughter, and she afterward was able to return to Martinique and open a boarding school, whereby she acquired sufficient influence to get her father elected as alternate to the National Assembly in 1848. At the time of his election Mazuline was a resident of Paris, living in a degree of comfort. Like Louisy Mathieu, he spoke rarely in the Assembly and then on inconsequential matters.[13] Twice in early 1849 he requested of the Assembly, and obtained, a leave from duties *(congé)*. In January he asked for leave for several days, and mid-March he asked for indefinite leave to make a voyage to Martinique "to make known to his brethren the good intentions of the government in their behalf." The mails were functioning normally, and there was no reason why the newspapers in the island would not have been glad to publish anything favorable to the island, but maybe he was getting nostalgic and here was a chance for him to make the trip as a dignitary. After all, others were asking *congés* of the Assembly and obtaining them; why not he?

Mazuline was back in the Assembly in mid-July, and wrote an ineffective protest against the election of Bissette on June 9 as deputy from Martinique. The letter went to the bureau in charge of election validations, which reported no sufficiently serious charge. The president of the Assembly announced therefore that unless anyone else had criticisms to make, the election would be recognized.[14]

This brought Bissette for a second time into the Assembly. He was to remain longer as deputy than the men already discussed, and to take a more active part, although even he was to leave something desired. He was absent from the session

[13] Martineau and May, *Trois siècles d'histoire antillaise*, pp. 242-43; *Moniteur universel*, CXXXIII, 2881, and CXXXIV, 147, 583, 1507.
[14] *Moniteur universel*, 19 July 1848, CXXXII, 2388.

when validation of his election in 1849 was discussed, and
more than once a defender had to say that he spoke for the
absent member or that one should not attack an absent member. Even when his election was confirmed, Bissette was often
absent, and he seldom spoke when he was present. His first
speech was not until May, 1850. It was occasioned by a
discussion of certain journals in Guadeloupe and Martinique.
He apologized that his first speech must deal with himself.
Then he told of an attempt made to humiliate him the year
previously when he was in Martinique. It was a parody of
his arrest and condemnation to the galleys in 1824. A dummy
figure representing him was to be carried through the streets
and afterward thrown into the room where his family was
assembled. His friends made a protest to authorities and the
affair was cut short, but it infuriated Bissette. The editor of
*Progrès,* a journal in Martinique, was arrested, with Bissette's
approval. Bissette also discussed the *Courrier de la Martinique*
and reasons why it was not suppressed. The speech was
personal in nature and showed that Bissette could not forget
his own sufferings.[15]

Bissette did not let the matter rest with a speech. He
published a letter in the *Courrier de la Martinique,* denouncing
the affair. In the letter he blamed the parody on Dorville,
Jouannet, and Cochinat, to whom he said rumor attributed the
prank. These three prominent citizens of the colony thereupon
sought to bring suit against Bissette, who was protected
against legal action by Art. 37 of the Constitution (colonial)
of 1818 and by some subsequent laws; hence it was essential
for the National Assembly to grant authorization to the court
in Martinique before the suit could proceed. A request to
this effect was made to the Assembly by Meynier, procurator
general of Martinique, and published in the *Moniteur universel* of June 12. The charge brought against Bissette was
defamation of character. No action was taken at first save to
appoint a commission to inquire into the matter. At length

15 *Ibid.,* 5 Feb. 1850, CXXXVIII, 413, and 4 May 1850, CXXXIX, 1509.

*[handwritten annotation at top: nature of remaining records limits what McC discusses, making it more imp than it was]*

on June 20 Pory-Papy brought before the Assembly renewal of the complaint and requested authorization for court action. It was pointed out that a commission to study the matter had already been appointed; Pory-Papy's request was sent to it. Bissette insisted that a new commission should be appointed, but he failed.[16]

The matter was brought up anew at the session of July 2, with the commission making its report and recommending refusal of authorization for pursuit. There was much discussion. Jouannet spoke at length, saying that he was director of the interior in Martinique at the time and never heard of the alleged parody, the justice of peace in the neighborhood had never heard of it, the governor never heard of it, even Bissette's nephew by marriage wrote a letter for the journal saying he had never heard of it, and the three men accused of fomenting it denied complicity and knowledge of it. Jouannet accused Bissette with inventing the whole story. Bissette replied in caustic language, at which he was adept, saying that he was in Guadeloupe at the time (not Martinique), but got his information from relatives and friends when he arrived in Martinique. He denied accusing the three men of responsibility for the affair, but wanted them to set forth what they knew. This they had not done. The commission's report was brought up for a vote, and the request for legal action against Bissette was turned down. The whole thing was a sorry affair which should never have occurred in the first place. Bissette was a hothead who took fire on the slightest provocation, and had long been used to making charges and countercharges. He was fortunate that the Assembly on this occasion rescued him from legal pursuit.[17]

Not long afterward in the Assembly there was another flareup of Bissette's temper. On July 11 the question arose as to whether or not martial law should be declared at Pointe-à-Pitre in Guadeloupe because of violence that had developed there following a great fire in May which had destroyed

[16] *Ibid.*, 12 and 21 June 1850, CXXXIX, 2022, 2128.
[17] *Ibid.*, 3 July 1850, CXL, 2272-73.

seventy homes. The debate developed into a discussion of racial relations and animosity. Schoelcher had introduced the matter and discussed it quite calmly. He ended by proposing that a commission of three, acceptable to both whites and Negroes, be sent to the Antilles to make an inquiry into conditions prevalent there, and he named eight men whom he placed in the category of being acceptable to all. These innocent remarks aroused the indignation of Bissette, who arose and expressed astonishment at their utterance. He was outraged that Schoelcher referred to whites, Negroes, and mulattoes. Such terms he called archaic; all colonials now were on one class. "I demand of the Assembly," he said, "the permission to repel certain words which the orator descending from the tribune has pronounced. Under the regime of slavery we understood perfectly that one still designated the colonial inhabitants by the terms of whites, blacks, and mulattoes. But today, under the regime of liberty and equality, these words are superfluous; we ought to endeavor to chase them from our memory, and it is astonishing that this be [by] a representative elected by the colony of Guadeloupe." Dain, Perrinon, and others joined in the discussion, but Bissette was reluctant to let anyone else have the floor. A deputy named Santayra rebuked him, asking if he considered himself speaking in favor of conciliation. Bissette then brought up the matter of his own sufferings, which paranoidally he seemed never to be able to forget.[18]

Perhaps Bissette's ill will toward Schoelcher lay at the bottom of it all. Since about 1843 he had been bitterly jealous of Schoelcher, possibly because of the latter's leadership in the emancipation movement. Mercer Cook relates the story of their quarrel and points out that Schoelcher twice challenged Bissette to a duel to settle their differences, but each time Bissette declined.[19]

On this occasion Bissette denied that there was ill feeling in the colonies between the races. He claimed to know be-

[18] *Ibid.*, 12 July 1850, CXL, 2369-73.
[19] *Five French Negro Authors*, pp. 50-52, 63-70.

cause he had recently been there. Save for a few trouble-makers, all fraternized well. Even white women were happy to sit at tables with former slaves, and he commented that the white women in the colonies were marked by more pride and haughtiness than the men. When they could sit at the table thus, he said, it was proof that the ancient prejudices had disappeared. He then went on to say that in the colonies some officials were inciting trouble, and he offered to give their names privately to the Minister of the Marine and the Colonies if these were wished. Some asked him to name the parties from the tribune, and others asked if he intended to become an informer.

Later, Dain spoke at length, disagreeing with Bissette on the matter of racial relations in the colonies. He asked why Bissette should declare that racial distinctions in the colonies should have been abolished and yet advocate martial law for Guadeloupe. Why, he continued, should the races, if so harmonious, be divided into different parties? Perhaps Bissette was speaking for the effect it would have in the colonies, Dain concluded, but he was unrealistic; conditions were simply not as Bissette pictured them.[20]

Thus his fellow colonial deputies, Dain, Perrinon, and a week earlier, Pory-Papy, had disagreed with Bissette on matters of fact. Indeed, Bissette was heavily dominated by sentiment and personal experience to the point of fanaticism. That he had ideals, even high ideals stemming from deep religious convictions, no one would deny, but he was ruled by emotion rather than reason, and this handicapped him as a deputy in the National Assembly.

Perhaps his long career as abolitionist had turned Bissette into a cynic, for in most of his speeches he acidly denounced others' motives. For an additional example, he spoke on July 29, delighted at the establishment of bishoprics in the Antilles and on Réunion. He considered it a matter of major impor-tance, and said that the colonies would benefit from the aid

[20] *Moniteur universel,* 12 July 1850, CXL, 2371.

of moral force supporting order. Religion, instruction, and justice were needed in this respect. As his speech proceeded, he discussed in particular the evil forces on the islands, and laid them at the doors of the political and judicial officials and government representatives in the colonies. He spoke of the harmonious spirit that prevailed in the first election after the emancipation of the slaves in 1848 (the election so criticized on the floor of the Assembly), but said that subsequently things had changed, due to the officials. (A week previously he had taken a different stand.) He declared that duty required him to present the matter to the Assembly, a matter that the Minister of the Marine and the Colonies seemed unaware of. The contest was one between liberty and anarchy—anarchy that led to despotism. "In the name of these ideas," he said, "in the name of humanity, in the name of France, whose interest and honor are engaged in the consolidation of the new order of things, I beg the government not to let fall the influence of dangerous officials in one of the balance scales where at this moment are suspended the destinies of the colonies."

This pompous statement was greeted by cheers from the rightists, but it drew a reprimand from the Minister of the Marine and the Colonies, who remarked that usually when criticisms of his department were made, he was given advance notice. He proceeded thereupon to deny that his ministry was supporting subversive officials. "The honorable Bissette," he stated, "comes to tell you among other inaccurate things that the bad officials of the Antilles have a point of support in the central administration. I repel this accusation with all the energy of my soul." He then defended the government in this particular. Among other things, he said, "Messieurs, we are unfortunately in the presence of passions exalted by misfortune; the colonists, ruined by a brusque emancipation that I dare even to call imprudent . . ."[21]

Bissette spoke with better grace on August 8 in opposing a

[21] *Ibid.*, 30 July 1850, CXL, 2614-15; article on Bissette in the *Dictionnaire de la biographie française.*

bill to put fetters on the colonial press. One might think from his criticisms of certain colonial editors that he would welcome this chance to shackle them, but he knew from his own experience as newspaper and review publisher that freedom was needed. He opposed the bill at some length, but ineffectively; it passed.

In February, 1851, Bissette spoke upon the matter of whether an extension of time should be allowed Frenchmen owning slaves in other lands to dispose of them. Schoelcher estimated that about twenty thousand Frenchmen in this category still possessed slaves in 1851. According to the law of 1848, such owners were to dispose of their slaves within three years. The date now approached when this interval would end. Two deputies proposed an extension of ten years for them; Schoelcher proposed a three-year extension; Bissette, one of two years. Bissette spoke in favor of his amendment, but it failed. The ten-year limit was passed, but it was to count from 1848, and not 1851.

After this Bissette spoke rarely. Never a strong representative, he had been interested almost exclusively in matters colonial, and even then on matters coming within his limited scope of interests. He had a good mind, wrote well, and had a certain degree of eloquence, but he permitted emotion and personal experience to rule his thinking. Though he spoke more frequently than some others from the colonies, he did not have the range of interests or effectiveness of Charles Dain or Perrinon.

Two high honors came to Bissette in 1851, to sweeten his later years. In March he was made a chevalier of the Legion of Honor, and in April a ship was named jointly for him and for Pécoul (the other deputy of that time from Martinique). He and Pécoul went to Le Havre to witness the occasion. The ship was to ply between Le Havre and Martinique, and was ready to set out immediately on her maiden voyage.[22] Unfortunately, we do not have the details of either ceremony.

[22] *Moniteur universel,* 14 March and 25 April 1851, CXLIII, 731, 1157.

Bissette by this time had come to be a well-known person both in France and in the colonies. The honors were deserved and a tribute both to him and his race.

Perrinon and Charles Dain enjoyed far less reputation than Bissette, but both spoke on a much wider variety of topics, especially on economic matters affecting the colonies, about which Bissette was silent.[23] Perrinon had previously been governor of Martinique, and in that capacity he had had earlier acquaintance with the budget, on which he spoke often in 1849. Dain, too, spoke on the budget, on taxes, on constitutional matters, and other topics. Jouannet, representative from Guiana (his race is not indicated), spoke often on various phases of finance affecting the colonies—taxes, banks, the budget, penal work.[24] These men were all more moderate in temperament and escaped the reprimands and tilts that Bissette encountered on the floor of the Assembly. They were more conversant with conditions in the colonies, having been there more in recent years than Bissette, who thought himself well acquainted with colonial conditions although he had scarcely been there since 1824.

If there were other men of color in the Assembly during these years, they have escaped notice. Dain of course was white, and perhaps Jouannet was also, but as colonial deputies they serve for contrast on certain matters. Of course it was not to be expected that the Negroes in that day would possess the education or political experience to make a showing comparable to the more favored whites. They were making their introduction in the political forum, and they did better than might have been expected.

Since 1848, Negroes have continually sat as representatives of the colonies in the French parliament, despite the changes in government. Forty-two sat in the lower house in 1956. Reference will be made later on to some recent participation of Negro representatives in the French government.

[23] Ibid., CXXXVII, 3191.
[24] See the index of the Moniteur universel for 1851, CXLV.

# NINE      LITERARY ACTIVITIES

*THE DESIRE* to write has ani-
mated a large number of French Negroes, and it is surprising
how many have been successful—surprising because many have
had little formal education, surprising because most of them
have lacked the literary background in their homes, surprising
because so many have exploited the one theme of race relations.
Good writers are commonly considered to be well trained in
rhetoric and well read in literature. But in the instances of
several Negro writers to be considered in this chapter, such
conditions did not prevail. On the other hand, these writers
had a vivid imagination, a feeling for literary artistry, and a
burning sense of injustice. Like the Old Testament prophets
they had a message to convey, and enough verve and skill to
make it appeal.

The earliest literary activity on the part of Negroes in France
was by Julien Raimond at the time of the French Revolution.
Raimond's writings, already described, were for political ends
rather than entertainment. His objective was to obtain for
the mulattoes in the colonies equal rights with the whites.
Seldom did he mention the Negroes, and then only after the
whites had refused to compromise with the mulattoes and
these last were obliged to join common cause with the Negroes.
It was literary effort that ruined Raimond financially. His
pamphlets reached no second edition, but that they had some
influence may be judged from the fact that on more than one

occasion he was asked to head a deputation appearing before French legislative bodies, and from his appointment under the Directory as one of three commissioners sent from France to investigate the government of Sonthonax in Santo Domingo.[1]

Other Negroes and mulattoes of the Revolutionary era likewise resorted to the publication of political tracts, printed in France. Among those to do so were Gatereau, Pinchinat, Besse, Rigaud, Bonnet, and Jastran. The most interesting thing about these pamphlets is that such a number of Negroes and mulattoes were capable of writing them, so severe had been the hand of repression in the colonies. All evidently had been trained by tutors, for other means of education were closed to them.

During the Napoleonic period there appears to have been a cessation of Negro literary activity in France. For one thing, the press was state-controlled; and for another, slavery was restored in the colonies in 1802. With this, Negro political activity, save in Santo Domingo, was virtually terminated. But with the Restoration a weaker hand than Napoleon's was at the helm of government, and in the 1820's and 1830's some famous *causes célèbres* involving free mulattoes in the colonies attracted public attention, and with them came further pamphlets crying against the chains of slavery, calling for freedom and equality. The brochures on the whole were well written and set forth good reasoning. The authors revealed study of the laws allegedly violated and a familiarity with the procedure of court appeal. In short, they had taken the pains to be well informed. Their writings, a total of six or eight brochures, were written not to entertain but for judicial and political ends. The topic continued to be the same as that of the Revolutionary Negro pamphlets—race relations.

The *Revue des colonies*, founded by Bissette in 1834, had some significance in the encouragement of literary effort on

[1] A chapter on him may be found in Cook's *Five French Negro Authors*, pp. 3-37, and likewise an article by the same author in the *Journal of Negro History*, XXVI (1941), 139-70.

the part of the young Negroes in France and in the colonies.[2] In it may be found the work of Louis T. Houat, probably the first French Negro to attempt poetry. In volume III of the *Revue*, for 1836-1837, Houat, at St. Denis on Réunion, had four poems: "Poésie à mon ami," "Le pêcheur," "Le convoie de la jeune fille," and "Le bengali." The first has no remarks on race or the slave question, but dwells on the beauties of nature, and is addressed to a friend A. L., identified as Auguste Lacaussade, a young mulatto on the island of Réunion.[3] The second describes the dangers of the sea for the fisherman. The third depicts the sad funeral of a young woman. The last, on a songbird in his cage, a bengali, much prized in the East, is the best of the four. Houat compares the poor little bird in its prison to himself, for he had written the poem while a prisoner on Réunion. All four poems breathe the contemporary spirit of Romanticism. Evidently they made some impression, for Houat later published them separately in booklet form. Houat revealed himself as a sensitive, reflective youth who was something of an idealist.

Houat spent the six years 1838-1844 in extensive travel in Russia, Italy, and Germany. On his return to Réunion in 1844 he published a romantic novel entitled *Les marrons*. The scene is laid on the island of Réunion, in the Indian Ocean; the date, 1833. Four slaves, all but one of them from Madagascar, enter into a plot to run away, with the idea of finding safety with a tribe of the Salazes, where one of them has a grandfather as chief. Three are recaptured almost immediately, but the fourth, a Câpre,[4] eludes his pursuers by a sort of miracle and comes upon two Negro runaways and a white woman with

[2] There is a chapter on Bissette in Cook's *Five French Negro Authors*, pp. 38-71.

[3] Professor Cook has an article on Houat in the *Journal of Negro History*, XXIV (1939), 185-98.

[4] Lafcadio Hearn in *Two Years in the West Indies* (New York, 1923), pp. 246-47, speaks of Câpres as red, cinnamon, or chocolate in color, and remarks that they insisted on being of red (Indian), not black, descent. Littré and other lexicographers and encyclopedists fail to explain this racial term. It is even omitted by Moreau de Saint-Méry in his very elaborate chart on mixed races in his *Description . . . de la partie de l'Ile de Saint-Domingue*, I, 96-100.

her mulatto child in a cave. There for some time the refugees continue to live as cliffdwellers. One of the two Negroes found in the cave is an old man, a sort of Robinson Crusoe on the island, gifted with much knowledge and very resourceful. The story of each of these persons is related at length, providing a splendid opportunity to depict the cruelty of slavery and the social life on the island. Eventually the hideout is detected; armed men close in on the runaways; and one of the Negroes is strangled and the Câpre is marched away to prison. Meanwhile, the three Madagascans have made a second attempt at flight, this time to Madagascar, but again they are captured. Tried in court, they are condemned to death. The day of execution arrives, the crowd, the prisoners. Suddenly a rescue party of about a hundred Negroes, gathered by the Câpre who has escaped from prison, dashes in and rescues the Negroes. Then the Negro thought to have been strangled at the cave appears on the spot; he had merely fainted instead of dying. Melodramatically, the heroes are avenged and the villains vanquished. From first to last, the novel reeks of Romanticism: it portrays the beauty of nature and the cruelty of man; and its heroes are guilty of no wrong. A precursor of *Uncle Tom's Cabin*, it failed to get the reception Houat wished, and thenceforth he attempted no novels.

After eighteen years of silence, Houat, now an enthusiastic spiritualist, materialized in 1863 with a volume entitled *Etudes et sciences spirites*, and subtitled *Morale, philosophie, médecine, psychologie*. He had become a member of the Society of Homeopathic Medicine in France, an organization of physicians that followed the bizarre medical ideas of Dr. Samuel Hahneman of Germany. Houat published three medical treatises, and read a paper before the International Homeopathic Congress in 1867. His last years were spent as a physician at Pau, in southern France. It is to be regretted that Houat did not continue further in poetry, where he had early revealed some capacity.

Another mulatto writer in France at this period was also

from Réunion—Auguste Lacaussade (1817-1897). Sent to Nantes for education in its lycée in 1827, he spent seven years there; then he returned to his native island to begin a career as a notary. But life on Réunion was boring, in fact fettering, after a long stay in France, and he longed to return. His family at last agreed to furnish him the money to study medicine at the University of Paris, and soon he was on his way. He began the study of medicine well enough, but found dissection distasteful and after a time decided to change his interests to poetry, in which Victor Hugo, his hero, was then the lion. In 1839 came his first endeavor at publication. It consisted of a small volume of verse, dedicated to Hugo, and was entitled *Les Salaziennes*. It passed unnoticed. In 1842 he published a translation of Macpherson's *Ossian* (entitled *Oeuvres complètes d'Ossian*) that was considered "one of the best."[5] The work revealed that he was an accomplished translator of English and led to a job as secretary to Sainte-Beuve, in which he long continued. Already introduced to some of the prominent literary figures of the day, he now found closer ties, and his success as a literary personage became more assured. He returned to Réunion in 1842 and remained there for three years, during which he married, but thenceforward he lived in Paris and considered himself French.

Lacaussade contributed to various literary reviews, including the *Revue contemporaine*, and when the *Revue européenne* was founded in 1859, he was named director. This periodical ran until 1861, and its contributors included the leading French literary men of the day. Lacaussade himself contributed only a few fugitive poems and articles, however. This was his one and only role as editor.

In the meanwhile, he had published, in 1852, a volume of poems, *Poèmes et paysages*, for which the Académie Française awarded him the Bordin Prize. Again, in 1862, he was

---

[5] "M. Auguste Lacaussade," *Revue des colonies françaises anciennes et modernes*, I (Paris, 1897), 97-100. See also the chapter on Lacaussade in Cook's *Five French Negro Authors*, pp. 101-22.

given the same prize, this time sharing the honor with Léon Halévy. This second award was for Lacaussade's poems entitled *Epaves*.[6] In 1875 he published a collected volume of poems, entitled *Poésies de A. Lacaussade*. And later, in 1888, he published a French translation of the poems of Leopardi (*Poésies de G. Leopardi*), for which the Italian government gave him the Cross of the Order of Saints Maurice and Lazarus.

Lacaussade therefore was a poet who received some recognition from his contemporaries. His poems employ the rhyme patterns of nineteenth-century poetry. There is much of the spirit of Romanticism, much reference to Greek and Roman mythology, a low opinion of woman (who is weaker than man and voluptuous), resignation to suffering and mistreatment, a love of solitude and nature, of flowers, birds, wine, and dances. Lacaussade also wrote some patriotic poems centering around the War of 1870-1871. He was bitter toward the Germans, whom he called "Huns," "Teuton ravagers," and "Vandals of another age." France, on the other hand, was the land of "progress, the arts, and light."[7] His "Siège de Paris" is a poem of praise to the city's noble defense. Many lines could be quoted for illustration, among them these:

"Devant ces murs d'airain que la foudre illumine,
Vainqueurs, vous avez reculé!
    Ce n'est pas avec vous, c'est avec la famine
    Que Paris a capitulé!"

One poem, "Une victime de Sedan," commemorates the loss of a childhood friend, Lieutenant Colonel Hyacinthe Rolland (born on Ile Bourbon, later Réunion), who was mortally wounded in that battle. Lacaussade had come to regard

---

[6] Cook, *Five French Negro Authors*, p. 106. The article in *Revue des colonies françaises anciennes et modernes*, I, 99, however, reports that the Bordin prizes were for Lacaussade's *Epaves* (1861) and his *Anacréontiques* and *Automnales* (1875).

[7] *Poésies de A. Lacaussade* (Paris, 1875), pp. 201-203. From his poem, the "Cri de Guerre."

himself as French, and the collapse of France before the German onslaught wounded him as deeply as if he had been born in France. There were times when he showed himself sensitive on the matter of his race, and he often alluded to the beauty of nature on his native island. But more than any Negro writer thus far described, he took the role of a Frenchman, not of a colonial resident in Paris.

Two other nineteenth-century Negro writers from overseas deserve mention. One was Victor Séjour (1817-1874), from New Orleans; the other, Alexandre Privat d'Anglemont (1820-1859), a native of Sainte-Rose, Guadeloupe. Séjour was a natural son of François Marcou, a mulatto from Santo Domingo, and Eloisa Farrand, a New Orleans quadroon. Christened Jean Victor Séjour Marcou in New Orleans, he later shortened his name. His father was ambitious for him and sent him for education first to the Sainte-Barbe Academy in New Orleans, run by a well-trained mulatto, and afterward to a college in Paris. Séjour remained in Paris, aspiring to follow the role of Alexandre Dumas and Victor Hugo, as dramatist. He wrote twenty-one plays that were presented on the Paris stage. Some were in verse, others in prose, and all were saturated with the Romantic spirit of the time. For a period his plays were popular, but with the change of taste for grandiose spectacles, he had much difficulty in marketing his last plays. In consequence, he died almost penniless in a charity hospital of tuberculosis. All his plays were written in French; only one, *Les volontiers de 1814,* dealing with the Battle of New Orleans, had an American setting. Some were built around prominent historical characters like Richard III, Philip II, and Cromwell; but others dealt with lighter themes, as *L'Argent du diable, Noces vénitiennes,* and *Mystères du temple.* Almost without exception they were five-act plays, and he is reported to have polished their wording right up to the minute of their presentation. In fact, it is reported that he introduced changes in the fifth act of one play after it had been started, and had to have a rehearsal of this act during the intermission following the fourth act. An admirable desire on his part for perfection, but how the actors must have disliked him! Yet a southern American writer of that period was proud to claim him as a Southerner.[8]

About the same time that Séjour went to Paris, four other young men of mixed blood from New Orleans, all freemen, also went to the French capital for their education and became permanent residents. All became poets of much merit. A selection of their work, as well as a poem by Séjour, was published in 1845 in an anthology entitled Les cenelles ("Holly Berries"), in which twelve other authors were represented. The collection was judged sufficiently important to be edited and republished in the United States in 1945, with a foreword by Professor H. Carrington Lancaster. The French mulattoes contributing to the volume were Armand Lanusse (also the editor of the first edition), B. Valcour, Camille Thierry, and Pierre Dalcour. Short sketches of all are given in the preface of the centenary edition.[9]

Privat d'Amblemont, likewise a mulatto from New Orleans, was sent early to Paris for his education, and save for a brief trip home for business (he took the same boat back to Europe after twenty-three hours!), spent the rest of his life in the French capital, which he loved dearly. His father owned a sugar plantation, which an older brother managed, and from which Privat long drew revenue sufficient to live handsomely. He spent several years at the Collège d'Henri IV, receiving his baccalaureate, and proceeded to enroll in the faculty of medicine at the University; but his duration as a medical student was brief, due, it is said, to his enchantment with literature and the arts—rather, with the café society of writers

[8] Article by Edward Larocque in the Dictionary of American Biography, ed. by Dumas Malone, XVI (New York, 1935), 565-66; Roi Ottley, No Green Pastures (New York, 1951), p. 88; Grand dictionnaire universel du XIXe siècle, XIV, 498; James Wood Davidson, The Living Writers of the South (New York, 1869), p. 501.

[9] Creole Voices: Poems in French by Free Men of Color. First Published in 1845, ed. by Edward Maceo Coleman (Washington, 1945). The other mulattoes contributing were all residents of New Orleans, it appears.

and artists. His was a happy, idle existence until in time his revenues dwindled and he was obliged to earn some money. Thereupon he took to writing for a number of newspapers and periodicals, his contributions consisting of light essays on quaint corners and personages in Paris. Saturated with the spirit of Romanticism, he found charming all that was odd and old, no matter how dilapidated or smelly. A volume of these essays he collected and published in 1854 under the title of *Paris anecdote,* with preface and notes by Charles Monselet. It was much read, reaching a fourth edition by 1886. An atheist, Privat would allow no priest to see him when he lay dying from tuberculosis in 1859, and ordered that his body "be taken directly to the cemetery without passing by the church." In 1861 a friend edited another book of his scattered articles, under the title of *Paris inconnu,* with two brief biographical sketches of the author. The essays are light and gossipy; to some degree they remind the reader of Mercier's *Tableau de Paris.*[10]

All the above-described Negro writers were born overseas and came to Paris to live. There were, however, two Negro writers who were born in France, never visited a French colony save for Algeria, and had the interests of the colonists very little at heart. They were French through and through. These were Dumas *père* and Dumas *fils,* who ranked among the major literary personages of the century.

Alexandre Dumas (1803-1870), known as Dumas *père,* was the son of General Alexandre Dumas of the French Revolution, and the father of Dumas *fils* (1824-1895), actually Alexandre Dumas III. On the remarkable dynasty André Maurois has recently written an excellent history, entitled *Les trois Dumas* (Paris, 1957). The first of the dynasty was a mulatto, the second a quadroon, the third an octoroon, the last two having white mothers. The mother of Alexandre Dumas *père* was the

---

[10] The Library of Congress has copies of both works. The bibliographical sketches of him at the outset of the second work were written in 1859 by Victor Cochinat and Alfred Delvau, friends of Privat. A brief sketch likewise is found in the *Grand dictionnaire universel du XIXe siècle,* XIII, 187.

daughter of a hotel owner in the small town of Villers-Cotterets. She had married his father, then a lieutenant colonel, in 1792, and remained in her home town while her husband fought in France, Italy, and Egypt. Her husband returned in broken health after the Egyptian campaign and eighteen months' imprisonment in an Italian military prison, to die shortly after the son's birth. He had plotted against Napoleon in Egypt and thereby forfeited Napoleon's support and the chance of a pension. The boy grew up in the most straitened circumstances, with education of the most limited form. His mother and aunt taught him to read and write; later he attended a college in Villers-Cotterets taught by the Abbé Grégoire for a short time, and learned a little Latin and grammar. He also acquired beautiful penmanship, which later served him well when as a youth he decided to go to Paris. He was able to find employment as a secretary to the Duc d'Orleans, to whom he received an introduction through the aid of General Foy, a friend of his father. Dumas was adroit in making use of friends to aid him in making contacts when he had need of them. His realization of when to seek them and the use to make of them when opportunity came was almost astuteness. If Dumas had little formal education, he had a keen mind and was a straight thinker. He knew when others could help him and he was quick to pick up knowledge from whatever source. He became a widely read man, but he read only books that appealed to him. He did research to obtain information for his plays and novels, but for minute or faithful detail he cared not the slightest. The era of Romanticism seemed made for him, and he could alter any story to suit his whims and to delight his audience and his readers. To them, the alterations were only so many improvements.

Dumas had become interested in vaudeville and the theater even before leaving Villers-Cotterets. A trip to Paris to see Talma, the great actor, play in *Sylla,* and a conversation with him, set him afire to go to Paris to live and, if possible, to become a playwright. He approached his mother; she gave him a liberal part of the slender sum her husband had left them; and he set out for Paris. There he became secretary to the Duc d'Orleans at the slender salary of 1,200 francs a year —though at that time the sum seemed big to him. He worked long hours, from 10 a.m. to 10 p.m., save for respites at meal-times. An older friend in the Duc's office recommended to him a course of reading the classic authors, and he set out devouring Aeschylus, Plautus, Molière, and Schiller. When he could, which was rarely, he attended the theater. Some vaudeville pieces that he composed brought him extra cash. But he aspired higher.

A painting that he saw of Giovanni Monaldeschi being killed at Fontainebleau by order of Christine of Sweden led him to investigate the story. The story of a former lover now jilted, it seemed to him the basis for an excellent play. So he wrote *Christine* (1828), a drama in five acts, and then came the problem of getting it accepted by some theater. He inquired of friends; they told him that it was imperative, for quick action, to have a literary friend sponsor it. Whom among the *literati* did he know? Only one, a certain Charles Nodier, a minor writer beside whom he had sat at the theater when Talma played and with whom he had entered into conversation. Nodier on that occasion had been expelled by the police for getting irritated at the performance. Dumas wrote him reminding him of the occasion, and asked his aid. Few men could refuse Dumas—and few women either. Nodier agreed. Dumas was given the proper introduction, his play was accepted, subject to some verbal changes, and it was to be presented at the Théâtre Français. Everyone thought highly of it and was enthusiastic, save for Mademoiselle Mars, distinguished actress who was to play the leading part, who was dissatisfied with her lines. When Dumas refused to alter the role to suit her, she proceeded to scuttle the performance.

Dumas began at once to write another play, *Henri III et sa court*, which was accepted by the same theater and played

(1829). He had profited from his earlier experience, and this play had a role more pleasing to Mlle Mars. He had the ingenuity to induce the Duc d'Orleans to attend and bring a party of twenty or thirty aristocrats. For thirty-eight nights the play ran, a great success, and Dumas became overnight famous.

From then on, throughout his life, there was a procession of plays, and after some years had passed, a procession of romances, for Dumas came to learn that bigger profits were made from successful novels than from successful plays. He was never allergic to making money. He made a fortune during his lifetime, but as fast as he made it he spent it—on women, parties, and other things. Generous to a fault, his pocketbook was open to all who approached him. He had always some new mistress, and sometimes several at the same time. Several children were born, all out of wedlock; some he recognized as natural children, others he did not. His son, Alexandre Dumas *fils*, he acknowledged after seven years had passed. His only marriage, in midlife, was anything but a success, and both parties shortly went their own way, with their own lovers. Aside from his eroticism and his improvidence, he was a man of the most radiant personality, loved by virtually all who knew him.

The Romantic age seemed to be made for Dumas. He chose, in general, historical themes both for play and novel, made gripping stories from them by letting his imagination run riot where essential to add to the interest, and was never fettered by historic fact. A multitude of plays and novels resulted, the most celebrated being one of his earliest novels, *The Three Musketeers,* that took the reading public by storm, and that continues to be read avidly throughout the world, especially by the youth. His second most famous work was his *Count of Monte Cristo,* a gripping story based upon a report in Jacques Peuchet's *Mémoires tirés des archives de police de Paris* (Paris, 1838). Peuchet had been archivist for the police. There was thus a historic foundation for the story, but not for the details that Dumas inserted. Dumas had the fantastic touch that could glamorize and entertain, a very fertile imagination.

Dumas made use of a very capable person, a former professor from a Paris lycée, Auguste Maquet, to aid him in writing. Exactly how far this aid went, no one knows. Maquet was highly trained for literary work and did much of the research and the drafting. Maurois, who has made extensive research for his book, is of the opinion that Dumas planned the works, left the drafting to Maquet, and added the finishing touches, perhaps after the manner of Rubens in painting. He never questions the master hand of Dumas, however.

Dumas also wrote works other than novels and plays. He traveled widely from time to time, to Spain, Algeria, Italy, Switzerland, the Netherlands, Germany, and Russia, and wrote a multivolume travel account, *Impressions des voyages.* In Italy at the time of the Garibaldi Expedition in 1860, he accompanied Garibaldi in his own little boat, the *Emma,* with a young wench aboard dressed in admiral's uniform, his latest mistress. She was an embarrassment to Garibaldi and the Italians, but what could they say when they needed help from every quarter? Happily she became pregnant and soon left when Dumas refused marriage. From the start Dumas saw the opportunity for a good story out of the expedition, and as a result he gave the world his widely read and fairly accurate *Mémoires de Garibaldi.*

Dumas prevailed upon the government of Louis Philippe to believe that a new theater was needed in Paris. He said that there were only two of any merit. The government accordingly set up a third in 1847, the Théâtre Historique, with Dumas as director. For about a year all went well, but the Revolution of 1848 caused its fortunes to sag, and in December, 1849, Dumas resigned, leaving the sinking ship, already deeply in debt.

He also had disastrous experiences with a newspaper and with a chateau. The newspaper, entitled *Le mousquetaire* after his great novel, was founded in 1852 with a capital of 30,000 francs, a fairly respectable sum for that period. For a time it ran well, appearing punctually, but shortly no salaries were forthcoming. Dumas tutoyered everyone and this carried the enterprise for a time, but this was not enough grease to keep the wheels running long. The staff dwindled, subscriptions dropped, and before many years the paper became defunct. Dumas' experience with a gaudy chateau, costing him 200,000 francs or more, built at Saint-Germain-en-Laye was likewise a disaster. He entertained lavishly, inviting several hundred guests to an opening dinner, in a style worthy of Fouquet at Vaux. The meal was served by a fashionable Parisian caterer. Dumas and his splendor at Saint-Germain-en-Laye were the talk of Paris—which of course pleased him greatly—but financial difficulties arose, creditors besieged him and sought court action, and he had to take to hiding—after selling the bizarre chateau for a trifle.

In his last days, in Normandy, Dumas even published a cookbook. An epicure who loved good food and who became fat from indulgence, he had long been a collector of recipes. If he were served a new dish that delighted him, he would rush back to the kitchen, compliment the cook, and ask for his recipe. And so there came forth, in 1869 or 1870, his last book, a *Dictionnaire de cuisine*. He had brought to Normandy a cook to aid in its preparation. The work is illustrative of the imagination, the resourcefulness, the tastes of this remarkable personage.

Dumas was decorated with the Legion of Honor, and several foreign countries awarded him the ribbons of their orders. Alone among the high honors which might have come to him but did not was the election to membership in the Académie Française. Perhaps this was due to coolness toward him both by Louis Philippe and Napoleon III, for he had strong republican tendencies. It may be mentioned that he played something of a comic opera role in both the Revolution of 1830 and that of 1848, and he was not reluctant to express his strong republican sentiments on many occasions. With the coming of the Third Republic, however, Dumas was to receive recognition in another form, in part compensation, by the erection of a monument to him on the Place Malesherbes, Paris. He is there depicted seated in a chair, and at his feet a tableau, in metal, of a group of readers absorbed in one of his books.[11]

Dumas *fils* was like his father in that he had a limited education, was something of a roue, traveled extensively but made Paris his home, took no part in the church, and amassed a fortune from his writings. But in other and more numerous respects he differed from his father, in finding that writing came more slowly and with greater effort, in being far less prodigal with his money (especially after his forties), in making a success of his marriage, in being more a reformer than an entertainer, in leaning to introspection and reflection, in preferring realism to romanticism, and finally in being elected to the Académie Française. This is not to suggest that Dumas *fils* stood on the same plane as his father; probably no one would make such a claim. Dumas *père* was too outspoken a man for election to the Académie, where, as one author has put it, deportment was an essential.[12] Dumas *fils*, though he lived to be slightly older than his father and was very productive, did not match his father either in the number or the quality of his works. The father had a touch of genius that the son lacked, and a radiant personality that surpassed the son's.

And yet the son had a better formal education. Dumas *père* tried to give him education of the best quality, sending him first to a M. Vauthier, then at nine to the Pension Saint-Victor, a boarding school, for six years, and afterward for two years to the Collège Bourbon (today the Lycée Condorcet). The son did not, however, complete the course of training at the latter, nor was he a brilliant student.[13]

Tired of studies, young Dumas persuaded his father to send

[11] The best study of Dumas *père* is to be found in Maurois, *Les trois Dumas*, but like most biographies it is somewhat laudatory.
[12] J. Lucas-Dubreton, *The Fourth Musketeer*, pp. 104-105.
[13] F. A. Taylor, *The Theatre of Dumas fils* (Oxford, 1937), pp. 4-5.

him to Marseilles, where he idled many months and made a number of friends in café society.[14] Later on, however, this period was perhaps nonetheless valuable to him. After the stay in Marseilles, he traveled to Spain and Algeria (1856) with his father.

Already young Dumas had been quite a libertine. One of his mistresses, Alphonsine Plessis, who called herself Marie Duplessis, was reportedly a girl of remarkable beauty and personality. The mistress of a series of nobles, she derived from them a handsome income. Oddly enough, she willingly deserted these wealthy patrons for Dumas *fils* during a period of several months, prior to the Algerian trip, although the money he could give her in return was but a pittance. A sufferer from tuberculosis, she died when only about twenty-five, while Dumas was in Africa. On his return to Marseilles, he heard of her death and was greatly saddened. The more he reflected on her, the more idealistic she became to him, and on returning to Paris he wrote, with her the central figure and heroine, his greatest book, *La dame des camelias* (1847). Like others of his books, it is partly autobiographical, although he changed names and events to suit his fancy. He then proceeded to put it into drama, although his father did not think it could be done. It was accepted by the Théâtre Historique, but before it could be presented, the Revolution of 1848 had begun and the theaters were emptied by more exciting events out-side.[15] It was then laid aside until 1852, because of difficulties with the censor. When it finally was presented, there were those who denounced it for idealizing a courtesan.

By accident, Dumas *fils* had set for himself a theme on which most of his subsequent plays were to touch—fallen women and their unhappy lot. Two plays he wrote shortly afterward carried out a similar plot—*La dame aux perles* (1852) and *Diane de Lys* (1853). These, with some disguise, recorded his

[14] Maurois, *Les trois Dumas*, pp. 162-67.
[15] *Ibid.*, pp. 189-235. Verdi's opera *La Traviata* is based upon this novel.

amours with the young, beautiful, wealthy Countess Nessel-
rode, married to the son of the celebrated Russian Minister of
Foreign Affairs. To break up the liaison, the husband had been
forced to take her back to Russia, and Dumas had followed
them through Belgium and Germany to the Polish frontier,
where entry was refused him.[16]

Dumas *fils* later married a Russian woman, a Princess
Naryochkine, by whom he had two daughters, Colette and
Jeannine. They appear to have had a happy household,
although Dumas seems to have pursued other women whenever he chose. Late in life, he shamelessly left his dying wife
for a mistress, whom he at once married, shortly before his
own death at the age of seventy-one.

Dumas *fils'* relations with women were of vital significance
for the reason that he chose, more especially after 1865, to
make his life a mission of preaching for better treatment of
woman. He denounced the double standard in morality then
prevalent, the handicaps woman faced before the law, and
the cold shoulder society gave to the woman who bore a
child outside marriage. More than once he had difficulty with
the censorship, and some of his works were banned by the
church. Bishop Dupanloup, himself of illegitimate origin,
sympathized heartily with Dumas *fils'* ethics, until his church
spoke and forced him to silence.[17]

Behind Dumas' theme lies the story of his own illegitimacy,
his humiliation at school from taunts by his schoolmates, the
shabby treatment of his mother, Catherine Labay, by his
father. Always a gloomy, sensitive youth, he was very intro-
spective. George Sand, his close friend who called him "Son"
and had him call her "Mama," reported that for several years
in the early 1860's he harbored the thought of suicide. He was
morbid, proud, somewhat dictatorial. He was polished in
society and was clever with the women, but he had many

[16] *Ibid.*, pp. 249-90.
[17] *Ibid.*, p. 401; Taylor, *The Theatre of Dumas fils*, pp. 40-41.

enemies, especially men, who dubbed him "Le fils peu prodigue."[18]

In passing, it may be said that Dumas *fils* was a superior playwright and novelist, but not of the topmost quality; an excellent artist, but one who did not develop his characters well in all respects; a moralist with some glaring inconsistencies. Like his father, he was little interested in the colonies or the problems of the Negroes. Only a single novel *(Georges)* by Dumas *père,* and none by the son, was directed toward improving the status of the Negro race. Nor did their known trace of Negro blood handicap either of them, whether professionally or socially, although an occasional critic of Dumas *fils* referred with contempt to his Negro origin.[19] Both father and son moved in the circle of the leading French writers of the day.

A small niche perhaps in the record of Negro literary activity of the nineteenth century belongs to one who was not a writer but the inspiration of a noted French writer. Jeanne Duval was mistress of the morbid poet Charles Baudelaire (1821-1867), who called her his "Black Venus." Reportedly she returned his warm devotion with complete indifference, but she was "the inspiration of some of the most graceful and sensitive poetry in the French language."[20]

The twentieth century has seen an increase in the number of aspiring Negro writers. All save one, however, appear to have been born in the colonies, either in Africa or the West Indies. And for nearly all of them the major theme, as for the colonial-born Negro writers of the nineteenth century, has been their race. The old topic of race relations and race discrimination still, alas, is exploited, but the twentieth-century Negro is becoming prouder of his race and writing

18 Taylor, *The Theatre of Dumas fils,* pp. 20, 46, 49; Maurois, *Les trois Dumas,* pp. 338, 433.
19 Taylor, *The Theatre of Dumas fils,* pp. 50, 202; Cook, *Five French Negro Authors,* pp. 80, 82-83, 92, 94.
20 Ottley, *No Green Pastures,* p. 73; *Dictionnaire de biographie française,* V, 835-38.

on its culture, habitat, and background, as seen in Africa. Here and there appear fantastic claims for African Negro culture of the past.

Perhaps the leading Negro writer of the twentieth century resident in France is René Maran, a native of Martinique who has lived subsequently and longer in French Equatorial Africa and regards himself as being a product of it. Born of Negro parents at Fort-de-France, Martinique, in 1887, he was taken at the age of three to Africa. There the climate did not agree with him, and accordingly, when he was seven, his parents took him to France and placed him in a boarding school near Bordeaux. They themselves returned to Africa and three years passed before he saw them again, at which time he did not recognize them. On completing his studies at this school, he continued them at the Lycée de Bordeaux, where he graduated in 1909. He then returned to Africa, obtaining a position in the colonial service. There he remained for ten years, and they made a tremendous impression on him, for most of his many novels have African settings. He has shown himself a lover of the jungle and its wildlife.[21] During this period in Africa, while World War I was being fought, he witnessed frightful starvation of the natives from famine, and also the corruption of French officials.

After the war, Maran returned once more to France and, save for fleeting travels, has lived there ever since. His earliest book of verse was published in 1909, while still at Bordeaux. In 1921, still an unknown author, his novel *Batouala,* written in Africa, won for him the celebrated Goncourt Prize, adjudged by the French Academy. Ottley calls the book an indictment of French colonialism.[22] As time has passed, Maran has softened and come to think of himself as French. Professor Mercer Cook, who knows him well, tells of his efforts to stay apart from other Negroes in France, having suffered some

---

[21] For these biographical details, see Cook, *Five French Negro Authors,* pp. 126-29. He is not described in *Who's Who in France* or other current biographical dictionaries, perhaps because of his reticence.

[22] *No Green Pastures,* p. 89.

unfortunate experiences from them.[23] Maran's attitude is easily understood. Many Americans long resident in France try to avoid the tourists among their fellow countrymen.

As a poet, Maran has attracted little attention, but since winning the Goncourt Prize in 1921, he has been a marked novelist. More than one of his writings has reminded readers of La Fontaine's treatment of animals. For example, there is *Bacouya le cynocéphale*, the story of a monkey with a dog's head. The creature has the power of thought, and these thoughts are communicated to the author. The scene is laid in Africa, and the jungle, the animals, the insects, the birds, the ants, the tornadoes are all set forth in vivid description.[24] Maran writes in a romantic, almost poetic, vein.

His *Savorgnan de Brazza*, published in 1951, depicts a legendary man of the Congo region, a sort of Paul Bunyan. About thirty years of age, he goes about aiding the oppressed and the feeble, and punishing the guilty. In consequence, he exercises great power over the primitive Africans.[25]

For his many works of fiction, which number ten or twelve, Maran was awarded in 1950 the Grand Prix de la Mer et de l'Outre-Mer. He has also written some verse and many articles for periodicals. He lives in the Latin Quarter of Paris, married to a French wife, and he moves in a small circle of intimate friends, chiefly whites. He avoids publicity, and even honors. Professor Cook was present on one occasion when he refused a member of the Chamber of Deputies permission to recommend him for the award of Legion of Honor.[26]

After Maran, the most distinguished contemporary Negro author in Paris is Léopold Sédar Senghor. African-born and educated in part at Dakar, in part at Paris, he subsequently

[23] *Five French Negro Authors*, p. 124.
[24] *Chroniques d'outre-mer: études et informations*, published by the Ministère de la France Outre-Mer, June 1953, p. 87.
[25] *Ibid.*, Feb. 1952.
[26] *Five French Negro Authors*, pp. 124, 125, 133; *Chroniques d'outre-mer*, Feb. 1952, p. 90. Ottley (*No Green Pastures*, p. 89), reports that the Grand Prize was for Maran's *Bête de la brousse*. On other prizes that have been awarded him, see Mercer Cook, "The Negro in French Literature: An Appraisal," *French Review*, XXIII (1950), 382.

taught at lycées in Tours and Paris, and for many years now he has been a professor at the school for colonials in Paris (Ecole Nationale de la France Outre-Mer). He has distinguished himself both in politics and in literature. Though he apparently has attempted no novels, he has published several books of verse and various essays. One of his books of verse is entitled *Chants d'ombre.* The poetry therein is of high quality; sonorous and soothing, it displays a wide vocabulary and is pleasant to read. Without rhyme, it is more like poetic prose. Fundamentally it greatly resembles the Hebrew poetry in the Old Testament Psalms, a second line repeating the thought of the first, with variations. Often there is repetition of words or thought within a line, and sometimes the repetition runs through several lines. In this collection Senghor wrote on various subjects—moods of the human spirit, the memory of friends and relatives, Negro social life and customs, and temporal events, like "Vacances," "Neige sur Paris," "Départ," "Visite," and "Liberation." Over and over he makes allusions to African places, streams, forests, and social customs. Though French in expression, he is African in soul. Nowhere is he cruel or angry, but on the contrary, peaceful, languid, meditative, more pagan than Christian, more African than French. Another poem of length is to his good friend, the poet Aimé Césaire.[27]

Among Senghor's essays is one entitled "Vues sur l'African noire, assimiler ou non être assimilés," published at Paris in a book of essays in 1945. In it he discusses in philosophical terms and with great show of knowledge (for he is a widely read man) the African and European civilizations. He presents an exalted view of the African, which he would place on much the same plane as the European, insisting that since about the tenth century, the culture of portions of Black Africa has been at a high level. He does not indicate in what respects this culture existed save in social and religious matters. He argues for the exchange of cultural ideas between Africans and Euro-

[27] *Chants d'ombre* (Paris, n.d.), pp. 11-13, 39-50, 69-75.

peans of today. He is not an advocate for the assimilation of either race or culture, but for the separate existence of each, which he considers can be aided and improved by mutual contact.[28]

In 1948 Senghor had an important part in the publication of an anthology of Negro poetry written by contemporaries living either in France or the colonies.[29] The work, edited by Professor Charles André Julien, Professor of African Studies at the Sorbonne, carried a foreword by Jean Paul Sartre as well as an introduction by Senghor. Professor Julien observed in a preface that this collection of verse was a sufficient refutation of the claim that the Negro is incapable of intellectual development—a notion which Schoelcher had argued against in the 1840's. Senghor in his introduction stated that the work was assembled for the celebration of the Revolution of 1848, in which the slaves were freed in the French colonies. He had been called upon by Professor Julien to make the selection of poems. At first he thought of publishing many poems by a few poets, but after some reflection, he decided upon the selection of a few poems by many poets. The reason for this decision, he observed, was the difficulty of choosing the few outstanding poets. He admitted that "the contribution of the Negroes to poetry is yet modest"; nevertheless, he considered it already impressive. He omitted poems by René Maran, considering him better at prose than poetry. He also hesitated to include Madagascan poets, since certain of them (Hovas) consider themselves Melanesian rather than Negro. Yet he did include them. Concluding his introduction, he said, "And now, let the Negroes sing!"

The book is so arranged that the poets are treated by colonies—Guiana, Martinique, Guadeloupe, Haiti, North Africa, and Madagascar. One to four poets for each colony is included, and a brief biographical sketch of each author precedes his

28 The essay occupies pages 55-98 of the booklet *La communauté impériale française*, with introduction by Tingitanus (Paris, 1945).
29 *Anthologie de la nouvelle poésie nègre et malgache de la langue française* (Paris, 1948).

poems. Not all the writers have lived in France. Those having dwelt in France at one time or another were Damas, Césaire, Niger, Roumain, Senghor, Diop, and Rabémanjara. The selections vary in number, from two to fifteen. For several, ten or more poems are given: Damas, Césaire, Senghor, and Rabéarivelo. It is to be observed that all of the writers, in being listed by colonies, are considered as colonials first and Frenchmen second. That also represents their train of thought.

Léon G. Damas is mentioned as born at Cayenne in 1912. After study at the Lycée Schoelcher at Fort-de-France in Martinique, he went to Paris and studied law. He has subsequently traveled widely, has served as a deputy for Guiana in the French parliament, and has published some anthologies of Negro poetry. His *Black Label* is a protest against the difficulties met by his people from the whites.[30]

Aimé Césaire, one of the leading Negro poets in France at the present time and also one of the leading Negro deputies in parliament, was born at Basse-Pointe, Martinique, in 1913. After study at the lycée of Fort-de-France, he went to Paris for further work at the Lycée Louis-le-Grand, the Ecole Normale, and the Sorbonne. A professor until 1945, he subsequently has served as deputy for Martinique. Senghor calls him a poet of passion. Césaire was a Marxist and sang of the Negro as proletariat and of the white as capitalist. He has written several books of verse.[31]

Paul Niger hailed from Guadeloupe, where he was born in 1917. After secondary-school training on the island, he went to Paris. His "Petit oiseau qui me moquais ou le paternalism" (Little Bird That Mocks Me, or Paternalism) is not bad, but most of his poetry may be designated as simply poetic prose.[32]

Jacques Roumain, a native of Port-au-Prince, Haiti, died in 1944, but for twenty years he had lived in Europe—Switzerland, England, France, and Spain. It is reported that he knew well the languages of these countries and their diverse cultures.

[30] *Ibid.*, pp. 18-25; *Chroniques d'outre-mer*, June 1956, p. 67.
[31] Julien, *Anthologie*, pp. 55-82; *Who's Who in France, 1955-1956*, p. 323.
[32] Julien, *Anthologie*, pp. 91-104.

During World War II he lived in Paris and assisted in the founding of the *Revue indigène*, a periodical run by Haitians during the Occupation. He was very sensitive on the race question. A Marxist, he came to limit his love of people to the proletarians. Senghor likens him in many respects to Césaire. His "Bois d'ébène" and his "Nouveau sermon nègre," two of his four poems included in this collection, are Marxist throughout, saturated with race consciousness and bitterness at the sufferings experienced by his people.[33]

Alone of the poets in this anthology, David Diop was born in France—at Bordeaux in 1927, the son of a Senegalese and a woman from Cameroun. His childhood was marred by much sickness, and he is reported to have spent it partly in the hospital, partly in the schoolroom, in France, Senegal, and Cameroun. His five short poems reveal a persecution complex. He writes as though he lived in the days of slavery and suffers the worst ills of that period. Such is his poem "Le temps du martyre" (The Time of Martyrdom), where he, his father, and his mother are depicted as subject to the most brutal treatment at the hands of "the white." Such, too, is the spirit of "Souffre, pauvre nègre" (Suffer, Poor Negro), in which he depicts the Negro as whipped, worked sweaty throughout the livelong day, his children suffering from hunger, and his wife called to her master's bed. Of course the days of slavery, when such conditions prevailed, are now more than a century past, and lingering thought on them denotes morbidity. Another of his poems, "Un blanc m'a dit . . ." (A White Told Me), with lines that run (in translation):

> "You [Tu—a term of contempt] are a Negro!
> A Negro!
> A dirty Negro!"

displays the same racial hatred. No doubt there are some whites who descend to such attitude and language, but this is certainly unrepresentative and does not improve racial

[33] *Ibid.*, pp. 111-20.

relations. Diop, however, appears to be the most bitter of the group.

The sixth of these Negro poets to have sojourned in France was Jacques Rabémanjara, born at Tananarive, Madagascar, in 1913. He studied at the Jesuit college in his native city, and then entered colonial administration. The outbreak of World War II found him in Paris, where he had gone on a business mission to the Ministry of the Colonies, and he was obliged to remain there for the period of the Occupation. With time at his disposal, he proceeded to take a licentiate in letters at the University of Paris. He also did some writing. His literary career in fact had begun earlier, at Tananarive, where he had founded a *Revue des jeunes*. The two poems by him here quoted reveal no race feeling whatever. The second, "Chant XXII. A mon ami, M. De la Roche . . ." was written in a civil prison in Tananarive in 1947, where it would seem that the poet had participated in the Madagascan uprising, but there is no bitterness.

Of the ten poems by Senghor here included, four had appeared already in the *Chants d'ombre*. All the ten are serene, meditative, liquid. Racial feeling is absent.

Of the book as a whole it may be said that the poetry is fair. Most of it is modern, with little or no attempt at rhyme, and with the verses of unequal length. Several of the writers reveal bitterness toward the white race, which seems a bit odd in a book published to impress the French. Where did they acquire it? Perhaps a Marxist affiliation partly explains it. But it seems to be more prevalent in those poets here included who have been to France, where eating of the Tree of Knowledge awakened them as never hitherto to racial discrimination back home. In this connection it may be said that in all times Negro writers who have been to Europe have been among those crying the loudest against Negro treatment from the white. The book certainly is impressive in revealing the interest in poetic activity among the French Negroes of today. It augurs a more promising future.

# 184 THE NEGRO IN FRANCE

To encourage literary effort on the part of young Negro writers in France and in the French colonies, a prize has been established, entitled Grand Prix de la Mer et de l'Outre-Mer, set up by the National Association of Writers of the Sea and Overseas. In 1950 it was presented for the first time, being given to two writers from Black Africa, Ousmane Soce and Diop Birago. The award to the former went for his *Karem*, a Senegalese romance setting forth the African in world civilization and the reactions he makes. Diop Birago received the award for *Les contes d'Amadou-Koumba*, a series of tales and legends of his native Senegal. It gives the reader an introduction to the African family and African folklore.[34] The books were designed for French readers. In 1951 the award went to Joseph Zobel, a Negro writer in France from the Antilles, for his novel *La rue Cases-Nègres*, depicting Negro life in his native village. A young professor in a Parisian lycée, Zobel had written an earlier book, *Diab-La*, much along the line of the latter book, attracting some attention.[35]

Other prizes are open to young Negro writers in France. Two are reported to have been carried off by Clément Richer, a young Negro writer from the West Indies. In 1939 he received the Prize of Humor for his *Ti-Coyo et son requin;* later, for two other books, he received the Prize Paul Flat of the French Academy. He has been referred to as "a young writer of the Antilles who has obtained in France, from his literary beginnings, the most flattering successes." One of his books is *Len Sly*, the story of a planter who lived at Fort-de-France and had grown up by the sea. It was published in 1950.[36]

Another young Negro writer in Paris, Camera Laye, published in 1953 *L'enfant noir*, an autobiography. It records the story of a young Negro come to Paris from Guinea in 1920 after graduation from a technical school in his own country. Laye became a technical student in Paris, attending courses

[34] *Bulletin d'information de la France d'outre-mer*, published by the Ministère de la France Outre-Mer, April 1950, p. 67.
[35] *Chroniques d'outre-mer*, Feb. 1951, p. 31.
[36] *Ibid.*, Jan. 1951, pp. 31-32.

at the Conservatoire Nationale des Arts et Métiers and the Ecole Technique d'Aéronautique et de Construction Automobile, in the hope of becoming an automobile engineer, and yet finding time to write this autobiography. The book not only recounts his own past, giving pictures of his home and parents in Africa, but also describes his stay in the Latin Quarter in Paris and tells of his aspirations. Laye did not come to Paris until 1948 in actuality, landing at Orly, and it is reported that all he had by way of baggage was a map of Paris in his pocket.[37]

It is remarkable that while many Negroes resident in France have written fiction and poetry, and some drama, few have attempted to write history. The sole Negro historian of note in France is J. E. H. Lémery, senator from Martinique prior to 1940, who wrote a *Histoire de la Révolution française à la Martinique* and *De la paix à la guerre d'Hitler*. Similarly, the Negro in France seems to have evaded the other fields of scholarship and reflection for the belles-lettres.

One American Negro who has made France his home in recent years deserves mention in this chapter inasmuch as his long residence there entitles him to be called a French writer as well as American. This is Richard Wright, the well-known novelist who has written on racial themes. Born in Mississippi in 1908, he received his early and apparently only formal education at a Seventh-Day Adventist school at or near Natchez. At fifteen he began work at Memphis, and later took jobs in Chicago and New York, becoming a writer for newspapers and magazines, among others, the *Daily Worker*. For twelve years reportedly he was a Communist, but later he pulled out of the Communist Party and today is an active member of the American Church in Paris. In 1938 he won a prize of $500 for his *Uncle Tom's Children,* the first of his significant novels; in 1939, a Guggenheim fellowship and and the Spingarn Medal, given to the American Negro of the Year. One novel by him rapidly followed another, the better

[37] *Ibid.*, Nov. 1953, p. 100.

known being *Native Son* (1940), *Black Boy* (1945), and *White Man, Listen* (1957). *Black Boy* is reportedly the story of his own life in the South. All his books deal with the racial problem and the mistreatment of the Negro. He holds a bitter memory of his past, but oddly enough, he is married to an American white woman. He lives in Paris, the paradise in this world for the Negro, and writes books for the American reading public—for virtually all his books have been written in English and with an American setting. His one book on Africa, *Puissance noire,* telling of a trip he made to the Gold Coast, was criticized by a French reviewer, who said that Wright did not understand Africa at all. His latest book, *The Long Dream* (New York, 1958), continues to hammer away at racial conflict in a Mississippi small town. In all his works it is the racial problem over and over in one aspect or another.[38]

Many American Negro authors have visited France or dwelt there for brief periods, but they have no claim to being French, not even the philosopher and onetime American Negro Rhodes Scholar Alain Leroy Locke, who reportedly spent all his vacations from Howard College visiting France and who has a bigger claim than the others to consideration here.

Not to be omitted from this chapter, however, is mention of the French Negro literary journal *Présence africaine,* begun in 1947 and directed by Allioun Diop, a well-educated young Negro from Senegal. Diop's wife and other collaborators, all Negro, assist him in its publication. It is designed to promote the well-being of the Negro race throughout the world. On an average, five thousand copies are printed. Once the circulation was greater in France, but Diop has reported that now the circulation is greater in the colonies. At first an annual, it has subsequently been published more frequently, but it is not yet a quarterly. Each issue is devoted to a single theme,

[38] *Who's Who in America, 1958; Twentieth Century Authors,* ed. by S. J. Kunitz and V. Colby, First Supplement (New York, 1958), pp. 1111-12; *Chroniques d'outre-mer,* Jan. 1956, p. 11; *Présence africaine,* n.s., Dec. 1955–Jan. 1956, pp. 115-17; Louisville *Courier-Journal,* 23 Nov. 1958; *Harper's Magazine,* Nov. 1958.

and represents much thought and planning. The articles are by well-informed authors and reach a high level. Its tone is that of loyalty to France, and yet it is strongly colonial in spirit and views independence in the distance.

Thus it is seen that the French Negro has been alert in the literary field. Many have already distinguished themselves, and the future will perhaps outshine the past. It is interesting to reflect that they have all written in French, an adopted language. The Negro nationalists may one day regret this.

*Does he return to this point?*

*More generally chronological with topical interruptions*

# TEN     SERVING UNDER THE TRICOLOR

*I*N AN EARLIER Chapter the story has been told of Negro participation in French wars since the middle of the eighteenth century, sometimes fighting as units, sometimes as isolated soldiers in white units, often in the role of drummer or bugler. Not until the time of Napoleon were they organized overseas for service in France; some were sent to France from the West Indies for military duty in 1799.[1] It was the beginning of Negro troops for continental use from that quarter. Not until 1819 were troops raised in Senegal, and then only for domestic usage. From 1819 until 1849 Negro soldiers were enrolled in Senegal, Madagascar, Guiana, and other French colonies. By the mid-nineteenth century their usage had become common, despite much desertion, lack of morale, and difficulty in enlistment due to slavery. Few, however, it would seem were taken to France. They were segregated from the white troops, even in the hospitals, where their odor was said to be offensive to the whites.[2]

The number of Negro troops brought to France before the midcentury is unrecorded, but in the Crimean War 40 percent of the French soldiers that served reportedly were Negroes, and an Algerian contingent of troops stationed in Paris for several years after 1854 "was almost entirely composed of

[1] Faure, "Le garnison européene du Sénégal," 29-30.
[2] *Ibid.*, 30-93.

Negroes."[3] Some of the officers of this contingent, too, were Negroes.

In the Franco-Prussian War of 1870-1871 Negro troops also served in large numbers. Most of them, as those in the Crimean War, were in Algerian regiments of sharpshooters or infantry. They took part with distinction in a series of engagements and sieges: Wissembourg, Froeschwiller, and Sedan; Strasbourg, Thionville, and Bitche. Besides the Negroes from Africa, others from the West Indies had a part in this war, notably in the Wissembourg, Froeschwiller, Bourget, Toury, Artenay, Mazières, and Héricourt battles, and in the siege of Paris. They were termed "valiant defenders."[4]

Lieutenant Colonel, later General, Charles Mangin went to the point of giving figures for the Negroes participating in this war. Three Algerian regiments forming a part of the Army of the Rhine in 1870 comprised some 7,800 men, and a regiment enrolled in the Army of the East numbered about 1,200. Reportedly a third of these troops were Negroes. Mangin states that there were also several squadrons of spahis, totaling about 9,500 men, with the Second Army of the Loire, of whom 2,500 to 3,000 were Negroes. Accordingly, close to 6,000 Negro soldiers fought for France in this war. The loss of the war was not due to them, Mangin reports, for they acquitted themselves bravely.[5]

Some of the soldiers sent to Mexico in the 1860's were Negroes, and all of the contingent with Captain Marchand at Fashoda in 1899, it would appear, were Negro troops. These last had set sail from Toulon on May 30, 1899.[6] They had later marched across the African sands.

[3] Mangin, "Soldats noirs en Europe," 457. There were 309,268 French troops in the Crimean War, according to F. Burot and M. A. Legrand, Les troupes coloniales, statistique de la mortalité ([Paris, 1897]), p. 104. Of these, 95,165 died. The British sent 97,684 men, and lost 22,182. The French lost approximately one-third of their men, the British one-fourth.

[4] Victor Basquel, Coloniaux en avant! C'est pour la France (Paris, 1920), pp. 27, 29.

[5] "Soldats noirs en Europe," 458-59.        [6] Ibid., 460.

During the 1890's there arose to prominence a quadroon general, Alfred Amédée Dodds. General Dodds (1842-1922) acquired a reputation for his conquest of the African colony of Dahomey in 1892-1893. Born at Saint-Louis, Senegal, of Anglo-French ancestry on his father's side, and of a mother of mixed blood, he was sent to France for his education, which he received at the lycée of Carcassonne and the military school of Saint-Cyr. Leaving the latter in 1862 as second lieutenant, he requested to serve in the infantry of the marine. Through intelligence and bravery he rose rapidly in rank. During the war of 1870 he served with the Army of the Rhine, was captured, escaped, joined the Army of the Loire, and December 24, 1870, was decorated Chevalier of the Legion of Honor. In 1871, he was sent to Senegal, where he remained on duty until 1883, save for a year in the late 1870's spent in Cochin China. In Senegal he was raised in rank to lieutenant colonel and decorated Officer of the Legion of Honor. In 1887 he was made colonel and given the post of Superior Commandant of Senegal. Made Commander of the Legion of Honor in 1891 and stationed at Toulon, he shortly afterward, in April, 1892, was placed in charge of the French posts in Bénin and designated as director of the expedition against Béhanzin, native king of Dahomey. After "a series of brilliant combats and operations," he forced this king to flee. For this exploit he was made brigadier general and Grand Officer of the Legion of Honor. Later he was given a tour of the French colonies and made inspector general of colonial troops. From 1904 to 1914 he served on the French Superior War Council. In the War of 1914-1918 he evidently took no part, being over seventy years of age.[7]

That possibly only one man of Negro blood could have reached the rank of general in the French army in the hundred years since Napoleon contrasts to the proliferation of Negro generals of the 1790's and early 1800's. This in no way is a

[7] Fr. Desplantes, *Le général Dodds et l'expédition de Dahomey* (Rouen, 1894), pp. 39-49, 127.

reflection upon the relative merits of the Negro soldiers, but upon the circumstances. The number who rose to prominence in the earlier periods could never have done so save for the chaotic conditions brought on by the Revolution and the distance from France.

In the War of 1914-1918 the Negro legions were the saviors of France. The vast numbers that came and the great contributions they made were above all the outgrowth of efforts since 1907 made by the distinguished General Charles Mangin, whose statue stands today in Paris by the Hôtel des Invalides at the head of the Avenue de Breteuil. Mangin had repeatedly pointed out to the army leaders the valuable military resources in manpower that lay in the twenty million or more Negroes making up the colonial empire, and the need of drawing on them heavily for defensive purposes. Though he got the support of General de Lacroix, Vice President of the Superior Council of War, he found little support from others, and from 1910 he resorted to writing in an endeavor to awaken the general public to his point of view. The large numbers of colonials that did volunteer for service when the war came has accordingly been regarded, in large part, as due to his initiative and foresight.[8]

As it turned out, 275,000 colonials from Africa fought under the French flag, 215,000 of whom served on European soil. Of the 275,000, some 135,000 were from the Negro provinces. The total number of African Negroes that served was therefore larger than this last number, for many soldiers from Algeria and the Arab provinces were also Negroes. Alphonse Séché in his book on the Negro effort in this war comments that "if the organization of these resources had been realized before 1914, their contribution would have been four or five times greater and their transportation carried out before the submarine struggle reached its height. This million of excellent

---

[8] Alphonse Séché, Les noirs (d'après des documents officiels): l'armée noire, le loyalisme des Sénégalais, l'âme de Sénégalais, le campe de Fréjus, Berry-au-Bac, Dixmude, La Somme, Verdun, l'Aisne, les noirs sur la Côte d'Azur (Paris, 1919), pp. 8-9.

soldiers would certainly have shortened the war, lessened our losses, and modified the actual conditions of victory."[9]

Séché, of course, was wrong in attributing the origin of Negro divisions in the French army to General Mangin, for Negro battalions had served in the French army for a century or more. General Mangin was original, however, in suggesting that Negro troops be used on a large scale for aid in a European conflict. And far from France having difficulty in recruiting these men, it was done, so to speak, without effort.[10] Yet even so, when the war came, there were only two Negro battalions in France. These fought with gallantry in defending the sector near Reims. One was from Algeria, the other from Morocco. They were soon joined by some troops from Senegal. Writing in the *Revue de Paris* in 1915, the anonymous commanding officer of these troops praised their fighting qualities as equal to those of the Europeans. "These black troops," he said, "are excellent for the European war." Soon the French had five other Negro battalions to supplement the first two.[11]

As the war dragged on, there was more and more dependence on Negro soldiers. Never were they drafted; it was easy to get volunteers. In Senegal, where most of these troops were levied, a total of 24,000 were enlisted in 1914 and 1915, approximately 50,000 in 1916, and about 77,000 in 1918. In addition, Madagascar sent 46,000 troops during the years 1914-1917, and Somaliland sent a battalion.[12] In addition to the soldiers, many came as laborers, to load and unload vessels and perform other tasks of a nonmilitary nature. Pierre Khorat, writing after the war, reckoned at "nearly 850,000 colored [*i.e.,* nonwhite] warriors and workers" those whom France drew from all her colonies for military and for labor duty. He

[9] *Ibid.*

[10] "The Negro in the War: How French and American Black Troops Performed Deeds of Valor on Many Battlefields," *Current History Magazine,* XI (Dec. 1919), 536-37; Séché, *Les noirs,* pp. 13-17.

[11] "Troupes coloniales: nos forces ignorées," *Revue de Paris,* V (15 Sept. 1915), 270-71.

[12] E. C. Williams, "The Senegalese in the World War," *Howard University Record,* XV (April 1921), 313-14.

added that the French were pleased with their services.[13] An American student computed the number of colonials of all types who served France in a military way in the war at 545,000, and those who were killed at 115,400, or 20 percent.[14]

French African troops fought in virtually all the major battles and on all battlefronts after the First Battle of the Marne. They served in France and Belgium in the autumn of 1914; they were with the French at the Dardanelles in 1915; they fought at Verdun and on the Somme in 1916; they were on the Aisne in 1917. And "everywhere where the colonial troops and, in particular, the Negro troops attacked, on the Somme [and elsewhere], deeds of heroism were multiplied." Above all other places, it was at Verdun that they distinguished themselves most. There their gallantry in leaving the trenches and assailing the enemy in the open has been considered by one writer a vital factor in the retention of Fort Douaumont.[15]

The Senegalese suffered severely from the cold in the trenches. In the battle of Chemin des Dames in April, 1917, thousands of them had frostbitten feet, due to the snow and frigid weather and to their lack of experience with shoes. They were sent to the rear and disbanded. But this led to discussion of the question, "Why make them wear shoes?"[16]

Despite the severe European climate, the Senegalese fought with stubbornness. From all sides came commendation of their fighting qualities. American troops who got to France in the late period of the war returned home with praises of them. They were particularly renowned for their dexterity

[13] Pierre Khorat, "Colored Soldiers," *Living Age*, CCCXIV (Aug. 1922), 575-76.

[14] Williams, "The Senegalese in the World War," 314. Pierre Khorat supports the numbers in saying that nearly a million soldiers and workers were drawn by France from her Asian, African, and West Indian colonies during the war. "France and her Color Problem," *Atlantic Monthly*, CXXXI (March 1923), 407.

[15] "The Negro in the War," 538; Séché, *Les noirs*, pp. 20, 24, 81-93, 104, 150, 163-69, 178-80, 185; "L'utilisation des troupes noires," *Revue de Paris*, VI (1917), 873.

[16] "The Negro in the War," 538-39; Williams, "The Senegalese in the World War," 370.

with long knives, which they reputedly preferred in close combat. The story was passed around at the time that a Sudanese and a German met in a trench, and that the Sudanese made a slash at the German. The latter laughed derisively and said, "You failed to get me that time." "Shake your head," replied the Sudanese, "and you will find out." Another story related that the sleeping bunks of some Senegalese smelled so foully that their French officer undertook an investigation. Wrapped in a blanket he found a German head that one of the soldiers had cut off and planned to carry home as a trophy. Though these stories were no doubt wholly inventions of clever *raconteurs*, they depict well certain of the qualities of the Senegalese troops. They were crude, little civilized, and brave.

The Senegalese fought in segregated units of their own. Behind the front, they were often billeted by themselves and had their own hospitals. Thus on the Côte d'Azur were two Senegalese hospitals, one at Marseilles, the other at Menton. In the early days of the war, however, the sick and wounded Negro troops were placed here and there in various hospitals in France. "There was no small city hospital without its Senegalese." They drew attention and were amusing in their language, gestures, and caprices. The nurses became fond of them and tutoyered them. Later it was decided to move them to the south of France, possibly because the sunshine there would be more agreeable to them. Séché criticized their segregation in the hospitals at Marseilles and Menton, but it appears that the Senegalese themselves had no objections. The 200-bed hospital at Marseilles was in a school building behind the cathedral. Clean and well-equipped, it was staffed by ten sisters and ten soldiers who served as nurses under the supervision of four Red Cross women. At Menton, the hospital was in the Hôtel Carlton, a tourist resort on the seafront. Here only psychiatric cases were treated. Whereas the hospital at Marseilles was European in aspect, that at Menton was arranged to create a homelike atmosphere, with different halls decorated to depict the different colonies. Both hospitals were directed by a committee with headquarters in Paris.[17]

The Senegalese soldiers were encamped at Fréjus, where some 8,000 were inducted and trained. Their morale was high and their patriotism unquestioned. Séché interviewed fifty or more and without exception found them loyal to France and to their officers. He also cites several instances of their bravery. One concerned a night attack by a Senegalese company, for which their leader Mallet was given the Cross of the Legion of Honor.[18] In an article expressing appreciation of their services, the Parisian journal *L'Intransigeant* of August 1, 1918, told of a conversation at a recent ceremony near Verdun. Patté, Governor of the Colonies, was present, and at its close asked the colonel of a battalion of Negro troops if many of his men had received wounds. The latter replied that out of his 600 men, 598 had been wounded at least once, 170 twice, 94 three times, 75 four times, and 46 five times. The two who had not been wounded moreover were both wearers of the Croix de Guerre with two or three palms.[19]

The Germans were reported as contemptuous toward the Negro troops and incensed with the French for using them as soldiers, regarding them as of inferior race. Later the French used Negro troops in their army of occupation in Germany, stationing the Tenth and Eleventh regiments of Senegalese infantry at Mainz and Worms.[20]

Séché limits his consideration to the Negro troops from Africa. From the West Indies 34,000 came to fight in France, the far greater portion inevitably being Negroes. And in addition to those that fought, there were many others from Africa and the West Indies as factory workers and laborers. General Mangin set the figure of workers from all French colonies at 247,000, but this number included Orientals and Arabs. As for colonial soldiers of all types in the French

[17] Séché, *Les noirs,* pp. 235-45.        [18] *Ibid.,* pp. 27, 42-49, 98.
[19] Quoted *ibid.,* pp. 322-26.
[20] Basquel, *Coloniaux en avant!,* pp. 330-31.

army at the moment of the armistice, he estimated the number at 600,000. Of those killed, the percentage was 15.8 for the men, 22 for the officers.[21]

The French writers limit their discussion to the Negro troops from French colonies, but great numbers from the United States also fought in France. Professor John Hope Franklin places the number at 50,000; an earlier writer had estimated 80,000. Many of these troops served as stevedores in the ports of Le Havre, Brest, Saint Nazaire, Bordeaux, and Marseilles, unloading United States supplies. In September, 1918, alone, they unloaded 767,648 tons.[22]

The United States Infantry regiments 369, 370, 371, 372, and the 92nd Division consisted of Negro troops, with their higher officers whites. All fought with distinction, though the 92nd Division arrived later and saw less fighting than the others. The four regiments were stationed with French troops here and there from Belfort to Belgium, and fought bravely.[23] The 369th Regiment arrived in France early in 1918, moved up to the fighting front in April, almost a month after landing, and set a splendid record, described in some detail by Professor Franklin, who says: "It was the first unit of the Allied armies to reach the Rhine. The regiment never lost a man through capture, a trench, or a foot of ground. It saw the longest service of any American regiment as a part of a foreign army." In recognition of its heroism at Maison-en-Champagne it was awarded the Croix de Guerre as a unit, and 171 of its officers and men were recommended for this medal individually and for the Legion of Honor.[24]

21 The names of all colonials who died and those who received honors for fighting are found in Victor Basquel and Alcide Delmont, *Le livre d'or de l'effort colonial français pendant la Grande Guerre, 1914-1918. Publié sous le patronage du Comité d'Aide et d'Assistance Coloniale par l'Institut Coloniale Français* (Paris, 1922 et seq., 3 v.). Volume I gives the names of those from Guadeloupe, Guiana, French India, Martinique, French Oceania, Réunion, Saint-Pierre, and Miquelon.

22 John Hope Franklin, *From Slavery to Freedom: A History of the American Negro* (New York, 1947), pp. 452, 454; "The Negro in the War," p. 536.

23 Jerome Dowd, *The Negro in American Life* (New York, 1926), pp. 199, 234-36.

24 *From Slavery to Freedom*, pp. 454-55.

The 371st Regiment, drawn from the cottonfields of the South, likewise set a "brilliant record," winning the Croix de Guerre as a unit and having 146 of its men cited personally. Of the 92nd Division, 43 enlisted men and 14 officers were awarded the Distinguished Service Cross. All in all, "the feats of the Negroes were similar to those performed by other American soldiers," says Professor Franklin. He gives many examples. General Pershing is quoted as saying that the 92nd Division had rendered service and bravery second to none since its arrival on French soil.[25]

Casualties were high. In the 92nd Division, 208 men were killed in battle, and 40 others died of wounds. Besides them, 551 received lesser wounds and 672 were gassed. The 371st Regiment suffered 113 men killed in action, 25 mortally wounded, and 859 wounded to a lesser degree.[26]

While it was common practice for the Negro colonial troops to fight under French officers, there were a few Negro officers. Captain Helidore C. Mortenol, a Negro naval officer from Guadeloupe, was reportedly in charge of the air defense of Paris throughout the war. He had served in many parts of the world with distinction. Another Negro officer, Lieutenant Colonel D'Alenson, was for a while chief of staff at Verdun to General Nivelle.[27]

The Negro troops in the American forces served in segregated units, even as did the French Negroes. They made no complaint on the matter, but apparently some white American troops objected to their unsegregated social life. The French paid little heed to warnings that Negroes were rapists, however, and continued to entertain them in their homes. Robert B. Moton, successor to Booker T. Washington at Tuskegee, was asked by the United States government to go to France and

[25] *Ibid.*, pp. 457-59; Dowd, *The Negro in American Life*, pp. 234, 236.

[26] Franklin, *From Slavery to Freedom*, pp. 458-59.

[27] J. A. Rogers, *World's Greatest Men and Women of African Descent* (New York, 1935), p. 64; William H. Ferris, *The African Abroad . . .* (New Haven, 1913, 2 v.), II, 850; J. A. Rogers, "The American Negro in Europe," *American Mercury*, XX (May 1930), 4. Mortenol had been trained at the Ecole Polytechnique.

investigate in this particular. He found the cases of rape rare. For all the 12,000 men in the Negro regiments of the 91st Division, according to Professor Franklin, only seven were charged with rape, and in but two cases were the men found guilty. Professor Dowd, however, states that fifteen cases were charged against troops of the 92nd Division, and that its reputation for disorderliness caused General Bullard to request it be the first division sent home after the armistice.[28]

During the summer of 1920 several editorials appeared in the Parisian journal *L'Intransigeant* expressing appreciation of the Negro effort during the war. One, in the issue of July 20, written by the deputy Jean Fabre, was entitled "La France Immortale. Les Noirs." Written in reply to German criticism of French Negro troops occupying the Rhineland, Fabre asserted that they had displayed their valor on the battlefield and shown themselves loyal to France. They demonstrated the falsity of the charge that the French were only mediocre colonizers. The French had been able to draw heavily on their colonials for troops in the recent war, and these had responded with true affection. The colonies, he declared, had sent 535,000 troops to the front for combat, and 310,000 workers for jobs in the rear. Of course, not all had been Negroes. Fabre listed as having crossed the sea in this enterprise "180,000 Senegalese, 175,000 Algerians, 50,000 Tunisians, 35,000 Moroccans, 49,000 Indo-Chinese, 41,000 Madagascans, 2,000 Somalis, and 1,000 indigines of the Pacific." Of this number, 115,000 had fallen in battle beside the French. With her colonies and with the cooperation of Belgium, France could offer the resistance of about a hundred million men to Germany. He was certain that France could continue in the future to count on colonial aid.

On July 14, 1920, the Senegalese troops in Paris had a part in the great parade that customarily marks Bastille Day, and *L'Intransigeant* the next day carried a long article describing it. General Mangin, wearing the Grand Cordon of the Legion

[28] Franklin, *From Slavery to Freedom*, pp. 460-61; Dowd, *The Negro in American Life*, pp. 232-33.

of Honor, was in the reviewing stand at Vincennes to receive the salute of these troops.

Throughout the years 1920 and 1921 African troops were commonly seen on the streets of Paris. References to them in the papers were not frequent, but *L'Intransigeant* of June 18, 1920, carried an account of a contingent being sent from the Rhineland to quell a revolt in Morocco, and in the same journal on June 16 were several stanzas of rhyme in appreciation of the Senegalese.

On the eve of World War II, Negro troops were back in the news. *L'Intransigeant* of January 2, 1939, carried a picture of Senegalese soldiers boarding a troopship in Marseilles preparatory to sailing for Djibouti, their machine guns being carried in mule-drawn carts. The same journal in its issue of January 5 had an article referring to "our admirable colonial troops," and describing the parade that morning at Gabès before the reviewing stand of Daladier.

In World War II fewer Negro colonial troops served in France than in World War I, due in large part to the French military collapse of June, 1940. Even so, many Negro troops were in France for the period of the war. They were made prisoners by the Germans and were returned to their homes only after the war. Marius Montet, Minister of France Overseas, attended ceremonies in Marseilles on April 20, 1946, celebrating the sailing of 3,500 Senegalese troops and some 560 civilians, mostly wives and children, for their homes. In his speech to the soldiers, made aboard the vessel, he stated that already 40,000 Senegalese troops had returned home and that 20,000 others yet in France awaited return. He praised in high terms the fighting of these troops, commanded by General Leclerc, from the Libyan desert to the Rhine, indicating that they had come as French deliverers.

At least 6,000 Madagascan soldiers were prisoners of the Germans in France during the war.[29] Possibly the number who served on French soil was about 8,000 larger. Certainly

[29] *Bulletin d'information*, 30 July 1945, p. 10.

the *Ile de France* set sail from Cherbourg with 7,200 Madagascan soldiers and 1,000 civilians and arrived at Tamatave, Madagascar, on August 7, 1946.[30] In January, 1946, plans were under way to send 1,000 Madagascans and Réunionese at once back to their homes by boat from Marseilles. At that time it was stated that there would still remain 7,000 troops from Madagascar and 500 from Réunion.[31]

Besides the troops from Madagascar and Réunion, others from the West Indies and Indochina had been prisoners of war in France; a celebration in appreciation of their services was held at Agen on June 22-23, 1945. Several French dignitaries, including M. Giaccobi, Minister of France Overseas, were present, a sum of 25,000 francs was raised by an auction sale and presented them, and souvenirs were given to the individual prisoners.[32]

Throughout the last months of 1945 and those of 1946, in fact, a series of celebrations in various French cities were held honoring the colonial troops (chiefly Negro) who had been war prisoners or who had fought in the victorious French units in the late phases of the war. To detail them all would be tedious, but perhaps a few by way of illustration deserve mention. One was a memorial ceremony at Lyons on July 20, 1947, commemorating the seventh anniversary of the death of 200 Senegalese soldiers in combat at Montluzin. Various Negro deputies from Paris and other dignitaries were present.[33] Another, on November 11, 1946, was a memorial service at the Ecole Nationale de la France d'Outre-Mer in Paris, in honor of colonials fallen in the Wars of 1914-1918 and of 1939-1945. The service on this day was to become an annual affair.[34] On a third occasion, colonial troops had a part in the ceremony of relighting the flame at the Tomb of the Unknown Soldier, Place de l'Etoile, Paris, on June 23, 1945. Among the groups participating was a detachment that had made the celebrated

30 *Ibid.*, 26 Aug. 1946, pp. 22-23.        31 *Ibid.*, 28 Jan. 1946.
32 *Ibid.*, 25 June 1945, p. 7.             33 *Ibid.*, 11 Aug. 1947.
34 *Ibid.*, 2 Dec. 1946.

march from Tchad. Finally, the Protestants in Paris, in a religious service at their temple on the Avenue Ledru-Rollin, December 23, 1945, paid homage to three Madagascan teachers who had lost their lives in France during the war.[35] The French were very expressive of their appreciation to the Negro.

Perhaps the earliest and one of the most impressive services was held November 30, 1944, in the amphitheater of the Ecole Nationale de la France Outre-Mer, for Félix Eboué, Governor of French Equatorial Africa, who had recently died at his post. In November, 1940, as Governor of Tchad, he had refused to obey the orders of the Vichy government, following instead the call to resistance issued by General Charles de Gaulle. Eboué, born at Cayenne, Guiana, had studied in France at the lycée in Bordeaux and at the Ecole Coloniale in Paris, leaving the latter in 1908. From 1910 he held one colonial post after another, most of them in Africa but some in the West Indies. Maran relates a dramatic incident in connection with Eboué's appointment as Governor of Tchad. In the late 1930's Georges Mandel, Minister of the Colonies, invited Eboué to Paris, and offered him the governorship. War was likely, he said, and the African colonies would be endangered, but he considered that Eboué would be the man to hold them. He pointed out that Hitlerism held out nothing for the Negro race, and that he counted on Eboué to be a guide and lighthouse for his fellow Africans when the crisis should come. Then he abruptly bade him adieu: "I will not hold you longer. Go now to your great task."[36]

Eboué proceeded immediately to begin the construction of military roads across Tchad, so as to place it in better communication with the other French African colonies, the Belgian Congo, and the British territories. Moreover, he began recruiting the large body of troops that served in Libya in 1942, in Italy in 1943, in France in 1944, and in Germany in 1945. His

[35] *Ibid.,* 23 June 1945, p. 7, and 2 Jan. 1946, p. 3.
[36] René Maran, *Félix Eboué, grand commis et loyal serviteur, 1885-1944* (Paris, 1957), p. 87.

soldiers carried the Tricolor to Berchtesgarten in 1945.[37] To him was due the march of the troops across the Sahara to succor France.

The French did not forget his services. For the memorial ceremony in Paris in 1944, Eboué's widow and children were brought to Paris, various French dignitaries attended, and laudatory speeches were made.[38] Nor was this all. On May 4, 1949, the body of Eboué was brought from Egypt (he had died in Cairo) to Paris and placed in the Ecole Nationale, which he had attended as a student, and there lay in state until May 20, when in a notable ceremony it was placed, along with that of Victor Schoelcher, in the Panthéon. The greatest honor that France can bestow on one of her citizens was thus accorded the Negro Governor Eboué. It was recognition not only of what Eboué had done, but of what his race had done. And to make this more apparent, it was arranged that an honor guard of forty Negro soldiers would stand at the side of the casket of Victor Schoelcher, and that forty Negro students from the Ecole Nationale de la France Outre-Mer should stand beside that of Félix Eboué. The President of France, Vincent Auriol, was present, and a speech was given by M. Coste-Floret, Minister of France Overseas.[39]

On January 21, 1950, one further ceremony was held in honor of Eboué. This time a plaque was dedicated to his memory at the Ecole Nationale de la France Outre-Mer. After speeches by various distinguished guests, M. Monnerville, president of the Council of the Republic, unveiled the plaque, and a poem written on Eboué by one of the pupils at the school was read. Among the many dignitaries present was Madame Eboué, who since her return to France has been treated as a person of marked distinction even to the present.[40] Henceforth any Negro in the French Empire may consider that no honor is impossible for him to attain.

In addition to the French Negro soldiers, there were a

[37] *Ibid.*, p. 88.                    [38] *Bulletin d'information*, 4 Dec. 1944, pp. 1-2.
[39] *Ibid.*, 15 June 1949, pp. 14-18.                    [40] *Ibid.*, Feb. 1950, p. 23.

quarter million or more Negro troops from the United States during 1944-1945. Large numbers were used in ports at unloading supplies, but others participated in actual combat. The 761st Tank Battalion "saw service in six European countries," took part in the Battle of the Bulge, and gained great reputation. Similarly, the 614th Tank Destroyer Battalion had a fine service record in France and other European countries; the Distinguished Service Cross was awarded to one of its officers, Captain Charles L. Thomas, for heroism in a French engagement. "Negro units of field artillery were in France within ten days after the invasion. The 333rd [Battalion] fought through Brittany and Northern France and against vicious German attacks in the fall of 1944."[41] It is worth noting that the American Negroes liked France and considered the French hospitable.

Thus once more in many wars the Negro has fought for France. If the French people are especially cordial toward the Negro, as claimed or charged, there is a historic reason why they should be. French freedom and honor have frequently been upheld at the cost of Negro blood—much Negro blood. If France looks to the future and hopes again to have her Negro colonials fighting as allies in her cause in her next conflict, who can say that she is unwise? She has many times called upon them and has always found them faithful.

Whatever her fortunes or woes, her Negro subjects have been participants. *Le Figaro* of September 3, 1958, tells of a Senegalese soldier, aged twenty-three, being shot the previous day on the Rue de Metz in Paris, the victim of an FLN terrorist sharpshooter. He and four companions had been attacked without warning, and the attackers escaped. Taken to a hospital, he died. He is not the sole Negro soldier who has lost his life in this latest flareup of French troubles. But the French Negroes also share the honors and the benefits. Paris is their capital, and French their culture.

[41] Franklin, *From Slavery to Freedom*, pp. 566-67.

# ELEVEN     TO FRANCE FOR AN EDUCATION

*THERE ARE* no summary figures for Negroes who have studied in France, whether in the past or at present, and the acquisition of information on such students is difficult, due in part to the increasing tendency both in the ship lists of passengers and elsewhere since about 1840 to omit indication of color. During the present century a return to color reference has been made to some degree, at least in the press, as the "noirs" have become increasingly proud of their race and its accomplishments. Further, what information is available concerns chiefly Negroes who have gone from the French colonies and the United States for training, and little pertains to the Negro or mulatto who has been a native of France.

The French have always welcomed the Negro at their educational institutions, which have never been segregated. Under the Old Regime few Negroes were competent in education to enter the universities or even the secondary colleges; most were trained by tutors or guild masters. The Revolutionists in the 1790's, however, encouraged them to enter one or two schools already designated, and created a number of scholarships for gifted colonial youths whose parents lacked the means to send them to France. The sons of Toussaint Louverture and André Rigaud were among those benefiting. The Leclerc Expedition of 1801 and the renewal of slavery in the colonies, however, led to the closing of these schools to Negroes, and until the end of Napoleon's Empire it was rare for a Negro colonial student to come to France. An exception was Fernand Christophe, son of the distinguished Negro leader who later (1811-1820) was king of Haiti. While Leclerc was in Haiti (then called Santo Domingo), the elder Christophe broke with Toussaint and announced his cooperation with the French. At the same time he sent his ten-year-old son to France, under the custody of an aunt, to be educated. Young Christophe was placed in a boarding school at the Collège de Justice, and afterward, in December, 1803, in the Hospice des Orphelins. The aunt was placed in the Salpetrière, charity institution for women. Both aunt and nephew lived but a short time. Reportedly they were the victims of shabby treatment. Their ample funds somehow had disappeared. This change in their fortunes coincided with Christophe's perfidy, in turning to fight Leclerc and, later, Rochambeau.[1]

After the fall of the Empire and the end of the British blockade in 1814, travel between France and the colonies was resumed on an active scale. Once again many Negro and mulatto servants were designated on the ship lists as attending masters and mistresses, and many free Negroes and mulattoes who were traveling at their own expense were also named. Rarely, however, does one find mention of a Negro coming to France to study. No longer were little Negroes brought to France for training in the guilds (these no longer existed) or in Christian knowledge. The Revolution had brought an end to this. In the 1840's and later the ship lists do carry the names of many colonial students who were en route to France for training as physicians or engineers, some with state aid, but their color is not indicated and their names suggest that almost all were whites.

Sometimes the Negro students that went to France later

[1] Georges Servant, "Fernand Christophe, fils du roi d'Haïti, en France," *Revue de l'histoire des colonies françaises*, I (1913), 217-25.

acquired renown,[2] and biographical sketches have been trans-
mitted to us by encyclopedias or journalists. This happened
in the case of Auguste Lacaussade, of the Ile Bourbon, now
Réunion, who became a prominent literary figure in France
in the later 1800's. He went in 1827 to Nantes for study in the
lycée and remained there until 1834. After two years, he
returned for further study in France, this time at the University
of Paris, where he enrolled in the Faculté de Médicine.[3] Another mulatto who did well in France was Jules Mérentier, of
Pointe-à-Pitre, Guadeloupe, who read law at the University
of Paris and defended his thesis with success. Then he was
admitted as a barrister in Paris.[4] At the same time an even
more brillant showing had been made at the Collège Bourbon,
in Paris, by the mulatto Julien Girard of Guadeloupe. There
he had taken the first prize in Latin verse and the first prize
in Greek theme, the second prize in each of the three fields of
Latin theme, Latin translation, and French narration, and in
the broader University competition he had come off with the
second prize in Greek theme, the second accessit in Latin
theme, and the third accessit in Latin verse. This was in a day
when Latin and Greek were given great emphasis in the curriculum. It is interesting to follow the career of young Girard.
He remained in France and became a distinguished professor
of philosophy in several lycées, including Louis-le-Grand, re-
tiring in 1892.[5]

Bissette's *Revue de colonies* for September, 1834, named
four colonial "men of color" who had completed their medical
studies at the University of Paris. They were Antoine Clavier,
of Martinique; Virgile, of Guiana; Salesse, of Mauritius; and

---

[2] Some Negro nuns from Santo Domingo who were reared in France were
among the founders of a school in Baltimore in 1829 entitled the Académie
Saint-François, for young Negroes. Kate Brousseau, *L'éducation des nègres aux
Etats-Unis* (Paris, 1904), p. 33. During what years they were in France is not
indicated.

[3] *Nouvelle biographie générale*, XXVIII, 454-55; Cook, *Five French Negro
Authors*, pp. 102-103; "M. Auguste Lacaussade," *Revue des colonies françaises*,
I, 97-100.

[4] So reported Bissette's *Revue des colonies* (Paris, 1836), p. 95.

[5] *Ibid.; La grande encyclopédie*, XVIII, 967.

Merlet, of Haiti. The given names of the last three are omitted. Mentioned along with them was Eugène Clavier, who had been made a lawyer in Rennes.[6]

From the United States during the earlier half of the century came certain Negroes to study, destined later to play roles of some prominence. Foremost among them was the dramatist Victor Séjour (1817-1874), a freeman from New Orleans. His father ran a dry-cleaning establishment and was able financially to send his son to the Sainte-Barbe Academy in New Orleans and afterward to a college in Paris, in the 1830's. As Negroes from the first have done, Séjour fell in love with Paris and made it thenceforth his home. A poem entitled *Le retour de Napoleon*, published in 1841, was well received and marked his entry into the literary world. Shortly he became interested in drama, and from 1844 he wrote a long succession of plays that were presented on the Paris stage. He is one of the few Negroes of that period who have been honored with an account in the *Dictionary of American Biography*.[7]

About the same time as Séjour, there came to Paris as a student the future Negro inventor from Louisiana, Norbert Rilieux (1806-1894). Interested in science, he studied at the Ecole Centrale during the years 1830-1832, and even at this early period reportedly conceived of the principle of "multiple effect evaporation" which he was later to exploit in some inventions for refining sugar. In 1843 and 1846 he took out patents in Washington protecting these inventions, which had the double effect of improving the quality of the sugar and reducing its fuel cost. The inventions seemingly were profitable for him. Shortly before the outbreak of the Civil War he went back to France and made it his home thenceforth.[8]

Certain mulattoes of that era who were educated in France

[6] Page 58.  [7] Vol. XVI, pp. 565-66.

[8] A more detailed account of him may be found in J. Carlyle Sitterson, *Sugar Country: The Cane Sugar Industry in the South, 1753-1950* (Lexington, 1953), pp. 147-50. This author is indebted to his colleague, Professor Clement E. Eaton, for notice of Rilieux.

or in the West Indies served in the Native Negro Guards
organized at New Orleans in August, 1862, by General Ben
Butler of the Union Army. Within two weeks Butler had a
thousand volunteers. Among the junior officers that he placed
over them were Captain (later Major) F. Ernest Dumas,
Captain André Cailloux, and First Lieutenant Joseph Howard.[9]
Unfortunately, no information can be found on these men.

Another Negro, Jean Baptiste Pointe de Sable, referred to
as "the Haitian who founded Chicago," was educated in
France. Born in Haiti, he returned later to his homeland, and
thence went first to New Orleans and later to Chicago. Afterward he died in poverty in Missouri.[10]

The number of those studying in France in the second half
of the century was slightly larger than that in the first half.
Among them were uncertain cases of medical students from
Guadeloupe and Martinique in 1875. Four colonial students
had completed their training at schools in the colonies and
wished to take further medical study at Paris. Their families
were of limited means, and they applied for reduced transportation rates on French vessels. It appears reduced or free
tuition in France was also available to them. Two of the
students were possibly of mixed blood. One was Raphael
Cognet of Pointe-à-Pitre, Guadeloupe, the son of a man whose
first name was Aimé. Would a white colonist have borne such
a name? Was it not more likely that of a Negro? Small ground
for a decision, certainly! The second case is somewhat similar.
Charles Mégaldy of Fort-de-France, Martinique, wrote in his
application to the Minister of the Marine and the Colonies that
he was an orphan, the son of a father "who was European."
Of his mother he said nothing, implying thereby that probably
she was Negro. He claimed to be alone in the world, since
both parents were dead and he had no near relatives in the
colonies. At Nîmes he had some paternal uncles and aunts in

[9] Donald E. Everett, "Ben Butler and the Louisiana Native Guards, 1861-
1862," Journal of Southern History, XXIV (1958), 210-11.
[10] Journal of Negro History, XXXVIII (1953), 442-44.

mediocre circumstances willing to help him further his education, provided that he could get passage arranged to France. The statement that his father was European impressed one of the officials into whose hands it came, for he underscored the phrase in pencil. Mégaldy and the other applicants were granted passage to France on the understanding that they were to make preliminary payment of the cost of their meals for the voyage. This in effect would reduce the cost of their passage to their meals. The letters provide no other information, save that the French government was solicitous to give better medical training to colonial physicians than the colonial institutions provided.[11] Many medical students were permitted to go to France for this reason.

Other Negro colonials who attended French schools in this second half of the century included two future political personages, Joseph Eugène Henry Lémery, a native of Martinique, and Gratien Candace, of Guadeloupe, born in 1874 and 1873 respectively. Lémery attended the Lycée Louis-le-Grand and the Law Faculty of the University of Paris, and in 1898 received the license to practice law in France. Almost immediately he entered the field of politics, in which he came to have a distinguished career.[12]

Candace studied at the University of Toulouse, where he received the licentiate in science. Remaining in France, he at first taught technology, but later turned to journalism and collaborated successively in editing several newspapers and magazines. From this he went into politics, and as early as 1906-1909 was an undersecretary in the Viviani cabinet, one of the first Negroes to hold a French post. Thence until his retirement in 1940 he was continually a member of the French parliament, a member of numerous commissions, and a holder of more than one cabinet position.[13] His death came in 1953.

[11] Dossier of letters entitled "Guadeloupe et Martinique: Cognet, Lasalle, Megaldi, étudiants," Archives Nationales, Colonies, F5B113.
[12] Who's Who in France, 1955-1956, p. 1002.
[13] Dictionnaire de biographie française, VII, 1027.

Two American Negroes went to Paris late in the nineteenth
century or at the beginning of the twentieth century for the
study of the fine arts, the painter Henry Tanner (1859-1937)
and the sculptress Meta Warrick Fuller (b. 1877). Tanner
received most of his training in France and spent there most
of his years as a painter. Born into a Methodist bishop's family
at Pittsburgh, he resisted the wishes of his parents that he
enter the clergy and instead studied at the Pennsylvania
Academy of the Fine Arts. Afterward through the generosity
of the Hartzell family of Cincinnati, who were impressed with
an exhibition of his paintings in their city, he was enabled to
go to Paris for further training. There he enrolled in the Julian
Academy and studied for five years. In 1896 a grant by
Rodman Wanamaker made it possible for him to go to
Palestine for a study of the Holy Land. He had already turned
to drawing religious scenes, and the trip was designed to give
him further knowledge of the country and its atmosphere.
He returned to France to do much excellent work in this field
and to instruct several young American Negro artists in the
technique of painting.[14]

Miss Butcher says of Meta Warrick Fuller that her "career
as a sculptor was, next to Tanner's, the greatest vindicating
example of the American Negro's conquest of the fine arts."
She, too, took her preliminary art training in Pennsylvania.
Graduating in 1898 from the Pennsylvania School of Industrial
Art, she went to Paris and studied for three years further.
Some works displayed in the Paris exhibition of 1903 brought
her some attention, including complimentary remarks from
Rodin, under whom she had studied. Returning to the United
States, she married Dr. Solomon C. Fuller in 1909, and has
subsequently been engaged in art in this country.[15]

After the turn of the twentieth century, the number of

[14] Margaret Just Butcher, The Negro in American Culture (New York,
1956), pp. 217-19; Dowd, The Negro in American Life, p. 349.

[15] Butcher, The Negro in American Culture, p. 220; Who's Who in Colored
America, 1941-1944, p. 541; Who's Who in American Art, ed. by Dorothy B.
Gilbert (New York, 1956), p. 162.

Negroes going to France for study increased, both as regards colonials and United States citizens. Chronologically one of the first of these was Carter Woodson, celebrated founder and editor of the *Journal of Negro History*, who spent one semester at the Sorbonne in graduate study in history, and is reported to have "learned to speak fluent French."[16] This was apparently between 1908, when he took his master's degree at the University of Chicago, and 1912, when he received his doctorate at Harvard.

Alain Leroy Locke, another distinguished American Negro, made his acquaintance with France early in the century while a student at Oxford (1907-1910), the only Negro American Rhodes Scholar thus far. Later, from 1919 to 1938, he spent his summer vacations in Europe and made Paris his headquarters. The author of several books on Negro life in America and of others in philosophy, Locke was also on the board of editors of *The American Scholar* and a professor and lecturer at several American universities.[17]

From the colonies early in the century came to Paris to study Félix Eboué, the later distinguished governor of French Equatorial Africa who had so outstanding a role in the French Resistance Movement of World War II. Born in Guiana of Negro parents, he came to Paris for the study of law at the Ecole Coloniale, after which he entered the work of colonial administration.

Also at this time there came to France for study another colonial destined to play a great role in French political history, Gaston Monnerville. Born in Guiana, he came to France in 1912 on a scholarship and studied at the lycée in Toulouse, and later at the university of that city, where he took his training in law, receiving his doctorate in that subject.[48]

---

[16] *Journal of Negro History*, XXXV (1950), 344-45, XXXVI (1951), 78; *Who's Who in Colored America, 1941-1944*, p. 582.

[17] René Maran, "Le Professeur Alain Locke," *Présence africaine* (Paris [1949]), I, 135-38; *Register of Rhodes Scholars, 1903-1945* (London, 1950), p. 137.

[18] *Chroniques d'outre-mer*, Aug.-Sept. 1954, pp. 108-109. The dates for his study in Paris are not given here.

At the conclusion of World War I, the opportunity was afforded several hundred American soldiers to study for a period of several months in various French and British universities. Among those selected for this privilege, on American Field Service Fellowships, were a number of Negroes. They attended several French universities, including those of Paris, Bordeaux, Toulouse, and Aix.[19]

The War of 1914-1918 seems to have exerted on the part of the Negro, both colonial and American, great attractiveness for France and French culture. The Negro from far-off America or the French colonies was a different person after several months in France, where he was treated by the whites in a manner he had never known before. Tens of thousands of Negro soldiers had that experience. A few of the privileged were able to return in the years thereafter, but in most instances they merely passed on the word to friends and relatives, who have acted on their suggestion of going to France to study.

The Frenchman Paul Reboux, traveling to Haiti in 1919, found that "almost all Haitians of high society . . . make their studies in France, [and] almost all Haitians in government posts have sojourned there or dream of returning there." All Haitians, he said, loved France—"loved it as a sister."[20]

Among those coming to France from the colonies in the postwar period was the famous poet, deputy, and professor from Senegal, Sédar Senghor. After concluding his studies at the lycée in Dakar, he studied at the Lycée Louis-le-Grand and the Faculty of Letters at the Sorbonne. He passed the difficult examinations for the agrégation and became the first

[19] Franklin, *From Slavery to Freedom*, p. 460. They attended for periods during the war and afterward.

[20] *Blancs et noirs: carnet de voyage, Haïti, Jamaïque, Cuba, Etats-Unis* (Paris, 1910), pp. 133, 136. The occasion of this remark was his report of a visit to Kléber César, recent Minister of Public Instruction, who had sent his son, Aimé Fernand Césaire, to Paris for study at the Lycée Louis-le-Grand and the Sorbonne. The son later has served for many years as deputy to the French parliament from Martinique. See *Who's Who in France, 1955-1956*, p. 323.

African agrégé in France.[21] He was evidently not the first Negro agrégé, however, inasmuch as Julien Girard by virtue of his professorial positions and high distinctions must have anticipated him.

In the postwar period may be mentioned certain American Negroes of prominence who went to France for study. One was Robert L. Grière, later a professor of French at Fisk University and more recently receptionist to the vice president of the American Express Company in Paris. Born in Charleston, South Carolina, he moved to New York City at the age of twelve, and afterward attended the University of Buffalo. Thence he went to the University of Toulouse, where in 1930 he received the teachers' diploma. During the War of 1914-1918 he had served in France as army interpreter. His mother had studied in a convent school in France, and from early childhood he has read and spoken the language. He claims French ancestry, and France has been to him in a special way his second country, and her culture his culture.

Mrs. Anna J. Cooper, principal of a Negro high school in Washington, D. C., took her doctorate in Paris in 1925, after earlier studies at Oberlin College.[22]

The Negro scientist Ernest Just, Professor of Zoology at Howard University since 1912 and Professor of Physiology in the Howard Medical School from 1912 to 1920, spent eight years in Europe on Rosenwald Foundation funds working in the laboratories of leading scientists in Paris, Rome, and Berlin. A native of Charleston, South Carolina, he had attended Dartmouth College and the University of Chicago prior to his European researches, and had taken his Ph.D. degree at Chicago in 1916. He has written and published much in the scientific field, and besides serving as vice president of two American scientific bodies, in 1930 he was one of the editors

[21] Who's Who in France, 1955-1956, p. 1505; France d'outre-mer, Feb. 1957, p. 22.
[22] Who's Who in Colored America, 1941-1944, p. 133; Mercer Cook, "Booker T. Washington and the French," Journal of Negro History, XL (1955), 335. She began her study at Paris in 1911-1912.

of *Protoplasma*, an international journal, and a member of the French Société des Sciences Naturelles et Mathématiques. He died in 1941.[23]

To be sure, those described here are but a few of the many Negro students who attended French schools; they are those who subsequently acquired some renown. In the early 1920's, especially in Paris, a large number, possibly hundreds, of Negro students were to be seen on the streets and in the cafés of France. In their dress and bearing they were indistinguishable from the French. They were of the middle and professional class, apparently in very comfortable circumstances. This was still true in the 1950's of the vastly greater numbers to be seen, not only in Paris but in other French university cities as well.

Most American readers are aware of the fact there are no dormitories at the French universities and lycées, but that the students find their own lodgings out in town. In the late 1920's and subsequently, however, a series of elegant lodging houses, to all intents and purposes dormitories, have been erected on the Boulevard Jourdan under the name and control of the Cité Universitaire. There several thousand students of both sexes are housed and fed, and there find delightful social life, marked by much freedom. Two of the houses at least are open to Negro students. There are also some university-maintained eating places for students, where those with registration cards can have meals cheaply, due to the fact that they are subsidized by the government. Students seeking rooms, too, are aided by a university bureau which supplies them with information relative to places available. While the students are left to shift for themselves to a degree that is foreign to the greater number of students in American colleges and universities, they can get aid also if they will seek it.

During the 1920's and 1930's the Julius Rosenwald Foundation made it possible for several score young professors, artists,

23 *Who's Who in Colored America, 1941-1944*, p. 303; *Journal of Negro History*, XXVII (1942), 127-28.

and graduate students, Negro and white, natives of the South or living in the South, to go from the United States to Europe to pursue further their professional training. Among them a number went to France. Mercer Cook, Professor of Romance Languages at Howard University and one of the board of editors of the *Journal of Negro History,* was a Rosenwald Fellow to France and the West Indies in 1937-1938. He was likewise a Fulbright Fellow to France in 1950-1952.[24] Another was Roi Ottley, Negro newspaper correspondent overseas during World War I and later author of *No Green Pastures,* who held a Rosenwald Fellowship to Europe in the late 1940's.[25]

World War II brought an interruption to colonials and Americans studying in France. Some residents there at its outbreak were able to complete their studies, but had to remain until its termination and to be repatriated with government aid. Those without families in France were returned in advance of those married.[26] Since the conclusion of the war, however, there has been an amazing flood of Negro students, both from the French colonies and the United States. No figures have been published, and none seem to be available. Here again the sensitiveness to mention of color is still in force and handicaps historical research. There must be at the present five or six thousand.

Dr. Robert O. Mead, Director of the Foundation des Etats-Unis (the American hall for students) at the Cité Universitaire, estimated in 1957 that of the six thousand students residing at the Cité some 500 to 1,000 were Negro. It is doubtful whether this number would embrace half or even a third of the Negro students attending institutions of higher learning in the city. The number attending institutions of this category in the provincial cities might run into several hundred each, the southern institutions drawing more than the northern. Negro

---

[24] *Directory of American Scholars,* ed. by Jacques Cattell (3rd ed., New York, 1957), p. 149; *Journal of Negro History,* XXXVII (1953), 137.
[25] *No Green Pastures,* pp. vii-viii.
[26] *Bulletin d'information,* 16 July 1945, p. 12.

students are conspicuous on the streets, in the cafés and restaurants, and wherever one goes in France, whether in Lyons, Aix, Toulouse, Bordeaux, Nantes, or Le Havre.

Approximately 2,500 of these Negro students are now in France on scholarships, much the greater number coming from the French colonies. The number of scholarship holders has rapidly risen since the last war. In 1948 the number of *boursiers* from the colonies then studying in France was reckoned at 500, excluding some others who held scholarships of lower income. The 500 holding regular scholarships received 102,000 francs each a year, or 8,000 francs a month, with the residue payable for the summer vacation. The smaller scholarships (the number not indicated) carried on an average 45,000 francs each year, payable in ten equal sums. Three hundred and ninety-seven of the 500 *boursiers* came from the West Indian colonies of Martinique, Guadeloupe, and Guiana, and from the island of Réunion. The 500 regular scholarships represented a total cost of 36,075,742 francs, and was paid in part by the colonies and in part by France. Their winners were chosen on a competitive basis, and were required to agree in writing that they would serve for at least ten years in public teaching when they had completed their training.[27]

The sum granted to these *boursiers* has varied from time to time with the decline in value of the franc. In 1948 there was a call for increase in allowance so that the *boursiers* could live adequately on their stipend; by 1957 it was 30,000 francs a month. The scholarships represent an endeavor on the part of the French and colonial governments to train colonials for professional posts, and especially for teaching. Endeavor has been made to select students on their merit, and not on the basis of family influence. To succeed in this, it has been necessary to provide stipends sufficiently large to cover all expenses of the students while in France. And yet there have been times when the stipends have been delayed in payment and inadequate to meet the cost of living. Much complaint

27 *Ibid.*, 15 April 1948, p. 42.

has come from the boursiers in consequence. The complaint has been justified, but the fault has not been intentional on the part of the government. Not all boursiers from the colonies, to be sure, have been Negroes; some no doubt, especially from the West Indies, have been white.

One of the Madagascan students at the Ecole Nationale Supérieure des Beaux-Arts, who obtained his diploma in architecture in 1945, was graduated with distinction, being one of the four highest among the forty-three receiving diplomas. Evidently a Hova, he bore the long name of Razafy-Andriamihaingo. In 1948 there were said to be one hundred Madagascan students in France.[28] This was a large number for a distant colony. It was all the more significant because shortly following the war, Madagascar was in rebellion for approximately a year, seeking independence, and the insurrection was suppressed with some difficulty. Apparently animus against France was not widespread among the Madagascans. A congress of Madagascan students was held in late July, 1948, in Montpellier, eighty delegates being present and the city playing the role of host.

In the post-World War II period there have been several organizations to which the colonial students belong and in which they have taken fervent participation. This is one of their most interesting activities in France. They are highly organized and extremely sensitive of their colonial status. The government has considered it expedient to keep them under observation to see that they do not overstep the bounds of propriety. This, in turn, has led to some chafing on their part. They do not appear to have taken part in the activities of the FLN (Front of National Liberation) of the Algerians, but they have been accused of some flirtation with the Communists.[29]

It is only natural for students at college to gripe; an earful

[28] Ibid., 3 Dec. 1945, p. 7, and 15 Sept. 1948.
[29] Complaints of the African students may be found in Les étudiants noirs parlent, constituting vol. 14 of Présence africaine (Paris, 1953), p. 75. This volume also tells of the student organizations.

can be had on any American campus. It is all the more reasonable to expect that the Negro students in France would have their grievances. Not only are they far from home, without the opportunity for weekend or even annual visits, but they are alone and find many rooming places, and even some restaurants, closed to them. There are few Negro girls for them to date, for few young Negresses get the opportunity to go to France. Among the fifty-nine *boursiers* going from Togoland and Senegal to France in 1947, only six were young women.[30]

While most of the *boursiers* were to become teachers, some were to train for other professions. Of the above fifty-nine, for example, four were to study agriculture and four veterinary medicine. They were destined for various schools, almost all of a secondary level, in line with their professional interests. Evidently it was designed that they were to be separated, so that they would not have the opportunity to become a clan and live to themselves. All institutions of higher learning which take overseas students have to combat this tendency to group together. Although imperative for the student's own good, separation from his fellows adds to his isolation and loneliness.

The Negro student in France complains that a vast number of lodgings are closed to him, and also some cafés and restaurants. In short, there is a certain amount of discrimination. This allegedly is not because of race bias, but because of the habits of the Negro students. Albert Franklin complained that the French government interfered in many ways with the African students in France, taking away their meeting rooms and their places of residence because many of the students would not subscribe loyalty to France. The government of French West Africa, in turn, had bought some hotels in Paris for housing African students at cheap rates.[31]

The colonial students prepare in France for all the professions. In March, 1951, twelve pharmacy students came from

[30] *Bulletin d'information,* 15 Jan. 1948, p. 31.
[31] *Les étudiants noirs parlent,* pp. 75-76, 79.

the colonies to study at the Ecole de Santé Publique.[32] In June, 1958, eleven African students arrived in Paris to study technology, and the margarine industry in particular.[33] They were the second such group to arrive that year. In 1954, according to Gérard Marin, in the first of a series of four articles on colonial students in *Le Figaro* (issue of April 20, 1955),[34] there were at Paris 163 medical students among the *boursiers*, 146 students of science, 102 students of law, 16 students of agriculture, 7 students of veterinary medicine, and only one student at the Ecole de France Outre-Mer (a fact which Marin disliked). He stated that there were then, in 1955, about 1,700 colonial *boursiers* studying in Paris, of whom approximately 1,150 were training for technical and secondary (or college) teaching jobs. Breaking down this latter figure, he placed the number of those studying for the positions in secondary teaching *(enseignement supérieure)* at 750, and the number of those destined for teaching technology at 400. Many of the African students, he remarked, were simply the sons of rich fathers, without scholarly ambition or inclination. Marin was far from assured that the results would prove beneficial. He complained that among the *boursiers* in Paris one would find only four engineering students, four former students of law, and one physicist. Many *boursiers* of the past had not returned to their homeland, he stated, but had remained in Paris, whose charms for them were too great.[35]

Marin criticized the restless attitude of the Africans who tired of their colonial ties with France and wished for severance. A considerable part of these students, he stated, "make a sharp crisis of nationalism and even of misguided racism, the infant maladies of peoples." In this, he added, they were supported by the Communist Party, always ready to exploit

[32] *Chroniques d'outre-mer*, April 1951, p. 6.
[33] Their picture and a caption in *Noir et blanc*, 6 June 1958.
[34] These articles were entitled "Etudiants d'outre-mer: avenir de l'Union Française."
[35] *Le Figaro*, 20 April 1955. The subsequent installments appeared in the issues of 21, 23, and 27 April. All displayed a certain amount of pessimism that the results would match the hopes.

nationalist movements. He considered that nationalist aspirations dominated the minds and hearts of the African students
and hurt greatly their work in Paris. This nationalism he
found to be less evident among the students from Senegal than
among those from Madagascar, Cameroun, and the Sudan.
Those from Guinea, the Ivory Coast, and the West Indies he
found to be calm and little concerned.[36]

Some of the African *boursiers'* dissatisfaction in the past,
he stated, was based upon their slowness in getting their
checks from the government, but he asserted that this would
be corrected in the future. He expressed the wish that for
mutual better understanding, some volunteer families in France
would agree to receive these students in their homes for the
first few days after their arrival. "Thus the delicate first taking
hold of the young black in the metropolis will be facilitated,
[and] some barriers will be suppressed from the outset."[37]

This wish for reception of the young Negro *boursiers* in
the homes of the French had already been expressed as early
as 1951 by Dr. Aujoulat, Secretary of State for Overseas.
Saying that these students came from Africa by the dozens on
each plane and boat, he reckoned their total in France at that
time as "around 3,000, possibly more." They represented
forty million people in the French colonies. He asked the
people of France as a gesture of good will to open their homes
to these students, so that they might get to know the charm
of true French life instead of getting their impressions from
the cinema or the bistros.[38]

Subsequently, much has been done in this respect. For
several years now, groups of students brought to France on
scholarships or for brief periods of summer study have been
entertained for two weeks or a month in the homes of French
families, and afterward have been taken on a tour of a section
of France at government expense. Much money and effort
have been spent in this direction. Only rarely does mention

[36] *Ibid.*, 23 and 27 April 1955.          [37] *Ibid.*, 27 April 1955.
[38] *Chroniques d'outre-mer*, Nov. 1951, p. 5.

of it find its day into the French press; occasionally one finds a reference in *Le Figaro,* but more is to be found in the bulletins of the Ministry of France Overseas. As an example of this sort of entertainment, twenty-two young Africans were brought to France on a student exchange plan in the summer of 1956, after a proposal offered by M. Houphouet-Boigny, well-known deputy from the Ivory Coast. The boys were to be carefully selected for the observation of agriculture in southeastern France, and were to be brought from Dakar in two groups of eleven each. They were to land at Toulouse, and thence go by train to Lyons, where their hosts would meet them. They were given a hearty welcome, and for three weeks they were left alone with these families. These homes had been chosen with care, and teachers selected to explain things to them. Often in the evenings the villagers would assemble with the students for discussion and for singing, and both groups reportedly enjoyed the meetings. The students were amazed at the long hours and hard work of the French farmers. They were surprised to see much land tilled which at their homes would have been regarded as unfit for cultivation. They asked many questions and were amazed at the technical procedures of the French. After these three weeks, they were taken on tours of the French Riviera and to many agricultural and industrial establishments of southeastern France. Afterward, their stay in France was terminated with ten days in Paris. The undertaking was regarded as a great success.[39] In the summer of 1958 a similar group of students, twelve to fourteen years old and from several African territories, made such a trip. They were given a carefully conducted tour, with speeches of briefing and congratulation.[40]

Other groups, not necessarily future farmers, have subsequently been received in France. One such was the group of pharmaceutical students in 1958. Admirable as these gestures of good will have been, it can hardly be expected that they

[39] *France d'outre-mer,* Feb. 1957, pp. 41-43.
[40] *Le Figaro,* 18 June and 10, 11, and 15 July 1958.

can be adopted on a scale sufficient to care for all the many hundreds of Negro students who come each year to France to begin their studies. According to *Chroniques d'outre-mer* for June, 1956, there were 2,450 scholarships held during the academic year just ended by French colonial students. These scholarships represented the sum of 1,100,000,000 francs. The cost to France already was great; could more be expected of her?[41]

In addition to the students, chosen groups of adults from the African colonies likewise are invited to France as guests of the government to study conditions along their line of interest. In October, 1955, three Guinean ricegrowers were flown to France, at French invitation, to observe the ricegrowing at Camargue in the Rhone Valley. Since World War II, ricegrowing has become very widespread and profitable in Provence and Languedoc. After an intensive study of the ricefields, these guests were taken on a short visit to Paris, and then were flown back to Guinea.[42] At first on the trip they wore their African garb, but this attracted so much attention that soon they decided to discard it for European dress.

Also in 1955 seven Nigerian chieftains came on invitation to France to study modern technical methods employed by the French in agriculture. Since World War II, let it be stated, the French have made not only a beginning but great progress in the use of tractors and other machinery, especially in Normandy, northern France, and the Rhone Valley. These Nigerians, of course, were British colonials. They had just

[41] This same source places at 6,000 the number of overseas students in France (p. 9). This may refer only to colonials. The number of overseas students from all countries attending French institutions in the academic year 1957-1958 was reckoned at 16,877 by *France actuelle*, a periodical published by the Comité France Actuelle, a private association of French businessmen, 1 June 1958, p. 8.

A later publication by the French government, entitled *Madagascar, Birth of a New Republic: Ten Years of French Economic Assistance* ([New York?, 1960]), says that during 1958 more than 620 scholarships were given Madagascan students alone for college-level studies in France (p. 11).

[42] *Chroniques d'outre-mer*, Dec. 1955, p. 59.

visited Britain, and after their visit to France they planned to see Holland and the United States before returning home.[43]

Fifty-seven notable colonists from the Camerouns came to France on a visit of twenty-six days in the summer of 1952, thirty in one group and twenty-seven in the other. Both were to study agricultural and industrial methods.[44] In May, June, and July of the same year thirty-seven African grade-school teachers were in Paris and other French cities studying the schools and school methods. Most of the time was spent in Paris, but a twelve-day tour carried them into the Loire Valley, Auvergne, Dauphiné, Provence, and the Cote d'Azur—in short, the picturesque chateau region, the Rhone Valley, and the lovely Riviera. On returning to Paris, July 16, a three weeks' conference began, with eminent speakers addressing them and discussing various problems and methods. In every city visited they were taken on guided tours—as to the coal mines and abattoirs of Saint-Etienne—and they could not have returned to their homeland without being more informed and better teachers.[45] In 1953 forty African teachers went through a similar experience, the conference being planned by the Ministry of France Overseas and the Ministry of National Education. The tour of France was varied somewhat from that of the previous year, and at the conference were also forty white instructors who expected to spend their lives as teachers in the colonies.[46]

It has been exceedingly difficult to find rooms for all the Negro students coming to Paris, or for that matter for the French, American, and other students coming there. Housing in Paris has been at a great premium ever since the last war, and the ordinary American family going there for a prolonged visit has found the housing problem a nightmare. It is not a

---

[43] *Paris-Presse l'Intransigeant,* 21 and 22 Aug. 1955.

[44] *Chroniques d'outre-mer,* July 1952, p. 43.

[45] An elaborate account of their stay in France is given *ibid.,* Nov. 1952, pp. 13-15.

[46] *Ibid.,* July-Aug. 1953, p. 25.

surprise to learn that the African students have had difficulty in this respect. To alleviate their situation, the French government erected for them a large residence hall or dormitory at the Cité Universitaire, designated the Maison de la France d'Outre-Mer. Eighteen months in construction, it was inaugurated with much ceremony and *éclat* in 1951. Equipped to care for 249 students, it accommodates 161 in single rooms and 88 in double rooms, all equipped with single beds. A certain number of beds are at the disposal of each colony. The building also has a large study room, a cafeteria, a reception hall, and a library; in charge of the building is a director, appointed by the Rector of the University.[47]

The idea of segregating the Negro colonial students, however, drew sharp criticism, the complaint being that this prevented them from getting to know better the French people and French culture. Their education, it was held, should consist in acquiring not only book knowledge, but also an understanding of French life and manners.[48] It was accordingly proposed that some students from France proper should be permitted to live in the building with them. The dormitory also came in for criticism two or three years ago for the laxity prevailing whereby students were able rather freely to bring girls into the building for immoral purposes. The resulting exclusion of girls from the building was followed by a student strike, but to no avail.

Another building for African students in Paris was opened in 1956. For the use of students from Equatorial East Africa, the Foyer des Etudiants d'A.E.F., on the Rue Platon at considerable distance from the University, is a place of assembly for study and social purposes, rather than a residence hall. It was dedicated on March 22 with an elaborate ceremony in which participated several high officials from the Ministry of France Overseas and from the University.[49]

[47] *Bulletin d'information*, Dec. 1950, pp. 3-5; *Chroniques d'outre-mer*, Jan. 1952, p. 42, and April 1953, p. 19.
[48] *Chroniques d'outre-mer*, June 1954, p. 13.
[49] *Ibid.*, April 1956, pp. 25-26.

Three problems facing the colonial students in France were pointed out in a report made to the forty-fifth Congress of the National Union of French Students at Strasbourg in the spring of 1956. The first concerned lodgings; the second, meals, especially for the Moslem students, into which category falls the major portion of the Negro students from Africa; and the third, vacations. The two or three weeks' vacations at Christmas and Easter and even the three months' vacation in the summer are not long enough for the Negro students from overseas to go home. Consequently their vacations are expensive and nonproductive, unless they use them for travel, which few do. The scholarships which many hold do not include money for travel, as some overseas scholarships held by American students do. The majority of Negro students in France, however, are probably not on scholarships and are more affluent in means than those with them. Even these, however, do not appear to indulge in much European travel.

A considerable number of American Negro students, teachers, and artists have been recipients of Fulbright grants. Others have gone to France from the United States on the funds of other foundations. They have done creditably. One closely associated with the Negro students remarked that in general they do about as well as the white students from the United States who come there. In ability, seriousness, and accomplishments they rate as well. He spoke highly of what they had achieved at the University of Paris. Their humor has rendered them popular both with American and French students. They are cordially received, and there is no problem about dating. The American Negroes do not mix so well, however, with the French colonial Negroes, with whom they have little in common. They have a tendency to do better academically than the colonial Negro, probably being better prepared for their work at the University.

Most of the American Negroes, this informant added, pursue language studies, hoping to become teachers of French literature. A good many American Negroes, as well as whites, come to Paris to study medicine, as there are no bars to exclude them, at least for the first year. Then comes the weeding-out process. As for the other sciences, not many American Negroes pursue them; nor are they pursued by many from the French colonies.[50] Engineering is more popular, because of the hope of a good economic return.

The American Negro students, according to this authority, take no part in French politics out of lack of interest; but the French African students, especially those from Algeria and Morocco, do, and have caused much trouble. The French Negroes in large part are "Christian Progressives," a group not communistic but tending in that direction.

Another authority said of the French Negro students that they did well in their studies. He himself had taught a number of them and found that they range from mediocre to excellent. Almost all the professional men in the colonies, he remarked, have been trained in France. France is therefore their cultural mother. He was of the opinion that the Negro colonial students in France are contented and take no part in riots or in the encouragement of African nationalism, as some others have indicated. He denied that the Negro deputies in Parliament commonly vote with the Communists, as has been asserted, although he indicated that they do occasionally. He denied that these leaders wish independence from France, but rather desire to remain within the framework of the French empire. Asked about the religious complexion of the Negro African students, he commented that many are Protestants. Nearly all the Madagascan students are Protestants; particularly is this true of the Hovas. Some study theology in France, but the government does not provide them with scholarships as it does in the case of students desiring to enter professions serviceable to the state. This commentator also asserted that no racial bias exists among the French.

It would be more accurate to say that racial animus is rarely found among the French except for those who have lived in

[50] *Chroniques d'outre-mer*, May 1956, p. 16.

the colonies. Yet even the native French sometimes display strong feeling and the desire for segregation. A young Canadian teaching for a year in Paris remarked that she met a young Negro at the theater and afterward gave him a date, whereupon her French landlady came to her and commented that the better girls in Paris do not associate with Negroes. Others in casual conversation asserted that they consider the Negro inferior to the white in intelligence.

The lack of racial feeling in France—and its presence among those who have had colonial contacts—may be explained by the observation that animus toward any ethnic group is more commonly found where this group exists in rather large numbers alongside another group that considers itself the dominant one. In this respect France may face some distant trouble, for the Negro is coming to France, for study, for residence, for travel, in increasing numbers. The Negroes are eager for education and for those assets, political, economic, and cultural, that will enable them to create stronger homelands and to improve their condition economically. This goal of comfort and pleasure drives an increasing number to desire to remain in France, where they marry, the most of them French girls. Coming from homelands with a greatly inferior culture, they naturally throw aside much of it to espouse that of France. The French culture becomes theirs, even as the American culture has been adopted by the Negro of the United States. There are reasons why France should welcome this opportunity to spread her culture, reasons that will later be discussed. But for it to happen, there must come more interracial mixing, and the process may not always continue as free of problems as at present.

# TWELVE    ENTERTAINMENT AND SPORTS

*WHILE EDUCATION* is the greatest magnet drawing Negroes to France, there are also others, some professional, some diversionary. The most influential is music. Jazz, spirituals, and even classical music every year bring many Negroes, especially from the United States, not to study but to practice a profession. The French government permits them to do this and apparently to remain as long as they desire, but for some years prior to the De Gaulle regime a law prohibited the taking of more than about 30,000 francs (less than $100) out of France. But regardless of the money carried home, the visit to France has been worth a vast lot to any Negro, for in no other country can he have a more enjoyable time. Negroes take pride in impressing the French, and they have done so in many ways.

Jazz has been perhaps the leading Negro contribution in music. The first Negro jazz band in France reportedly came from the United States in 1918. It was the Fifteenth Regiment Band, and its leader, Jim Europe. Ever since then, Paris has had "Le Jazz Hot."[1] One of the outstanding early composers and conductors of jazz was Edmund Jenkins, who in 1924 wrote and played in Paris *Charlestonia: A Negro Rhapsody for Full Orchestra.* Many of the orchestra leaders of that day composed their pieces impromptu, but not so Jenkins.[2] By 1927 André Levinson, a French writer, could state in the

[1] Ottley, *No Green Pastures,* p. 100.
[2] Butcher, *The Negro in American Culture,* p. 84.

*Theatre Arts Monthly* that the French were captivated by jazz and Negro music, and also by the Negro dance.[3] Steadily in the period between two World Wars in this century Negro jazz was gaining popularity in France. It seemed unbelievable that such could take place in a country so endowed with artistic appreciation and trained in musical criticism. But it did. Even André Gide, the later Nobel Prize winner, is reported to have taken piano lessons from a Negro. Was it jazz?[4]

Since World War II the attraction of jazz for the French has continued to mount, and perhaps no American city has had more jazz orchestras to visit it than has Paris. And these seem to have been largely Negro. All or nearly all have been from the United States. In late 1955 a train of fifteen coaches, with its coterie of American Negro performers, made a tour of French cities, exhibiting performances of Negro art in many forms—orchestral playing, singing, dancing, buffoonery. Among them were the dancer Valerie Blake, the singer Fredye Marshall, and the humorist Beatrice Redding. *Paris-Presse l'Intransigeant,* an afternoon journal that gives much attention to Negroes and their activities, carried an article by Emile Vuillermoz on this "Apollo Jazz-Train" and a picture of Beatrice Redding.[5] The article, descriptive in nature, was appreciative in tone. No account, unfortunately, was given of the reception the jazz train met in the various French cities.

Among the many Negro jazz musicians who have been in France within the last few years may be mentioned Louis Armstrong and Velma Middleton and their troupe, who gave a concert at Roubaix, in the largest auditorium in northern France. Their audience, estimated at 2,200, contained some persons who had come from nearby Lille and Belgium, and also some that had come from Torquay in Britain. For two hours they played. The troupe later went to Paris, where the reception was seemingly less enthusiastic.[6]

In January, 1956, Lionel Hampton with a troupe of jazz

[3] *Ibid.,* p. 95.    [4] Ottley, *No Green Pastures,* p. 102.
[5] 23 Dec. 1955.    [6] *Paris-Presse l'Intransigeant,* 2 and 19 Nov. 1955.

players, singers, and dancers came to Paris, three months after
an unfortunate accident had befallen the company. The car
or bus in which they were riding had turned over in a wreck
and eight were hospitalized. Much space was given to this
orchestra in two issues of *L'Intransigeant;* under a picture of
Hampton was the epithet, "Jupiter the Thunderer, made in
USA."[7]

The year 1957 saw the jazz singers Diahann Carroll, Ella
Fitzgerald, and Eartha Kitt in Paris, all on different programs,
and Errol Garner, the reputed leading piano-jazz artist of
that year. Their pictures with appropriate captions appeared
in the press.[8] Ella Fitzgerald was described as "the greatest
lady of jazz at the present time," Diahann Carroll as a
"ravishing mixed-blood who without seeking this effect distills
the purest and most sincere romanticism of the Negro spirit-
ual,"[9] Eartha Kitt as "armed with a club and a smile [she did
wear somewhat more] . . . comes to repeat a performance
applauded on Broadway . . . in 'Shinbone Alley.'" The jazz
artists are given a surprising amount of newspaper publicity,
the photographs of all the "stars" being presented—a far cry
from pre-World War I days. Negroes, like all humans, enjoy
publicity, and the press apparently finds it advantageous to
cater to them, for they have already come to be an important
minority.

Even the staid, government-sponsored *Le Figaro,* commonly
regarded as the leading morning newspaper in Paris, devotes
liberal space to descriptions and pictures of Negro jazz artists,
entertainers of other types, and political personages. As an
example, much space was given in two issues in 1959 to the
participation of a celebrated New Orleans band in the ap-
proaching Cannes Festival.[10] Photographs and a cartoon were
included. Of course it would be ridiculous to imply that

---

[7] *Ibid.,* 18 and 21 Jan. 1956.

[8] These show Diahann Carroll in *Le Figaro* of 15 Nov., Ella Fitzgerald in
*Match* of early May, p. 94, Eartha Kitt (dressed to reveal her shapely figure)
in *Le Figaro* of 14 June, and Errol Garner in *Le Figaro* of 3 December.

[9] *Le Figaro,* 23-24 November.          [10] 29 April and 4 July.

the French journals give such "coverage" merely to please the Negro population; it is more sensible to conclude that it is given because of general public interest in it.

It is interesting that while jazz is sometimes referred to as a reversion to African music, the natives of Africa only rarely bring jazz bands to France.[11] They also on occasion bring dancers, fire-eaters, and other entertainers.[12] Ofter the African students at the French universities give programs for the public, presenting their native songs, dances, and folk tales, for French interest in things African much transcends jazz. During both World Wars of this century African troops stationed in France gave many public entertainments. American Negro troops have similarly given concerts, and indeed an American Negro ballet company sometimes goes to France, as did one from New York in late 1957.[13] Surprisingly, no entertainers seem ever to come to France from the West Indies.

Less frequent than the jazz troupes but equally popular are the singers of Negro spirituals, also from the United States. The French have long shown an interest in these spirituals. Fisk University of Nashville sent in the 1860's its first troupe of "Jubilee Singers" to France to raise funds for that institution. For seven years these singers gave concerts throughout Europe.[14]

From time to time other troupes of the "Jubilee Singers" have visited France. In September, 1956, a score of these singers from Fisk University went to France aboard the *Liberté*. They gave a concert aboard ship and later twenty-one concerts in France. Before returning in December they

[11] An African orchestra, conducted by Maurice Sonar Senghor, played for several months in 1957 at the Théâtre du Palais. The instruments used were all African. *Présence africaine*, n.s., Dec. 1955–Jan. 1956, p. 112.

[12] *Le Figaro*, March 1954 and 25 Nov. 1957; *Chroniques d'outre-mer*, March 1956, p. 31. The author of the article in the latter publication says that "if one judges by the numerous encores [at the concert], the folklore of black Africa has conquered the Capital of the French Union." The French Union was, while it lasted, the French equivalent of the British Commonwealth of Nations.

[13] *Le Figaro*, 14 Oct. 1957.

[14] Brousseau, *L'éducation des nègres aux Etats-Unis*, 72.

made a tour of several European countries, giving a total of sixty concerts. Certain of their performances were broadcast over the radio to perhaps millions of listeners.[15] Those who heard them praised them. In June, 1957, another troupe of singers, the "Golden Jubileers," were billed for a concert in Paris.[16]

Early in his career Paul Robeson visited France and sang spirituals for the entertainment of the French. While on vacation on the Riviera in 1924, he visited the little town of Villefranche-sur-Mer, and there engaged an Italian fisherman to take him along in his boat as he went to his nets and gathered the entrapped fish. As they went, Paul sang and captivated the fisherman, who on their return insisted that he sing for his wife and friends. In a gesture of good will, Paul bought the fisherman's catch for the morning and treated the villagers to a picnic. It was on this same vacation that he met Claude McKay, a Negro poet from the West Indies, and was advised by the latter to visit Russia and to enter the field of opera, not limiting his interest to spirituals. The advice was taken, as the world knows.[17] In 1928 he again visited France and sang at Paris, and has perhaps visited it often since then.

Occasionally Negro singers in France can be found in classical music roles. A concert by Marian Anderson in Paris in the winter of 1956-1957 packed a large auditorium, and the French cheered and called for encores with a madness that was astounding. That she delighted an audience of highly critical musical devotees was absolutely clear. Miss Anderson, it may be added, has been in France many times and often sung to French audiences. Perhaps there is no Negro musician of any note in this country, whether instrumental or vocal, who has not given a concert in France.

[15] See under "Historical News" in the *Journal of Negro History*, XLII (Jan. 1957), 86. This writer was on the same boat with them en route to France.
[16] *Le Figaro*, 4 June.
[17] Shirley Graham, *Paul Robeson, Citizen of the World* (New York, 1946), pp. 170-78.

In French operas and musical concerts Negroes often have their parts. In a performance of *Der Rosenkavalier* of Richard Strauss, at the Paris opera house in 1957, a little Negro boy took the role of a page. He had no part in the singing, but as attendant to a noble lady, he added color to the eighteenth-century setting, bringing chocolate and carrying the silver rose.

The journal *Le Figaro* in its issue of March 16, 1955, told of an operetta, being written at that time by Albert Willemetz and Jean Le Seyeux for presentation at a Paris theater, in which all the parts would be taken by Negro singers and comedians. Its title had not been chosen. Similarly, the printed announcement of the American Church in Paris for May 5, 1957, announced "an American Negro folk opera" entitled *Cousin Esther*, which was to be given that week at the Cultural Center of the Cité Universitaire and at the Cultural Center of the American Embassy. Participants in both instances no doubt were to be either Negroes or whites resident in France.

That things African have their vogue in Paris nowadays may be seen not only by the popularity of Negro music but even by the presence in shop windows of Negro dolls, Negro art objects, sometimes even Negro wax figures for exhibiting dresses. To no small degree the Negro is still a curiosity, even as he was in the eighteenth century. One will find Negroes employed in diverse roles in many of the night clubs, such as the Folies Bergères, the Lido, and the Moulin Rouge. One will find them also in the choir of the American Church on the Quai d'Orsay. In short, Negro participants will be found in nearly every form of music and entertainment.

Some are found in acting. A troupe of Negroes from the United States presented *Porgy and Bess* at Paris during several seasons in the early 1950's.[18] During the "Great Week of the University" of Paris in the spring of 1957, Negro students took part in extracts from the opera *L'Astrée*, written by Colasse in 1691. In particular they sang the "Song of Mahdi," an African

[18] *Présence africaine*, n.s., Dec. 1955–Jan. 1956, p. 112.

selection in which singing is intermingled with dancing.[19]
Dorothy Dandridge had a leading role in a French film made
in 1957, entitled "Revolters from L'Espérance." She played the
part of Carmen Jones in this story of slavetrading in 1830.
*Le Figaro* referred to her as a "celebrated black actress."

The success attained by the Negro in music, dancing, and
acting is partly attributable to early practice. The Negro from
his childhood sees that what has endeared him to the world
is the music which has been cultivated by his race and with
which he has grown up. Thus he is encouraged—not least by
his own people—to develop what talent he has and to practice
what skills he can learn.

In the French theater, Negroes have thus far taken little
part. The great American Negro actor Ira Aldridge (1805-
1867), who established his reputation in the role of Othello,
played in Paris as in the other leading European cities. While
in Paris, he was entertained lavishly by Dumas *père* at the
Reservoirs in Versailles.[20] Since his day, however, only two
Negroes are reported to have acted on the Parisian stage:
Habib Benglia, from French West Africa, who played in
*Emperor Jones* in 1950, and Georges Aminel, a West Indian,
who played the part of Friday in *Robinson Crusoe* and a role
in Julien Green's *Sud* in the early 1950's.[21]

Sports, too, have afforded the Negro an opportunity to gain
recognition and prestige, in France as well as elsewhere. Let
it be said that the Frenchman is keenly interested in sports.
Most Americans think that the French are little interested in
athletics because their universities have the sanity to avoid
"bigtime" competition. The Frenchman in common with the
Europeans in general considers that sports are a minor feature
of university life, and that universities exist for intellectual
ends—the liberal arts and professional training.

[19] *Le Figaro*, 14 March 1957.
[20] Lucas-Dubreton, *The Fourth Musketeer*, p. 246. A biographical sketch
may be found in the *Dictionary of American Biography*, I, 160-61.
[21] Rosey E. Pool, "The Negro Actor in Europe," *Phylon*, XIV (Sept. 1953),
264-65.

Negro participants in sports in France seldom do so under the aegis of universities or lycées, but more commonly as representatives of their homeland, or some French city, or unattached. Their photographs frequently appear in the press, commonly taken in athletic garb and on the playing field. They are usually referred to in the press by nationality, race, or color, as Malgache, Senegalese, or American, or simply as "noir." Only the most fragmentary biographical details are given, the press articles being restricted to the athletic performances under consideration or to previous performances by the athlete concerned.

In the realm of amateur sports the most active field for Negro competition in France is that of track athletics. *Paris-Presse l'Intransigeant* of August 7, 1956, carried two pictures of the Senegalese Lo Ousmane, a six-foot, twenty-year-old boy from Dakar, high-jumping at Colombes Stadium on Sunday, the day previous, in which he set a new record for France at 1.97 meters. The journal stated that Lo Ousmane jumped barefooted inasmuch as he had not become accustomed to the use of spiked shoes. The pictures showed him taking off from his right foot and rolling over the bar, with his arms extended to break his fall. This was his first trip to France, and in this event he had defeated his fellow African, Thiam Papa Gallo, evidently a close competitor. Another Negro, a Madagascan named Jean Bouin Rabemila, carried off the honors for the "junior title" in the high jump in the Championship Meet of Universities and Schools (Lycées) in June, 1957, with a jump of 1.95 meters. This was said to be 28 centimeters above his own height. Rabemila had been in France previously; in 1955 he had set the high jump record in the junior division at 1.88 meters.[22] He also did well in the hop, step, and jump. In the 1957 meet he set the winning mark at 15.19 meters. He was only nineteen years of age.[23]

At sprinting, Negro athletes have done particularly well in France. The Senegalese sprinter Aboulaye Seye, designated

[22] *France-Soir,* 11 June 1957.     [23] *Le Monde,* 11 June.

by a French journal as the "revelation of the season," won the 200-meter event at a meet at Colombes, near Paris, on August 6, 1956. His time was 21.9 seconds. He represented a military athletic club of Toulon, and was considered in advance as a possible winner of the 100-meter and 200-meter events, in which he had set marks of 10.7 and 21.8 respectively. A picture reveals him as short and stockily built. The next year, at Lyons, Seye lowered his mark for the 200 meters to 21.4 seconds, only one-tenth of a second behind the French record for that distance.[24]

Other outstanding Negro sprinters in France at that time were two Africans, Joël Caprice, with a record of 10.9 seconds for the 100 meters, and Thiam Habib, who ran the 200 meters in 22 seconds. These two men undertook the two last laps of the 400-meter relay race at Colombes in September, 1957, in an international meet.[25] In this same meet, two American Negroes, Murchison and Stanley, also participated. They drew much attention from the press, due in part to the fact that Murchison was one of the holders of the world record for the 100 meters.

These are by no means the only Negroes who have participated in track athletics in France in the last few years, but they are among the outstanding ones and illustrate the recognition Negro athletes there are making.

In football, both rugby and soccer, Negroes also have participated with success. Sometimes a team from Africa or Madagascar journeys to France for competition. This happened in October, 1957, when a Madagascan team came to Paris. Le Figaro carried a picture of eight players and a short account of the team. Already in France they had played and beaten teams in Toulon, Nice, and Toulouse. Their coach was termed "professor."[26]

Other Negroes play on French teams. The crack team of

24 Paris-Presse l'Intransigeant, 5-6 and 7 Aug. 1956; Le Figaro, 5 June 1957.
25 Le Figaro, 8 Sept. 1957.                    26 5-6 Oct. 1957.

Saint-Etienne in 1957 had a Negro star named N'Jo Lea, and at least on two occasions his picture in play was given in *Le Figaro*. The exceptional quality of the team was illustrated by the fact that it reached the Cup of Europe Contest, and was there eliminated by the Glasgow Rangers.[27] At the same time Toulouse had a wingman in the Negro Brahimi. This team won the Cup of France.[28]

Active participation in football for the Negroes in France dates at least from the beginning of the century, and possibly earlier. Maran in his biography of Eboué relates that when the latter went to Bordeaux as a student in 1901, he and several other Negro students joined the Stade Bordelais Université Club and played football. Eboué himself was an excellent player, and so was his friend Camille Eutrope. Later, at the Ecole Coloniale in Paris, he played on the leading rugby team in France, and with him on it were four other students from Guiana. At this time a team of Negro players played and beat a white team in a game promoted by the sports editor of *Le Figaro*. Eboué was one of several Negroes from Guiana playing on the Negro team. He was also an excellent track man, running the 100, the 400, and the 800 meters. While at Bordeaux, he won the championship of southwest France in the 100 meters, and followed this by winning second place in the national finals at Paris.[29]

Prizefighting also draws heavily on Negro participants. Like football in France, and unlike track, it is a professional sport. It is a quick way for the winners to gain money, and most boxers seem to have success against at least some of their opponents. Here again as in track, not a few of the Negro participants hail from the United States. Moreover, Negroes have been boxing in France for several decades. Roi Ottley tells an interesting story of Siki, Negro pugilist of the 1920's. In 1922 a bottlewasher in a Toulon café, Siki was signed for a

[27] *Le Figaro*, 29 Jan. and 27 Sept. 1957.       [28] *Ibid.*, 29 May 1957.
[29] Maran, *Félix Eboué*, pp. 16-17, 20-22.

bout with Georges Carpentier for the world's light-heavyweight championship, the contest to take place in Paris. It was agreed upon in advance that Carpentier was to win, but when the fighting got under way, Siki forgot about his agreement and proceeded to knock out Carpentier. This did not suit the boxing men, and so the referee proceeded to disqualify Siki and declare Carpentier the winner. Thereupon howls of disapproval arose from the fans, of course to no avail. The French Boxing Federation supported the referee. This, in turn, led Blaise Diagne, a Negro deputy in the Chamber of Deputies, to shriek and charge racial discrimination. The matter was at length carried to the Chamber of Deputies, and "Battling" Siki was given his rightful title, which he held for almost a year.[30]

Another episode of some interest occurred in the spring of 1958, when a Negro boxer from Martinique, named Theo Mollet, after forty-six professional bouts found himself going blind, at the age of twenty-eight, and proceeded to bring suit against the French Boxing Association for the sum of 50,000,000 francs, equivalent at that time to $119,000 in American money. He also sued two physicians of the Association and his former manager, alleging that they knew of his condition and should have stopped him. The court appointed a committee of three physicians to investigate the merits of the case and report back to it.[31] The doctors were asked in particular to ascertain if injuries had produced the state of blindness. How the case ended is not known.

Many have been the Negroes in the boxing ring at Paris. To catalog them is needless. Some have hailed from the United States, as "Sugar" Ray Robinson in the early 1950's and "Tiger" Ralph Jones in 1956.[32] Ten thousand fans witnessed the latter's defeat by Charles Humez in the Palais des Sports. Representing Britain, the Negro prizefighter Hogan Bassey

[30] No Green Pastures, pp. 108-109.
[31] Le Figaro, 16 April 1958; Louisville Courier-Journal, 26 March 1958.
[32] Le Figaro, 21 Nov. 1956.

won a combat in 1957 at Paris with the Algerian Cherif Hamia.[33] Judging from a newspaper photograph, the Algerian was the more intelligent and alert, but Bassey had the muscle and staying qualities. From Brazzaville and Dakar, Africa, came one of France's Negro boxers, Idrissa Dione. Born at Brazzaville in 1929, he later went to Dakar, where he entered pugilism and became the Senegalese champion. Then he went to France for military service. That finished, he continued in prizefighting, married a French girl, and made Nevers his home. In 1956 he was still a professional boxer.[34]

The popularity of boxing with the Negro fans of Paris is revealed by an enthusiastic welcome given in 1938 to the heavyweight Negro pugilist from the United States, Leroy Haynes, on his arrival there aboard the *Normandie* for a bout with the French boxer André Lenglet. As reported in the Philadelphia *Tribune* of June 16, "the entire staff of the Adelaide-Hall-Hetty Flacks 'Big Apple' cabaret, including the orchestra, were on the quai to greet Haynes when he reached Paris." With them were a horde of sports fans, reporters, and photographers. Also there was a band which "blasted away a rousing welcoming," while behind the fighter "posed two brownskin beauties carrying the large sign: 'Adelaide Hall's "Big Apple" Cabaret Welcomes Leroy Haynes to Paris.'" Clearly this "rolling out of the red carpet" for Haynes was by his American supporters; it may readily be assumed that the French Negroes were supporters of the French champion.

In other sports—tennis, fencing, swimming, basketball (a sport rapidly acquiring popularity in France)—the Negro seemingly takes little or no part; certainly he receives no mention in the press for them. A large portion of the Negro athletes now in France have come with sports learned in their homeland, where perhaps these other forms are little exercised. A small group, most of them are limited in funds and of necessity live modestly.

[33] The Paris *New York Herald Tribune*, 24 June 1957.
[34] *Paris-Presse l'Intransigeant*, 11 Feb. 1956.

Not always in France have the Negroes resorted to Western forms of sport, but on occasion they have participated in games and exercises of African origin. Between the two World Wars in particular, when great numbers of them were encamped and trained in southern France, the colonial troops often exhibited their native sports. Mrs. Marguerite Harrison has recorded an animated account of a visit she and her husband made in 1929 to Camp Gallieni, at Fréjus on the Riviera, where several thousand African colonial troops were in training. The Harrisons attended the very exotic and colorful Colonial Fête, in which the Negro soldiers, in native garb that they themselves had made, participated in spear throwing and catching, wrestling, boxing, dancing, and mock ceremonies, to the accompaniment of tomtoms and shrieks and regimental bands. A mock Sultan of Dahomey and retinue, with much ceremony, was brought on the field, the Sultan riding a coal-black horse in his white robes, attended by an umbrella bearer and a body of nobles, witch doctors, warriors, dancers, and others, with the green flag of Islam. As the retinue circled the field, tomtoms beat calls to war, peons of victory accompanied by chants, and then wails for the wounded and dead. There followed a gymnastic exhibition in which several hundred Africans, wearing only loin cloths, took part. Finally there was an elaborate parade. As the exercises ended, a muezzin came out on a minaret and called the hour to prayer. All around, soldiers fell prostrate, now garbed in their uniforms, facing the east. Mrs. Harrison described the events as an unforgettable occasion, and remarked that France did not try to force an alien culture on the troops at Fréjus, but permitted them largely to follow their African customs, even to the point of bringing black magic with them.[35]

In conclusion it may be said that the Negro is fond of sport and that the French public is favorably attracted by the Negro

[35] Marguerite Harrison, "Black Magic on the Rivera," *Travel*, LIV (March 1930), 34-35, **56, 58.**

athlete, even as by the Negro entertainer. He is still of interest as an exotic creature, for the eighteenth-century fad for things foreign has not completely gone. The French moreover are greatly interested in world affairs and are singularly friendly toward other peoples. They provide an atmosphere that attracts people of other lands, and this has led to the remark, often quoted, that "everyone has France as his second country."

# THIRTEEN   OTHER SOCIAL ASPECTS

*WITH THIRTY* or forty thousand
Negroes in France,[1] one will find most of the aspects of modern
society presented, from riches to poverty, from pleasures to
vice and crime. Yet the evidence is fragmentary, weighed in
favor of those features which by their nature are matters of
public record. One must rely on personal observation, remem-
bering, however, that the eye is often deceived.

In general, there is little anti-Negro discrimination in France.
There appears to be no segregation as to residence save in
Paris and Marseilles, and in both cities it is limited in extent.
The dormitory for African students at the Cité Universitaire,
constructed by the French government and housing 249 students, represents a certain amount of segregation. So does the
Foyer for Students of French Equatorial Africa, on the Rue
Platon, though not a residence hall. The concentration of
Negro students in the Latin Quarter (near the University) and
in the Montmartre section, forced largely by educational and
economic circumstances, operates in the same direction. This
is far from stating that all the Negroes of Paris are concentrated
in these areas, for they are not. Those with jobs and living on
a more or less permanent basis are widely scattered about the

[1] Ottley (*No Green Pastures*, p. 80) estimated in 1951 that France at that
time had between 50,000 and 100,000 Negroes, and that they were centered at
Paris and Marseilles. He was well informed from residence in France, but
the present writer thinks that number too high. Monsieur Monnerville also, in
private conference, indicated a smaller estimate.

city; and Negro travelers from overseas stay in hotels here and there.

In Marseilles are also some tendencies toward segregation. A small Harlem of several hundreds already has been started near the Cours Belsunce, and several hotels and cafés in that area are heavily patronized by Negro students. In other French cities this tendency is less apparent, but their numbers of Negroes are much fewer. Even in them, however, the Negroes are to be seen largely concentrated in the university areas. With the coming of more Negroes to France—and the number is steadily growing—it seems inevitable that more and more segregation will take place. This will not be because the French have willed it so, but because of educational, economic, and other circumstances of modern society.

The Negroes from overseas indeed choose a considerable degree of segregation. Lonesome and desirous of friends, they huddle together in a group as foreign students from any country have a tendency to do wherever they are gathered; and this applies also to others than students. At the same time they mingle and intermarry with the whites much more than they do in the United States.

Much miscegenation is taking place and has taken place in France, from the eighteenth century to the present. Surprisingly numerous records of interracial intermarriages in the eighteenth century and afterward have been found in the archives. In all but a few instances it has been the Negro man marrying the French girl, and there have been definite reasons for this. In the first place, there have always been more Negro men than women in France, and they have had little choice of women of their own race there. But secondly, the Negro has found that he could get a white wife, more educated, more talented, and able to offer him better social contacts than a wife of his own race. The white women forming such marriages have been usually of the poorer class and have found that the Negro man could offer them a home and perhaps more economic advantages than they could obtain otherwise.

Usually these interracial marriages have been marked with harmony, and one often sees such families together, with their mulatto children, on Sunday afternoons, on the boulevards and in the parks; but sometimes the papers carry the story of murder or a fight that has occurred between these couples.

Anyone familiar with the excellent book by Jules Mathorez on *Les étrangers en France sous l'Ancien Régime* knows that many racial blends have entered into the formation of the present French population. One, a very minor strain, has been the Negro. How widespread this fusion has gone no one exactly knows, for the reason that no one has made a special study of it. Ottley alleges that due to miscegenation much Negro blood is to be found in Auvergne and also in Bordeaux; in fact, he asserts that it is to be found "even in the best families" at Bordeaux.[2] However, he cites no authority for the statement, and it may therefore be questioned.

Even though the Negroes are well received in France, they are not completely satisfied, saying that some racial feeling still exists. Ottley gives expression to this feeling, and one may find it stated in many of the writings on France by Negroes. Whether they can ever be completely satisfied remains to be seen. It is easy to pick out illustrations in every sphere of life and show that Negroes are treated on an equal basis with whites, but that does not necessarily eliminate the possibility of discrimination in other cases. In May, 1959, a New York mulatto night-club entertainer won a beauty contest at Cannes against fifteen girls from various European countries.[3] One might argue much from such a selection. A beauty queen from Africa, Miss Nigeria, was entertained in France in 1958 by Miss Paris with a cocktail party at the Elysées-Matignon, a distinct mark of courtesy and equality.[4]

Counterbalancing these marks of cordiality, however, was the unfortunate episode of June 2, 1958, in which some fifteen white youths in Paris administered a beating with metal-

2 *Ibid.*          3 Louisville *Courier-Journal*, 14 May 1959.
4 *Le Figaro*, 19 June 1958.

buckled belts to four Negro boys whom they found with a white girl at a subway entrance. One of the whites made an insulting remark to the girl, and the fight ensued.[5] A most unusual episode, to be sure, but it happened. Are the Negroes of France becoming numerous enough to arouse race sentiment to this extent?

From time to time there have been minor episodes in which either discrimination or dislike of the Negro has been manifest, although they have not been frequent. Early in the century, a physician making a sociological study of a mental hospital in Marseilles where both white and Negro patients were treated found that the two races in the institution were antagnostic to each other, and the basis of the ill will he traced in part to the odor of the Senegalese.[6] He said that the Senegalese were aware of their peculiar smell and had a proverb on it that ran as follows: "The Lord loves the Negro well; he recognizes him by his smell."

During and immediately after World War I, white American soldiers were often rude to Negroes in France, and some restaurants and cafés catering to the former were accused of closing their doors to the latter. One episode drew national attention and a rebuke from the French government. It concerned an insult by some Americans to Prince Kojo Tovolan Hoveneu, son of the last King of Dahomey. He was beaten rather badly and "ejected from a Montmartre café by Americans who objected to his color." Evidently the proprietor of the café collaborated with the Americans, for the Prince, a lawyer, took the case into court, won it, and the café lost its license. There were several such incidents. One involved the ejection of a Negro surgeon from an automobile taking some Americans from Paris to Rheims. The Negro protested, saying that for four and a half years he had been fighting with the

---

[5] Louisville *Courier-Journal*, 4 June 1959.

[6] Paul Borreil, *Considérations sur l'internment des aliénés sénégalais en France* (Montpellier, 1908), p. 33. His study covered the period 1897-1907, during which time Senegalese were treated in the institution, and their average stay was twenty-seven months.

French army, while most of the Americans had been at home. Further, he reported this insult to the Foreign Office, and Gratien Candace, Negro deputy, wrote an indignant article on the matter. The journal *Le Temps* carried an editorial condemning the American attitude and stating that France did not support inequality.[7]

Likewise, when the Nazis captured France in 1940, many stories of mistreatment were carried in the American Negro journals. There were reports of Negroes expelled from high office, of some forced to leave France, of artists banned from public performance, of men shot down on the streets for challenging authority.[8] It was reported that no longer were Negroes permitted to ride first class on the Paris subway (few did anyhow), that many restaurants, cafés, and even stores put out signs that they were closed to Negroes, and that many French people, to ingratiate the Nazis, closed their homes to Negroes.[9] After the war, the *Negro Year Book,* published by Tuskegee Institute, referred to all these charges and questioned their accuracy, saying: "It appears, that in most instances the Negro suffered no special disabilities."[10] This sober publication has long had the world's respect and is to be accepted as disposing of the matter. It estimated the Negro population of Paris under the Nazis at 15,000 to 20,000.

Of course, in both these last two episodes it was the Americans and the Germans rather than the French who created the trouble, but allegedly they found French cooperation. This last is described so vaguely as to be little tangible. And yet the French do not come off unaccused. Even Félix Eboué, the Negro Governor of Tchad, is reported by his biographer to have charged privately on one occasion that he had been passed

[7] *Literary Digest,* 1 Sept. 1923, pp. 40-44; Albert Guérard, "The Black Army of France," *Scribner's Magazine,* LXXVII (March 1925), 238.

[8] Data obtained from a dossier of newspaper clippings in the Howard University Library relative to Negroes in Europe, some without date or title of journal. One of the most sweeping articles was written by J. A. Rogers, just returned from Europe, and dated 26 December—evidently 1940.

[9] Pittsburgh *Courier,* 8 March 1941.

[10] *The Negro Year Book,* 1947, p. 581.

over in rating because of his color. His biographer discusses the matter at some length, but of course it is impossible to know the truth in the case.[11] An American Negro has charged that the French government, though it employs many Negroes, relegates them to minor jobs, giving the better positions to the whites. There seems, however, to be little basis for such an allegation.[12]

Although few Negro laborers are apparent in France, a Negro labor union existed in 1938, and an American newspaper carried an article on its move into "new and spacious headquarters" at 5 rue de la Banque. It was hoped that the headquarters might develop into "a real cultural center for the 'Negro' peoples of Paris."[13]

One sees in France Negroes in all roles. A record of observation includes two Negro priests on the streets of Paris, as well as several young Negro officers, evidently pursuing courses of study at the Ecole Militaire. At Nantes were many Negroes wearing military uniforms, some the uniform of the French air force. Elsewhere there was an occasional Negro sailor, but these were few. At the Folies Bergères four Negro men took parts in the show. At the Louvre two Negro men were employed as guards. Once or twice Negro women were employed as ticket punchers in the Metro stations. A single Negro shine boy was observed in Paris, stationed at a sidewalk café on the Champs Elysées. Even the American Express Company no longer has a shine boy, as in the early 1920's, nor are any found in the barbershops. A sole hotel porter or bellhop was seen, in the vicinity of the Louvre. At the Flea Market a Negro was employed at a booth selling Moroccan leather goods. En route to Versailles by train were a score of African students. On a chartered bus to Fontainebleau carrying Fulbright students were two or three American Negroes. At the Archives du Ministère de la France d'Outre-Mer in

[11] Maran, *Félix Eboué*, pp. 35 ff.
[12] San Francisco *California Eagle*, 26 Feb. 1937.
[13] Chicago *Defender*, 19 March 1938.

Paris was employed a Negro to fetch the materials wanted, and similarly at the Departmental Archives at La Rochelle another Negro was employed. In the reading room at the Bibliothèque Nationale several Negro students were commonly to be seen engaged in research, and on rare occasions a Negro was to be seen at the Archives Nationales. Even this casual record indicates that there were no occupations, such as porter, which tended to be exclusively Negro.

As already stated, Negroes are rarely seen in a menial position; they move in middle-class circles and their activities are varied. A Negro bishop from Uganda celebrated high pontifical mass at Lourdes before an estimated 80,000 pilgrims during the religious festival of 1958.[14] In early September, 1951, four Negro delegates from Chicago and New York to the Jehovah Witnesses' world meeting in the Netherlands were in Paris.[15] A Negro from New York named Julian, commonly called "The Black Eagle," arrived at Orly Airfield in early 1958 and was turned back by French authorities on the ground or suspicion that he was selling arms to the Algerians. He protested much, but without success.[16] More welcome were seventy-two Negro policemen and policewomen from New York who visited Paris in August, 1958, while on a European tour. They, too, went by airplane. While in Paris they were officially received at the Prefecture de Police.[17]

An interesting episode involved a French Negro who assisted the American army on D-Day, 1944. As told by Roi Ottley, Toni (Antoine) Montbrun, a young Negro from Martinique, was a hero on that occasion. Only twenty-three, he had been a sailor in the merchant marine for several years. At the outset of the war in 1939 he enlisted in the French army, was captured, but escaped, being turned out of prison after simulating a demented person. He got into the French Resistance Movement, and in advance of the Allied landings was

[14] Louisville *Courier-Journal,* 15 Sept. 1958.
[15] Philadelphia *Afro-American,* 4 Sept. 1951.
[16] *Le Figaro,* 31 Jan. 1958.                     [17] *Ibid.,* 5 Aug. 1958.

chosen by the leaders of that movement to direct the American tanks through the streets of Cherbourg to avoid mines and pillboxes. This he did with extraordinary success. Clambering aboard the first tank, he directed it to the German arsenal, and seizing a fallen gun, he did some fighting of his own. At the end of the day he reportedly had killed fifteen Germans and captured 197 "in the day's greatest individual feat."[18]

Another Resistance episode involving a young colonial of mixed blood from Haiti ended more tragically. Tony Bloncourt, descended from the mulatto writer and lexicographer Melvil Bloncourt, had gone to Paris after taking his baccalaureate at Port-au-Prince. In November, 1941, he took part in causing the derailment of the fast Chantilly Express, in which 450 Nazis were killed and an additional 1,200 were injured. For this, he and seven others were executed in March, 1942. In his last minutes before the execution he wrote a very touching letter to his loved ones in the colonies, bidding them to be brave, and signed it with his pet name.[19]

The criminal record of Negroes in France is not singular. They are not underworld figures, and almost certainly they have no criminal records prior to entry in the country. Their crimes are not numerous, and in most instances spring from anger. Examples may be found in the killing of a fifty-two-year-old French wife by her Negro husband, aged sixty, after a quarrel. The Negro was without a job, and his wife did all the chores about the home. Seemingly the quarrel arose from her complaints; he ended it by slashing her throat.[20] In another case, also in 1957, a Frenchman was walking on grounds of the American military base at Nancy on the night of July 4. Without provocation, it would appear, an American Negro soldier standing nearby suddenly pulled out his pistol and killed him. Since the incident took place on the American

[18] *No Green Pastures*, pp. 94-95.
[19] *The Haitian-American Anthology*, ed. by Mercer Cook and Dantès Bellegarde (Port-au-Prince, 1944), pp. 116-18. The letter is incorporated.
[20] *Le Figaro*, 26 July 1957.

military grounds, the matter had to come up before an American military court.[21] In a third instance, two Senegalese fought a duel with knives about 1:30 in the morning in the Bois de Boulogne over some matter. Both duelists fell in the water, and one of them drowned. The other pulled himself out, left the other, returned to his hotel, and later informed the widow of the drowned man of what had happened. In all three episodes one sees the same pattern of crime committed through impulse.[22]

A yet more tragic act of this type took place at Fontaine-bleau in February, 1957, when a Negro teacher in mathematics at the international school, a subordinate part of the Lycée Carnot, assassinated a young Dutch woman teaching in the same school. Early in the morning of February 20, the Negro, a native of Togoland, knocked at the classroom door of the young woman and handed her a note when she presented herself. It so happened that Mademoiselle Van Steyn had felt sorry for the young man, who appeared lonely, and had taken some walks with him. Misinterpreting her motives, perhaps, the Negro attempted to put friendship on a serious basis. Mademoiselle Van Steyn refused to do that and insisted that they must discontinue seeing each other. The note handed her on the morning of February 20 asked her in ultimatum tones that she revoke her decision. She read it and for an answer shook her head. Thereupon the African drew from concealment a long knife and stabbed her twice, in her chest and shoulder. She reentered the room, tottered two or three steps, and fell dead before her frightened pupils. The murderer proceeded to leave the building by jumping from a window and took refuge under a bush until arrested. In this episode, of course, lay the tragic features of interracial courtship when both parties are not able to regard the matter in the same light. Instances like this are very rare in France.[23]

Sometimes in recent years Negroes in France have been

[21] *Ibid.*, 1 Aug. 1957.                    [22] *Ibid.*, 28 Jan. 1957.
[23] *Ibid.*, 21 Feb. 1957; Paris *New York Herald Tribune*, 22 Feb. 1957.

involved in robbery. In October, 1957, two young Negroes attacked a taxi driver at a very early hour in the morning, striking and kicking him, so that he had to be taken to a hospital for treatment.[24] In another case, in 1939, a Negro and a Negress robbed a fifty-nine-year-old woman living at Vitry-sur-Seine. They struck her several times with a stick and a revolver, and then fled, taking with them 35,000 francs in coin and jewels valued at 100,000 francs. The Negro woman hailed from Brazil, where the French woman had met her some years previously and befriended her by bringing her to France and caring for her. It was probably she who learned of the valuables and plotted the action, for she and the Negro man were acquaintances. A white man also found leaving the scene of the crime on the same evening was able to establish an alibi.[25] At Grasse, near Nice, in early September, 1957, occurred another such instance. In this case as in the previous one, the robbed furnished some provocation for what arose. Two Dutchmen, one owning a suburban villa and the other his gardener, met two young Negro men in Cannes and invited them to dine the next night at the villa. The party ran until midnight, when the gardener proposed that it was time to leave. Thereupon the Negroes seized a bottle and a knife, demanded the money of the other two men, and obtained 20,000 francs. As they left, the host set up a cry. The Negroes then struck the gardener twice with a knife, leaving him in a grave condition, and escaped.[26] In both these two last crimes the persons attacked had apparently established the impression that they were easy prey. Kindness well meant is sometimes folly.

Still another Negro, an American cook, was charged in 1957 with murdering his mistress. Her body was found in the woods at Chinon, and the cook gave grounds for suspicion. Among these was the discovery of a kitchen knife under the seat of his automobile. The case was turned over by the French

24 *Le Figaro*, 19-20 Oct. 1957.    25 *L'Intransigeant*, 13 Jan. 1939.
26 *Le Figaro*, 4 Sept. 1957.

to the American military authorities who had the jurisdiction.[27] How it terminated is not known, but it was given much attention in the French press. The motive for the deed was not clear, nor whether a third party was involved.

The Negroes are not now regarded in France as prone to crime. In some official documents of the eighteenth century the charge flatly was made that they were responsible for an increase of crime of all types in France, although the records do not substantiate the allegation for that or any other period. The Negro in France today of course is quite different from the typical Negro there in the 1700's in that he is no longer from the servant class but from the upper classes of their people. Most of them are in relatively easy financial circumstances and need not resort to robbery, thievery, or prostitution. In a very large number of cases they have been selected for study in France because of intellectual qualifications. In any class of society there are those who get enmeshed in crime, and the French Negroes are not exceptional in any degree.

If some Negroes are found in crime in France, others may be found in humanitarian enterprises. Of these perhaps the most conspicuous example is Josephine Baker, a native of Saint Louis, Missouri, and now in her fifties. Miss Baker went to Paris in the 1930's and became a sensation as a nude dancer at the Folies Bergères and the Casino de Paris. She was designated the "Black Venus," although actually she was a mulatto or octoroon and light in color. She attracted even more attention by taking on leash a tamed puma on the streets of Paris. "Salting away" her money, she has become a woman of wealth and independence. Marrying a Frenchman named Bouillon, she decided to make France her permanent home.

She and her husband have long been wealthy, owning a home in Paris on the fashionable Avenue Victor Hugo and an estate with a chateau at Milandes, near Cahors, in Périgord. A French paper reported that Miss Baker purchased this latter property in 1950 with proceeds derived from the sale

[27] *Ibid.*, 2 and 3 Sept. 1957.

of some real estate in Paris. Her Périgord estate was reported to consist of 232 hectars (a hectar being approximately 2½ acres), and the chateau a structure of nineteen rooms, with five baths (more than most French chateaux have!).

One of Miss Baker's motives in buying this estate was to make it the scene of a model experiment in racial study. She planned to adopt and rear there several children of different racial backgrounds to show that children of hated races can do as well in life as those of favored races if given the same opportunities and treatment. By September, 1959, the number adopted had increased to ten. All the children carry the name of Bouillon and have both French nationality and that of their birth. At their majority they are to choose their permanent nationality.

In the meantime, the children are provided fairyland surroundings. Many improvements to her estate have been introduced by Miss Baker, and already by 1955 it had become a showplace. From April to October of that year a total of 160,000 persons had visited it. The place was equipped with a bar, a restaurant, a museum, and a parking lot to accommodate one hundred cars. For the children, there was a zoo, a miniature golf course, two bowling alleys, while a winter theater and a children's garden were planned for construction. The museum contained wax dolls representing various episodes in the life of Miss Baker from her childhood in Saint Louis to her reception by the Pope at the Vatican.

Certainly the enterprise is to be commended for its original and humanitarian features. Whether it will accomplish what Miss Baker has desired remains to be seen. It is a noble experiment planned to show that innate racial differences in capacity do not exist. But so much depends on whether Miss Baker has chosen children with the same degree of mentality, health, ambition, and determination, that the experiment likely will prove only what experienced teachers have long known: that different children have different abilities. The experiment will nevertheless have its values; it ought to demonstrate that children of different races can be reared together in harmony and friendship, and in this it will provide a magnificent illustration for those fighting racial prejudice. Many colleges and universities, of course, have long provided examples in this respect.[28]

Miss Baker has long since become a personage well known throughout France. Her stellar role at the Folies Bergères in itself acquired her that prestige. But she has carried it higher by her orphans' experiment and also by her lectures on racial problems. For she speaks from time to time in France on the matter of racial prejudice, and more and more is devoting her life to a crusade in behalf of eradicating racial hatred. In this crusade she finds the French quite sympathetic.

Thus the Negroes in France are to be found in all phases of the social life of that country, from crime to humanitarian enterprise, and in all forms of professional and economic employment. More and more visitors are making their homes there. No restrictions against permanent residence are imposed, and some of those remaining are from the French colonies, others from the United States. A certain amount of segregation exists, more among the newcomers; those who remain on a permanent basis tend to establish contacts broadly with the French population. The Negroes hope that interracial relationships will become even more cordial, but the universal tendency for peoples to eye large minorities with dislike raises doubt of this.

[28] For accounts of Miss Baker and her experiment, see Ottley, *No Green Pastures*, p. 73; *L'Intransigeant*, 3 Jan. and 11-12 Dec. 1955; *Le Monde*, 20-21 Jan. 1957; *Le Figaro*, 28 Oct. 1957; Louisville *Courier-Journal*, 26 Jan. 1958; Lexington *Herald-Leader*, 13 Sept. 1959. More recently she has been sharply criticized by Westbrook Pegler for some unkind articles on the United States which she had written for the Latin American journal *Critica*. See Lexington *Leader*, 14 March 1960.

# FOURTEEN    IN BIGTIME POLITICS


$SINCE$ 1789, Negroes have participated in French politics and shown themselves remarkably adept at it. Raimond and other mulattoes of the Amis des Noirs were successful in obtaining various advantages for the Negroes of the colonies, until by February 4, 1794, they had gained not only the right to sit in the French legislative bodies but also the abolition of the slave trade and even slavery itself. Thenceforth until the time of Leclerc's expedition in 1801, Negroes participated in the French government. Afterward they were absent until the time of the 1848 Revolution, but the writings of Richard, Fabien, Bissette, and Houat had some influence in molding public opinion on the issue of slavery in the colonies and possibly some small part in preparing the way for revolution. With the advent of the 1848 Revolution, Negro representatives from the colonies once again were admitted to the French parliament and they have seldom, if ever, been absent subsequently.

For nearly a century the number of Negro representatives in the French parliament remained small, rarely more than two or three serving at any one time. Even as late as 1937, reportedly only two sat in the Chamber of Deputies.[1] More liberal provisions in the Constitution of the Fourth Republic, however, brought a swelling of the number, and from 1946 to 1958, more than fifty Negroes sat as representatives, thirty to thirty-three as deputies and twenty-one or twenty-two as

[1] San Francisco *California Eagle*, 26 Feb. 1937.

senators.[2] These sat on the left, near or with the Communists, and sometimes voted with them. While on many matters they took individual stands, they generally voted as a bloc on all legislation affecting the colonies. With the establishment of the Fifth Republic under President De Gaulle, the number of Negro deputies and senators was greatly reduced, due to the African colonies voting for autonomy. Voluntarily, therefore, the Africans declined representation in the French parliament, but the older French colonies of the New World voted in general for departmental status (as a part of France), and continue to send their representatives, commonly Negroes.

Since World War I, several Negroes have sat in French cabinets, and since World War II, there has been hardly a cabinet without one. This has been due, almost certainly, to the important role exerted in these wars by Negro troops fighting to defend the republic and also to the recognized political and economic importance of the colonies. It is not to say that the men selected for the cabinet posts have been without talent; quite the contrary! Nevertheless, that is the way in which men for cabinet posts normally are chosen—by virtue of their importance in some political group whose support is essential to the government.

Thus far ten Negroes have sat as members of French cabinets, as ministers or undersecretaries. The first, Severiano de Heredia, a mulatto born in Havana, became a naturalized French citizen in 1870, served actively as a deputy in the French parliament from 1881 to 1889, and for several months in 1887 was Minister of Public Works.[3] Others who have held such posts have been Henry Lémery, Blaise Diagne, Gratien Candace, Gaston Monnerville, Gily Dabo Sissoko, Léopold Senghor, Joseph Conombo, Hammadoun Dicko, and Félix Houphouet-Boigny.[4] Of these the larger number have come from the African colonies, the others from the Caribbean. The

[2] Information given the author by the French Embassy in New York.
[3] *La grande encyclopédie*, XIX, 165; Rogers, *Great Men of Color*, II, 420.
[4] Information from the French Embassy in New York; Rogers, *Great Men of Color*, II, 414-20; Ottley, *No Green Pastures*, p. 93.

first African to sit in such a post was Blaise Diagne, who in 1917 had been sent by Clemenceau to recruit African troops on a large scale. In 1931-1932 he was Undersecretary of State for Colonial Affairs. Even earlier there had been two West Indian Undersecretaries, Gratien Candace, assistant to René Viviani, Minister of Labor, 1906-1909, and Joseph Henry Lémery, Undersecretary of State for Maritime Transport, 1917-1919, in the Clemenceau cabinet. The former was from Guadeloupe, the latter from Martinique. Later, in 1932, Candace was Undersecretary of State for the Colonies in the third ministry of Herriot. Lémery in 1940 was Colonial Minister in the Vichy government of Marshal Petain.[5]

Lémery's stand with the Fascists appears somewhat fantastic. The report was made in an American Negro newspaper at the time that he had been compelled by Nazi pressure to decline the office, but his biographical sketch in *Who's Who in France, 1955-1956* lists the honor.[6] A mulatto born at Saint-Pierre, Martinique, in 1874, Lémery was educated at Paris in the famous Lycée Louis-le-Grand and in the Faculty of Law. He was twice married to French women. He practiced law for a while in Paris, but after 1900 was almost continually in politics. From 1914 to 1919 he was deputy from Martinique, and from 1920 to 1940 a senator. In addition he was the author of several books. It would seem that though he made good use of his connection with Martinique, he was more a Frenchman than a colonial.[7]

Félix Houphouet-Boigny, deputy to the National Assembly from the Ivory Coast from 1947 to 1958, when his colony became autonomous, was a member of several French cabinets, continuously since 1956. He was long considered to be the

[5] Ottley, *No Green Pastures*, p. 93; Rogers, *Great Men of Color*, II, 414-20; *Qui êtes vous* (Paris, 1925), p. 144; *Who's Who in France, 1955-1956*, p. 1002; *Dictionnaire de biographie française*, VII, 1027.

[6] *The Negro Year Book: A Review of Events Affecting Negro Life, 1941-1946*, ed. by Jessie Parkhurst Guzman and others (Tuskegee Institute, Alabama, 1947), p. 581.

[7] See sketches in *Who's Who in France, 1955-1956*, p. 1002, and Ottley, *No Green Pastures*, p. 95.

258 THE NEGRO IN FRANCE

most distinguished Negro politician in the lower house from the African colonies, save possibly for Léopold Senghor (now the leader in the autonomous Mali Federation), and his political stand was a bit more agreeable to the French than that of Senghor, in that he dismissed completely from consideration any aspiration for colonial independence in the near future. A stalwart supporter of cooperation with France and the head of a party advocating such, he was also the uncontested political boss of the nineteen million inhabitants of the Ivory Coast.

Houphouet-Boigny is a physician by training. Born at the village of Yamoussoukio in Africa in 1905, he studied medicine at Dakar and in 1918 entered the Ecole Normale at Paris. While studying at Bingerville as a youth, he was attacked by a swarm of bees one morning, leaving his face badly scarred. This gives him a severe appearance, but he is reported to be of genial disposition. He is a large landowner and the president of a syndicate of African landowners on the Ivory Coast. Like many Negroes in France, he joined the Communist Party, but severed his connection with it in 1950. During World War II he was a member of the French Resistance Movement in Africa. He was a leader of the African Democratic Rally, a political party which he helped to form in 1946 and which in 1957 had nine members sitting as deputies in the French National Assembly, to form the largest African bloc. For a few months in 1958 he continued to hold a cabinet post under President de Gaulle, but gave that up when the Ivory Coast chose autonomy and made him first premier and then president in early 1959.[8]

Of equal stature with Houphouet-Boigny at least is Gaston Monnerville, once Undersecretary of State for the Colonies (in 1937-1938), and since the founding of the Fourth Republic in 1946 President of the Senate. Through the changes of

[8] *France actuel,* 1 Feb. 1957; a biographical bulletin on Houphouet-Boigny issued by the French Embassy in New York in Sept. 1959; *Current Biography Yearbook,* ed. by Marjorie Dent Candee (New York, 1958), pp. 205-207; *Paris-Presse l'Intransigeant,* 1 Feb. 1956, p. 5; and *Time,* 18 Feb. 1957, p. 19. The fullest account is that in *Current Biography Yearbook.*

fourteen or fifteen governments of the Fourth Republic he held this position, and is still there under De Gaulle, until whose coming he was, technically at least, the most stable official under the Fourth Republic.

Monnerville is a highly trained lawyer, a political figure of long experience, a man of gracious and dignified bearing, one who would command respect for these qualities alone; but he is more than that. A native of Martinique and the most dominant political representative from the French West Indies, he is ipso facto a significant man in government affairs at Paris, all the more so when he represents the slightly left-of-center political party of Radical Socialists. Like Houphouet-Boigny, he has an admirable war record. Resident in France during World War II, he was one of the leaders of the Resistance Movement, first in Provence and afterward in the Massif Central, and for this role he was given the Croix de Guerre, the Rosette de la Résistance, and the Legion of Honor (military). He, too, he is a thoroughgoing supporter of the French Community. Indeed, the West Indians have not been afflicted by the nationalist itch, but consider themselves about as completely French as if they had been born on European soil. From childhood they know no other language than French; they have no history and culture save as French colonials; and since the great Revolution of 1789, they have shared and benefited from all national stirrings. They do not wish to be separate; on the contrary, they are proud to be French and have no higher aspiration than to share in French achievement. Monnerville has attained so many distinctions that it is impossible, and even needless, to record them here. His name and photograph are constantly in the French press, for he is invited as a dignitary to most ceremonial occasions, and he is perpetually called on as a speaker, for he has the reputation of an accomplished orator.[9]

[9] The fullest sketch of him is a little brochure of four pages, entitled *Gaston Monnerville . . . President du Conseil de la République* (n.p., 1950), given this author by M. Monnerville's secretary. See also *Who's Who in France, 1955-1956*, pp. 1177-78.

One further Negro holder of a French cabinet post in the past deserves to be mentioned, Léopold Senghor, from Senegal, who in 1955 was Secretary of State for Scientific Research. Chataigneau, former governor general to Algeria and former ambassador to Russia, mentioned that as member of the body drawing up the Constitution of France for the Fourth Republic, Senghor was charged with editing the phraseology of that document. Chataigneau thought this a mark of high honor, and indeed it was. Here was a man born and reared in Africa, who learned French as a second language and came to France for his education. He became an agrégé, a professor, a poet, and a political figure. For many years he sat in the lower house of the French parliament, and after Houphouet-Boigny he was the most powerful political representative from Africa. He is not Communist and is highly regarded in France.[10] In 1959 he was elected president of the Legislative Assembly of the Mali Federation.

Of the other outstanding Negro leaders who have sat as cabinet members in Paris, it may be observed that they were deputies from Africa rather than the West Indies, and that they held their posts in the 1940's and 1950's under the Fourth Republic. Their choice represents on the one hand the prominence of the Negro contingent in parliament, and on the other the larger representation from Africa. For the population of the French West Indies is negligible in comparison to that of the many French African provinces. Possibly, too, the political ferment in these latter provinces made it more necessary for French recognition of their strength. It is also to be observed that even prior to World War I the French were making diplomatic gestures toward their Negro colonials, for two or three undersecretaryships were granted them.

Aware of their need of colonial cooperation, the French continued to confer various political honors on Negro deputies in the interim between the two World Wars. This was evi-

[10] *Who's Who in France, 1955-1956*, p. 1505. A short biographical sketch of Senghor was published by the French Embassy in New York in Sept. 1959.

denced in the election of Gratien Candace in 1938 to be Vice President of the Chamber. The courtesy was not ignored; in 1940 he retired from French politics, declining to participate in the Vichy regime. Candace was a man of importance not alone in politics but also in culture. A graduate in science at the University of Toulouse, and afterward a professor of technology and a journalist, he became one of the founders of the Colonial Institute, now designated the Ecole Nationale de la France d'Outre-Mer, and also of the Académie des Sciences Coloniales.[11]

The body of Negro deputies in Paris has included several who are writers or professors. Besides Senghor, who has qualified in both categories, Aimé Césaire, still a deputy from Martinique, is a writer of reputation, and Jonah Renaivo, a deputy from Madagascar from 1951 to 1958, a writer and professor. Césaire attracted some publicity in France by bolting the Communist Party after the Hungarian Revolt of 1956.[12]

The Negroes cannot complain that they have been neglected in regard to publicity, for the French press has given them attention much out of proportion to their numbers. This applies to politicians as well as to visitors of other types. Photographs have been very commonly included. Thus, in 1954, when Robert Buron, then Minister for France Overseas, gave an official reception for five Negro deputies from the colonies, an account with two photographs appeared in *Chroniques d'outre-mer*.[13] At this reception were many dignitaries to greet them, such as Monnet, Senghor, Anjoulat, and others. A week later, a similar reception was held for other African delegates newly arrived. There were more photographs, this time of Buron standing among the Africans wearing their native garb and headdress.[14]

Receptions have come to be so numerous for visiting Africans that they are clearly a studied point of French courtesy. No

[11] *Dictionnaire de biographie française*, VII, 1027.
[12] *France-Soir*, 25 Oct. 1956; *Who's Who in France, 1955-1956*, p. 1368.
[13] July 1954, p. 32.        [14] *Ibid.*, pp. 33, 34.

Negro dignitary can come to Paris without the "red carpet" being rolled out for him, and if he wishes to attend in his native African dress, so much the better: it will photograph well and give more color to the occasion. But the dress is not essential. The Emperor of the Mossis in July, 1958, came in white turban and giant white robe resembling a nightshirt;[15] but President Tubman and his wife from Liberia in October, 1956, chose European dress. The President came in cutaway coat and striped trousers, a gold chain across his breast and white gloves on his hands; his wife, in hat, white dress, and high-heeled shoes.[16] The premier of Togoland, Gronitzki, was received by President Coty at the Elysée Palace, appearing in plain day dress.[17] Koukou, small daughter of the Tubmans, got her photograph and a writeup of some length in the dignified *Le Figaro*. She was wearing a red felt bonnet tied on by a blue ribbon, and was holding in her hand a minature of the Eiffel Tower.[18]

It matters little whether the visiting African dignitary be French or otherwise; official courtesy is granted him. Kuvuma, prime minister of the British protectorate of Buganda, in Ouranda, called by Paris after an official visit to London and was accorded state recognition by the French. He was greeted on his arrival by the Ministers of Foreign Affairs and of France Overseas, and on the next day was dined at the Hôtel Crillon with representatives of the two ministries (including the ministers themselves). A cocktail party was later held in his honor at the Hôtel Plaza-Athénée, where a large number of officials came to do honor to Kuvuma, including President Auriol, the British ambassador, the director of the cabinet, and other dignitaries.[19] The French know how to put on a party, and they usually have good ones for the visiting Africans.

In recent years the government has taken occasion to invite numerous prominent Africans to Paris for the July 14 celebra-

[15] *Le Figaro*, 11 July 1958.
[16] *Paris-Presse l'Intransigeant*, 4 Oct. 1956.
[17] *Le Figaro*, 21 Nov. 1956.
[18] 6 Oct. 1956.
[19] *Chroniques d'outre-mer*, Nov. 1952, pp. 20-21.

tions, apparently underwriting their expenses, giving them a tour of several days or more, entertaining them with receptions, and all in all providing them a magnificent show and memories long to be cherished. The *Chroniques d'outre-mer* for July, 1956, describes a series of receptions held in Paris for 220 overseas delegates. Most of them were "grands chefs noirs" from the various French possessions, and wore their colorful native costumes. From all parts of Africa, from faraway Madagascar and the isles of Oceania, they came. For four days they were guests of the French government. A series of receptions was held for them at the Ministry of France Overseas, the Elysée Palace, and elsewhere. Perhaps the high spot in the celebrations was the reception for them by President René Coty at the Elysée Palace on the morning of July 12.[20]

Naturally these guests witness the great parades of July 14, in which overseas troops have their part—always a very attractive feature of the great show. A vivid impression was made by the cheering Algerian contingent in the 1957 parade, and also by the colorful Moroccan spahis. In this parade was a unit of Senegalese riflemen; also, there were some Negroes mixed with whites in paratroop and other units; and at least one Negro was in a band. Many Negroes, men and women, were among the multitude of spectators. For decades this sort of thing has happened in Paris. The Fourteenth of July is the gala event of the year, and the government has spared no expense or effort to make of it a bond tying the empire together. Not infrequently the government invites to be present some overseas soldiers of former wars, as in 1955, and these are honored with a reception.[21] In 1953 a group of young Africans from preparatory schools were asked to participate in the July 14 parade.[22] Thus an attempt is made to enlist the attention and participation of all ages of colonials.

[20] *Ibid.*, July 1956, pp. 31-33. For 1955 it was very much the same. See *ibid.*, July 1955, pp. 29-33.
[21] Old soldiers from overseas and their children were invited to a reception in the gardens of the Ministry of France Overseas on the night of 6 July. *Ibid.*, July 1955, p. 33.
[22] *Paris-Presse l'Intransigeant*, 15 July 1953, p. 8.

THE NEGRO IN FRANCE

Nor is Paris the only French city where the Negroes are honored in fetes. Black Africa was honored at Dijon on November 10, 1956. The ceremony was attended by Albert Sarraut, president of the Assembly of the Union Française, and others from Paris, white and Negro, and a banquet was served at a restaurant, Sarraut presiding. Native African dances and songs were presented, and speeches were made, some by African deputies to the National Assembly. The occasion was a fair in Dijon, and this event was one of its features.[23]

Sometimes opportunity is found most unexpectedly to honor the Negroes. Thus at the opening of the World Movement of Mothers on June 9, 1958, in Paris, Houphouet-Boigny was asked to preside. The event might have passed with little attention had not a Negro baby, fresh from Africa, seized the attention of the audience by squalling at the top of his lungs and preventing the audience from hearing Houphouet-Boigny, to the evident amusement of all. The baby in consequence drew a good writeup in staid old *Figaro* the following day, under the caption: "A Little Negro Baby and M. Houphouet-Boigny Inaugurate the Session of the World Movement of Mothers."

Nor are these little incidents without their political bearing. If they were, Houphouet-Boigny and Monnerville would not attend so many functions like the above. Even when *France d'outre-mer* of December, 1956, carried as it did the photographs of several Negro bishops with sees in French Africa and Madagascar, the matter was not unconnected with politics. This is all the more apparent when the article describing them is entitled "Les missions catholiques en face de l'évolution des nationalismes africaines."[24] Yes, France depends heavily upon the bishops for support; they are to keep the masses quiescent. For this same reason an event finds inclusion in the publication

[23] *Chroniques d'outre-mer*, Dec. 1956, p. 30.
[24] Pages 22-23. Four bishops are identified and their sees designated. In 1959 a Negro cardinal in French Africa was appointed, the first in Catholic history.

of the Ministry of France Overseas in which the papal order of Saint Sylvester was given to a young Negro army captain, Sekou Kone, in one of the rooms of the Ministry of France Overseas, by Monseigneur Bertin. The papal representative thanked the Ministry, the Administration, and all present for their collaboration in "the propagation of Christian civilization in the French Union."[25] Sometimes political and religious interests are thus closely related.

From time to time special commemorative services honor some historic event or person. Thus in July, 1956, it was arranged that the 220 colonials invited to France to attend the July 14 celebration should visit the battlefield of Verdun, where their soldiers had fallen alongside the French in 1916. The elaborate affair had been planned for a year. Many dignitaries were present to participate and show government attention to the delegates.[26] On July 31, 1946, another memorial service at the Cemetery Père Lachaise was held for the great emancipator of the 1840's, Victor Schoelcher. Many colonials from Guiana and the West Indies, especially Negroes, were present.[27] Schoelcher, it will be recalled, is to the Negro of the French West Indies about what Abraham Lincoln is to the American Negro. Naturally the centenary of the French abolition of slavery in 1848 could not go unobserved. Accordingly, on April 27, 1948, a magnificent celebration was held in the great ampitheater of the Sorbonne, with President Vincent Auriol and Premier Edouard Herriot both present. Among a host of other notables present were Daniel Boisdon, President of the Assembly of the Union Française, Monnerville, President of the Council of the Republic, the Ministers of Education, France Overseas, the Interior, and Senghor and Césaire, deputies to the National Assembly. Again Schoelcher was exalted in speeches. Afterward, in May, an exposition commemorative of the abolition of slavery was set up in the

[25] *Chroniques d'outre-mer,* July-August 1953, p. 27.
[26] *Ibid.,* Sept. 1956, pp. 39-40.
[27] *Bulletin d'information,* Aug. 1946, p. 18.

museum of the Ministry of France Overseas.[28] A similar celebration in late May, 1931, commemorated the centenary of
the passing of Grégoire. It, too, was held in the great amphitheater of the Sorbonne, with more than a thousand present.[29]

The French are very history-conscious. They love the story
of their past and realize its power to unite the citizenry in
ideals and aspirations. They honor those who have fought for
freedom, regardless of whether it has been for whites or
Negroes.

Cordiality toward the Negro has gone even to the point
where "twinning" *(jumelage)* between French cities and African
cities has begun. Various exchanges of cordiality have taken
place. The first African and French cities to twin were Bouaké,
on the Ivory Coast, and Villeneuve-sur-Lot. Ceremonies in-
augurating the condition were held at Bouaké during the
period March 18-22, 1958. Various African dignitaries were
present, the mayors of the two cities exchanged greetings,
and congratulatory messages came from Paris.[30] Hopes were
expressed that exchange of students between the two cities
might result.

The Africans are willing to reciprocate these exchanges of
cordiality. With few exceptions they are cordial toward France
and realize that their countries have much to gain, much to
learn, by French association.

Cooperation on a much more important scale has come to
exist since 1946 in what was called the Union Française, and
since 1959, the French Community. The former of these
organizations lasted throughout the existence of the Fourth
Republic, and grew out of a conference of French and African
leaders at Brazzaville in 1944, in which Eboué, the governor
general of Tchad, insisted that France must give more political
recognition to her colonial subjects. A new constitution for

[28] *Ibid.*, 15 May 1948, p. 23.

[29] Dr. Price-Mars, "La participation Haïtienne à la commemoration du
centenaire de l'Abbé Grégoire," *Revue de la Société d'Histoire et de
Géographie d'Haïti*, II, no. 4 (Port-au-Prince, Nov. 1931), 6-7.

[30] *Le Figaro*, 27 March 1958.

France should be drawn up, he urged, which should accord the colonies greater representation in the government at Paris. A new organization, moreover, should be created in which representatives of the French and the colonials should discuss together, in frankness, matters of imperial concern. The plan was devised more elaborately by Giaccobi, and adopted by two constituent assemblees sitting in Paris in 1945-1946.[31]

Composed of about 250 delegates elected by France and the colonies, the Union Française was a federation with headquarters in Paris that met periodically to consider matters affecting the French empire as a whole. Since only seventy-five of its delegates were colonials, France had no ground for alarm lest they would dominate the decisions taken. Moreover, it had no power of legislation, but only of discussion and recommendation. Legislation was left the prerogative alone of the French parliament. For a time the meetings of the Union were held in Versailles, but in July, 1956, it moved its headquarters to the Place d'Iéna in Paris. A large audience of approximately 3,000 attended that occasion. Presiding was its president, Albert Sarraut. One of the speakers was President Coty of France. This new body, in short, was a miniature United Nations Assembly, created in response to colonial demands.[32]

At the beginning of 1959 the Union Française was replaced by the French Community of Nations. This came about through the advent to power of General Charles de Gaulle. In an election of September, 1958, the colonies, or "territories" as now the French government prefers to designate them, were offered the choice of four positions: (1) immediate independence; (2) the status of a French department; (3) continuation of the status of an overseas territory, with repre-

---

[31] "Recommendations adoptées par la Conference de Brazzaville," by the Ministère des Colonies, Paris, 1945, republished in *Colonisation et communauté*, ed. by L. Bellpeer ([Paris, 1946]), p. 112.

[32] *Les étudiants noirs parlent*, pp. 134-35; *Bulletin d'information*, 21 Oct. 1946, pp. 15-16, and 10 Feb. 1947; *Chroniques d'outre-mer*, Aug. 1956, p. 15, and July, 1951, p. 27; *Le Figaro*, 16 Oct. 1957.

sentation in the French parliament; and (4) autonomy and membership in the French Community. While Réunion and the Caribbean possessions voted in favor of departmental status, and Somaliland and New Caledonia preferred continuation as overseas territories, Madagascar and all the territories of West Africa and Equatorial Africa save one took the last choice—Community membership. Guinea alone voted for complete separation from France and from the Community. Thirteen African states by this election thus voted themselves independence but union with France in the new federation—the Community. They have the power to leave it at any time. Their inclusion, therefore, is entirely of their own volition.

As members of the Community, the African states act together on matters of common interest, like imperial defense, foreign affairs, economic policies, education, and vital raw materials. The President of France is automatically President of the Community. Other members of its Executive Council are the premiers of the component states and the French cabinet members whose portfolios concern Community affairs. The first meeting of this Council was held in Paris on February 3, 1959; a fourth took place at Tananarive, Madagascar, July 7-8, 1959; and a sixth at Saint-Louis, Senegal, December 11-12, 1959. Meetings may be held either in Paris or in the capital of any of the member states. Besides the Council, there is a Senate composed of 284 members, representation being based upon the size of population. A Court of Arbitration is to settle disputes between member states and to interpret provisions of the constitution. Finally, there exists a small body of Advisory Ministers appointed to confer with the French government on important matters that concern the Community. Four Advisers were named in July, 1959, to serve for one year—Houphouet-Boigny, representing the Ivory Coast; Lisette, Tchad; Senghor, Senegal; and Tsiranana, Madagascar. The new organization is too young as yet for any judgment to be made of its success. Its leaders appear to be in large part former members of the French Chamber of Deputies, well conversant with parliamentary procedure and French ideals and needs.[33] The significance of this new organization is that it symbolizes the end of colonial status for those African territories which in 1958 voted for autonomy, even as for Guinea, which has left the empire completely. The autonomous republics, thirteen in number, at their own choosing have retained a slender tie with France; this they can sever at any time.

A prelude to these organizations, the Union Française and the French Community, was a series of Pan-African Congresses that began in 1919, at the close of World War I, and that have continued from time to time until the present. They have done much to fan the restlessness of the Negro people of the world. According to Professor John Hope Franklin, the first of these Congresses developed from American origins. The NAACP in December, 1918, requested Dr. W. E. B. Du Bois, one of its founders, to go to France "to investigate the treatment of Negro soldiers and collect information concerning their participation in the war." The idea of a congress occurred to Du Bois, and Paris seemed the logical place for it. Blaise Diagne, deputy from Senegal and a cabinet member, obtained from Clemenceau the privilege of holding it in Paris, and the Grand Hôtel was set apart for the delegates and the meeting. The congress took place in February, 1919, with a total of fifty-seven delegates present. Sixteen were American Negroes, twenty from the West Indies, and only twelve from Africa. Little was accomplished beyond giving expression to desire for democratic treatment and for future meetings.[34]

In 1921 a second Pan-African Congress was held at London, Brussels, and Paris, its promoters being Du Bois, Diagne, and Candace. It drew much hostile press comment at the outset, but this subsided after a time, and those who called the

[33] Details of the new organization may be found in the brochure entitled *Communauté* (Paris, 1959), published by the French government; also in articles 77-86 of the Constitution of the Fifth Republic, and in *Two Years of the De Gaulle Administration, June 1958–June 1960*, published by the French Embassy (New York, 1960), pp. 41-45.

[34] *From Slavery to Freedom*, p. 462. Ottley (*No Green Pastures*, pp. 95-96) charges that the "French Negroes manoeuvered the movement into virtual futility." They desired to remain French and not to oppose the French in their thought.

congress had another chance of proclaiming the aspirations of the Negro race. The main theme of the meetings seems to have been the claim of the Negro to equality with the white.[35] At this congress, expression was somewhat more unrestrained. Belgium was condemned for her administration of the Congo, and this naturally led the Belgian press to fight back. Later in Paris, Diagne made an unsuccessful effort to get the motion reversed or watered down. This congress also established a secretariat in Paris, in an endeavor to put their organization on a permanent basis, but it lasted only two years.[36]

A third Pan-African Congress met in London and Lisbon late in 1923, with eleven countries represented; a fourth was held in New York in 1927, with delegates from thirteen countries; but an attempt to hold a fifth Congress in Tunis in 1929, at the time of the world depression, drew opposition from the French government and had to be postponed. The French told the congress executive that they might meet anywhere in France, but not in Africa. Not until 1945 did the fifth Pan-African Congress meet, at Manchester, England, with two hundred delegates representing "60 nations."[37]

In 1955 the Communists called a world congress of non-whites at Bandung for the purpose of condemning colonialism and white rule in general.[38] Some French Negroes attended. Also in 1956 there was a World Congress of Negro Writers and Artists in Paris, with French Negroes participating. Again colonialism was the chief theme of the meeting, it would appear. The speeches delivered during the four days of the meeting were afterward printed in *Présence africaine.*[39] The Negroes have learned that it pays to organize and to proclaim their opinions.

[35] A 17-page brochure by Gratien Candace, entitled *Le deuxième congrès de la race noire en 1921* (Paris, 1921), describes the meetings. It also discusses the first congress.

[36] W. E. B. Du Bois, "Africa and the American Negro Intelligencia," *Présence africaine,* n.s., Dec. 1955–Jan. 1956, p. 42.

[37] *Ibid.,* pp. 43-45.

[38] *Présence africaine,* n.s., Oct.-Nov. 1955, pp. 82-85.

[39] June-Nov. 1956.

# THE FUTURE OUTLOOK

*IT IS DIFFICULT* for those who
have not been to France to visualize the status of the Negroes
there. Rarely are they servants. Most are of the middle class
and to some degree approximate American students and
travelers who go to France, though displaying more frugality.
They number thirty or forty thousand, one may estimate, with
two-thirds at least living in Paris, and the others in the port
and university cities, especially in the South. Several thousand
are students, on tenures running from one to five or six years,
and of these perhaps a third or more hold a scholarship from
the French or colonial governments. Of the other Negroes,
some are transients staying for a limited period, others settlers
pursuing a profession or holding a job. All are well dressed,
well behaved, and have some limited social intercourse with
the French, but in general they fraternize among themselves.

On the whole they have been well received, although at
present and throughout the past there have been some Frenchmen opposed to them. The government of Louis XVI thought
that their immigration should be halted and made efforts to
return as many to the colonies as it could. The government
of Napoleon followed in the same direction. Subsequent governments permitted their entry with reservations. Today all
can enter, since they are French citizens. But this does not
guarantee that the Negro immigrant will find housing easily.
Many of the French reportedly do not want Negro roomers
and offer easy excuses to refuse them. Much complaint has

272                                    THE NEGRO IN FRANCE

come from the Negroes on this point; they realize, or imagine,
that they have been given an evasion. Housing, however, has
been very short in all the major cities of France ever since
World War II, and even the French have had extreme difficulty
in obtaining rooms and apartments.

Such is the situation at the present. But what is the future
destined to bring? The Negro population will continue to
grow. Ever since World War I it has developed rapidly in
French cities, and especially in Paris. It appears destined to
continue. This assumption may be based upon the remarkable
economic development taking place throughout Black Africa.
There the cities, with their banks, stores, and manufacturies,
are being built along the latest European designs, and wealth
is accruing. A middle class slowly is developing, consisting of
merchants, property owners, and professional men. In the
United States, too, the Negro continues to gain in wealth and
education, and the number of American Negroes visiting
France for one cause or another continues to augment each
year. To the Negro race Paris is Mecca, and France the
Promised Land. The day may come when the number of
Negro tourists there will be formidable. Continued discoveries
of oil or uranium in large quantities in Africa could make it so.
Already the oil resources of Venezuela and Saudi Arabia have
eclipsed those of Texas, and in time those of Africa could do
so too. The day may come when hordes of Negro travelers
from Africa, the West Indies, and the United States will go
to France and bask on the Riviera.

More significant perhaps would be the development of a
large permanent Negro population in France. So far this
population is small and unnoticed. But should it continue to
grow, it will sooner or later attract attention and possibly
opposition. For one of the important factors in racial antagonism is that of numbers. It is partly the large number of
Negroes in Mississippi and South Africa that gives rise to the
problems in those areas. Why should that operate? Because
the whites fear domination politically, economically, or cultur-
ally in this day of racial assertiveness.

Of course France would have no such overwhelming body of Negro residents. There would be no danger of subversion in any of the above respects. Nevertheless, in states where Negroes are far from being in the majority their presence is resented, and this resentment grows with their numbers. The Negro is not the only race that meets resentment, for the Jew, the Indian, the Oriental all in turn have been the victims of bitter treatment here and there, and it is usually because of their numbers. In areas where they are few they are well received; where they are more numerous, they are commonly, but not always, the victims of ill will.

There is much to suggest that this will not happen in France. The Negro has been a vital support to France in the last two World Wars. Of this the French are very mindful and appreciative. Above all things they are desirous of maintaining their close political and economic relations with the Negro colonial and of having him as an ally in any future European war in which they may become engaged. There are fifty or sixty millions of these Negroes, and they are well disposed toward France. They are among France's most likely allies. On their part, these colonists, though wanting nothing so much as independence (which now indeed most of them have had since 1958), wish to continue their ties with France, realizing their need of Western civilization and of economic development, both of which they are conscious that they can best obtain through France.

Strengthening this friendship between mother country and colonies—if colonies they may still be called after the French Community of Nations has become a reality—is promoted in no other way so effectively as through the visits of the Negroes to France, and particularly through those of the students. Few are the French who go to the colonies, and they are chiefly officials. But the students who go to France and there spend several years, during the most impressionable period of their life, are numerous. Some work hard; others take it in leisurely fashion. They sit idly about the sidewalk cafés and drink their coffee or wine, discussing world problems and building fantastic dreams of how they will transform the world. Most of these dreams no doubt will come to naught, but others may come true. When these students go home, they will reflect on those pleasant days, and if storms come to France, they will be sympathetic. Most of them probably will take the side of France, as in the past their predecessors have done. Among them may be future Eboués. Thus the French policy toward the Negro is apt to pay off. It is the best investment in futures that France can make.

It may be observed that the Negro is extremely sensitive of his treatment by the whites anywhere in the world, and those who visit France are no exceptions. This writer has been surprised to find some of them critical of the French—critical that they are not cordially received in all circles, critical of their difficulty in getting housing and meals, critical that the French government does not turn over the reins of colonial government completely to the natives to run it as they wish. This last grievance, of course, no longer has validity since De Gaulle's offer to them of independence in the elections of 1958. It was theirs for the asking, and only one state, Guinea, asked for it. The others chose autonomy and continuance in the French Community. As French citizens they can come and go at their pleasure, and they have no subordinate status to rankle them. This should augur for a more cordial attitude on their part.

At the same time the Negro is emerging somewhat, both in France and elsewhere, from the feeling of racial inferiority. In the nineteenth century they seem to have shunned attention, and in France to have resented any reference to their color. While still the French courteously avoid the term "Negro" and use the expression "noir" (or "black"), the Negro likes publicity and takes a pride in his race. He is proud of the accomplishments of his race in art, literature, politics, learning, music, and the sports, as of course he has just reason to do. This self-confidence is increasing and should have its part in making the Negro less sensitive. For fundamentally he has gained vastly more from the French than they from him.

# INDEX

278